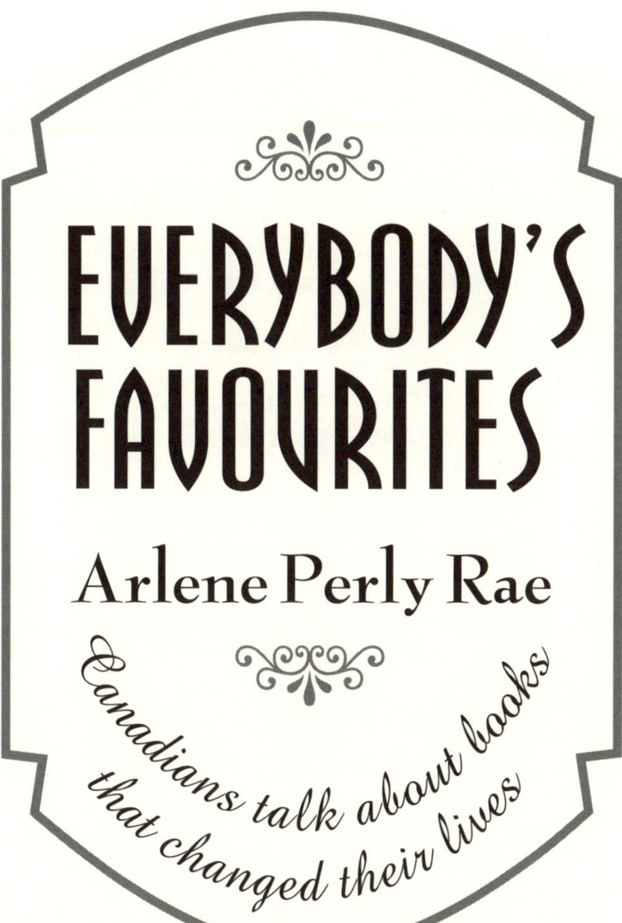
EVERYBODY'S FAVOURITES
Arlene Perly Rae
Canadians talk about books that changed their lives

VIKING

VIKING
Published by the Penguin Group
Penguin Books Canada Ltd, 10 Alcorn Avenue, Toronto, Ontario,
Canada M4V 3B2
Penguin Books Ltd, 27 Wrights Lane, London W8 5TZ, England
Viking Penguin, a division of Penguin Books USA Inc., 375 Hudson Street,
New York, New York 10014, U.S.A.
Penguin Books Australia Ltd, Ringwood, Victoria, Australia
Penguin Books (NZ) Ltd, cnr Rosedale and Airborne Roads, Albany,
Auckland 1310, New Zealand

Penguin Books Ltd, Registered Offices: Harmondsworth,
Middlesex, England

First published 1997

1 3 5 7 9 10 8 6 4 2

Printed and bound in Canada on acid free paper ♾

Canadian Cataloguing in Publication Data

Main entry under title: Everybody's Favourites:
Canadians talk about books that changed their lives

ISBN 0-670-87080-3

1. Children – Books and reading. 2. Celebrities – Canada –
Books and reading. I. Rae, Arlene Perly, 1949–.

Z1037.A1E93 1997 028.5'5 C96-932036-1

Visit Penguin Canada's web site at **www.penguin.ca**

In memory of my parents
Hannah and Albert Perly
and
for Bob, Judith, Lisa and Eleanor

You must write for children in the same way you do for adults, only better.

Maxim Gorky

In writing children's books I have the best of childhood over again and the best of being old as well.

Arthur Ransome

Books are the children of the brain.

Jonathan Swift

Whoever does not remember the old tales has lost the key that opens the door of life.

Patrick Kavanagh

A book is a garden carried in a pocket.

Chinese saying

The dreamer awakes, the shadow goes by
When I tell you a tale, the tale is a lie.
But ponder it well, fair maiden, good youth;
The tale is a lie, what it tells is the truth.

Ida Zeitlins Skazki

The oldest books are only just out to those who have not read them.

Samuel Butler

The person who does not read good books has no advantage over the person who can't.

Mark Twain

One's first book, kiss, home run, is always the best.

Clifton Fadiman

Contents

Acknowledgements

Many people helped make this book a reality, most of all the contributors. Remembering takes time and effort. Thank you to each person who responded for their generous and thoughtful participation. Thank you, too, to the parents, teachers and librarians who so often set them on their way. I gratefully acknowledge the permission given by a few of the contributors to reprint (and occasionally edit) excerpts from previously published material.

Special thanks to Timothy Findley for (unwittingly) planting the idea. In the late eighties I began reviewing children's books for *The Toronto Star*. Tiff sent over a celebratory gift, his long-time favourite children's book, *Wild Animals I Have Known* by Ernest Thompson Seton. As I waded through the mountains of new books published in Canada and other countries, Seton's classic stayed on my desk. Because of it other books recalled from childhood were constantly dancing in my head. I was curious about some books' enduring power to enchant and delight and yearned for an opportunity to link great books from the past with current children's literature. Soon the idea for this book evolved.

Thanks to everyone at Penguin Canada for their patience and encouragement—especially my editor, Meg Masters. Her gentle but consistent pressure, recommendations and support made all the difference. Thanks to Mary Adachi for gardening tips and delicious lunches but most of all for her good advice. Thanks also to Cynthia Good, Scott Sellers, Louise Curtis, Tedd Kelemen and Jem Bates.

Thanks to my typist, Elizabeth Way, who with an expert eye, read handwritten, computer-typed and fax-fuzzy contributions and then speedily rendered them "word perfect."

Thank you to all the helpful and knowledgeable people at the Toronto Public Library, Lillian Smith Branch, and to everyone at the Canadian Children's Book Centre—Charlotte Teeple, Jeffrey Canton, Judi McCallum and Yuen Chu—for information, catalogues and general assistance, especially gathering the awards lists. Thanks to Penny Dickens and Siobhan O'Connor at the Writers' Union for similar help reaching members across the country.

Thank you to Michael Levine for approving my contract. Thanks to Gloria Bishop, Christie Fletcher, Alison Gordon, Mike Katrycz, Maureen Kenny, Eleanor LeFave and Susan McCulloch (of Mabel's Fables), Karen Levine, Roy MacGregor, Nora McCabe, Mampta Mishra, Susan Morgan, Laura Mullen, Jack Rabinovitch, Maria Ralley, Judy Sarick (of The Children's Bookstore), Jennifer Scott and Judy Stoffman for a variety of calls and contacts. Thanks to Sonya, Charlie and Dillon for lugging books and papers back and forth between houses.

I am indebted to my niece, Kate Rae, for looking up elusive addresses and to Anne Shortell for checking out obscure facts (e.g., the author of *Lars in Lapland*) at the library and on the Internet. Thanks to Joel Cleroux for providing an impressive list of Canadian athletes. Thanks to Louise Dennys, Avie Bennett and Rick Wilks (publishers from other companies), who graciously eased access to "their" authors.

Thanks to Leslie Milrod for encouraging me to pursue this project and to Laurie Stevens and Inga Lubbock for taking on extra work to free my time. Thanks to Morgan Kenny for bringing poetry back into my life.

I am grateful to Stuart McLean for his generous advice early on, especially concerning the contents and composition of the request letter.

Special thanks to my friend and business partner, Molly Yeomans, for contacts, coffee breaks and all manner of moral support.

Speaking of moral support, thanks to many good friends who consistently offered encouragement—for the book and much more—Rosie Abella, Bea Bindman, Susan Camp, Ellen Cole, Kathy Cooper, Andrée Crépeau, Eva Czigler, Steve Doede, Bronwyn Drainie, Kathy Feldman, Graham Fraser, Marianne Grek, Beth Haddon, Susan Hauer, Wendy Hughes, Nina Josephowitz, Rhonda Katz, Deena Mandell, Evelyne Michaels, Margaret Tatham, Barbara Uteck, Cynthia Wine, Arlene Wortsman, Sonia Zanardi and Bill Zimmerman.

I am grateful for the encouragement of many family members, especially Ginny Rae-Peterson, Jennifer Rae, Patricia Anne McKinnon, Gary Conn, Laurie and Armand Jelilyan, and my infinitely generous and supportive sister, Jeannie Conn.

My biggest hugs to our three daughters, Judith, Lisa and Eleanor, for frequently reading books I suggested and for always offering candid opinions. Thanks to Judith for her translation, to Lisa for her metaphors and to Eleanor for her enthusiastic commentary. Thanks too for your love, sense of humour, flexibility and remarkable capacity to settle for pizza dinners at a moment's notice. You are the *raison d'être* for everything I do and my pride and joy.

My gratitude and love to Bob (a great reader and terrific source of recommendations) for always being there, motivating, soothing, and offering practical help with (your trademark) wit and wisdom.

Introduction

Some people say that it doesn't matter what children read as long as they do. Well sure, up to a point, but when there are hundreds of imaginative, beautiful and thought-provoking books there for the taking, why not head for the best? After all, every child deserves to see marvellous pictures and read great literature. At the very least they should be given a road map to show them the way. Children, like adults, are always on the lookout for good stories. I hope this collection of memories and recommendations will suggest to people of all ages a wide variety of reading opportunities.

It has also been said that books read while young make a stronger, more lasting impression. Graham Greene insists that "it is only in childhood that books have any deep influence on our lives." I'm not sure that's entirely true... there are lots of books I've read in the twenty-five years since childhood that have made a profound impression. Still, the question haunts me—were any quite as wonderful as that first beloved picture book read countless times? Or the consuming experience of lying in bed, following *Charlotte's Web* in all its humour and tragedy, read definitively in my father's resonant voice? Or, a few years later, secretly (and deliciously!) staying up all night to finish *A Little Princess* or, some time in my teens, sobbing helplessly from the enormous impact of *Gone with the Wind*? Maybe Greene *is* right after all. Certainly, to judge by the essays from contributors to this book, there *were* a great many books—some read rather long ago—that have affected people very deeply. Key books encountered when one is young and impressionable may be among the significant influences that shape personality, ideas and attitudes for years to come.

Today, an entire children's culture has developed that is (often for marketing reasons) very attentive to the needs and interests of the younger generation. Whether through targeted literature, music, drama, movies, TV, sports, fashion or the ever-expanding world of cyberspace (computers, video games, the Net, the Web and so on), the highly significant child/consumer is anything but ignored. This has not always been so. While children have long been celebrated for their innocence, they were historically often thought of as miniature adults (ripe for moulding into grownup ideas and customs). It is only recently that youth has been singled out as a phase of life different from adulthood in its manner of learning and development. In recent decades the emphasis, for both education and moral enlightenment, has been transferred to play and imaginative expression. Childhood is now generally acknowledged as a time with its own needs, interests and characteristics.

In contrast, for much of the two previous centuries most books for children in Britain, northern Europe, Canada and the United States were influenced by the strict moral code and restrictive spell of the Puritans. Readers of all ages (both then and now) may absorb John Bunyan's *The Pilgrim's Progress* (1678) as a powerful adventure, but it was originally intended and for years taught solely as a religious or spiritual journey.

Subsequently, tales for children were either earnest religious tracts or boring utilitarian lessons disguised as stories. Well-meaning educators in the eighteenth and nineteenth centuries lured unsuspecting children (yearning as always for fantasy, adventure, rich plot, humour, characters they could identify with, imaginative flights of fancy and other delights) into their "stories" with a few tempting openers. But very quickly these tales (and there were far too many of them published) would reveal their true and far duller colours. They would piously overwhelm their young victims with sermons, moralizing, dry lessons, patronizing tones, false sentiment, phony dialogue and impossibly too-good characters. These lessons were the official menu of children's reading and the staple of their educational diet until they were able to graduate to adulthood—and with any luck and opportunity, a wider variety of literary choice.

Paul Hazard, the noted French critic, eloquently described this "tasteless food" in his eye-opening text *Books, Children and Men*, an important contribution to the study of children's literature. "Virtue was never praised so much; useful advice was never so freely given; adolescence was never urged more eagerly to improve itself..." Having frequently noticed (with a wince) the restrictive lacy dresses and high-collared velvet suits decorating children in so many venerable paintings, I am in particular agreement with his further observation: "If for centuries, grownups did not even think of giving children appropriate clothes, how would it ever have occurred to them to provide them with suitable books?" Indeed they did not.

Fantasy and imagination, fairy tales, fables and rollicking adventure tales were for too many years looked down upon—denounced and condemned even—by self-appointed "wise" teachers. Their tendency to folk wisdom, fun, magical elements and entertainment was presented as a serious flaw. But these stories did not disappear. Far from it. They survived as an underground or subversive literature.

They prevailed through chap (cheap) books sold by pedlars, through songs, rhymes and the ballads of travelling minstrels. They were passed on from generation to generation through the oral tradition. Legends and fairy tales flourished in spite of trying times precisely because they were loved and demanded. They survived in family retellings, in grandparents' memories, on nurses' knees and guarded folklore collections.

Many Bible tales have long been enjoyed as simple stories—valued for character and narrative merit as much as for message. Animal stories, fables, wonder and folk-tales were told for centuries in the widest variety of languages and cultures. Hidden sometimes in family libraries as well as the stacks of the great universities were traditional legends, the great Greek and Roman epics, and romantic medieval tales of courage, loyalty and heroism.

In their private letters and journals many noted authors and composers confessed to an abiding love of adventure and fairy tales. Charles Dickens, for example, declared a boyhood crush on Little Red Riding Hood. He dreamed of marrying her when he grew up! Certainly his own enduring tales (*Great Expectations*, *A Christmas Carol*, *A Tale of Two Cities* and others) are celebrated for their literary quality, character development and the depth of human spirit they reveal, rather than anything like the sanctimonious promotion of a rigid moral philosophy or doctrine.

There has been, in the last one hundred and fifty years, the exciting emergence of a golden age of children's literature. Emphasis has moved almost entirely from the arid teaching of skills and morals to a far healthier combination of edification and delight (with a distinct emphasis on the latter). From the simplest ABC or counting book through picture and chapter books, short stories, novels, history and non-fiction for young adults, the highest goal has become a celebration of the imagination. This has created for the young twentieth-century reader a verbal and visual feast. The best and most talented writers, illustrators, editors and publishers are happily preoccupied with furthering the trend. But there are so many books and such varying quality and options now available that it may be difficult for interested adults and children to determine, on their own, where to look and what to read.

For *Everybody's Favourites* I asked people to recall stories, often read or heard years ago, that meant something to them, "to think of a special book, read as a child or teenager, that woke them up, stirred their soul or changed their life." Despite the (formidable) competition for a child's time and attention, it is my belief that few activities remain as engrossing, intimate and ultimately satisfying as a key encounter with that special book. The question is—which ones? I decided to ask people to reflect upon that specific question. Were there pivotal books that stood out or made a difference? If so, what made them memorable? The answers are grouped loosely, according to theme. The contributors are a cross-section of well-known Canadians.

Remembered favourites connect with individuals in a highly personal way. Like other happy memories, a positive connection with a particular book locks it in memory and in a valued place. It remains treasured despite the passage of time. In some mysterious way favourite books become partners with people in unique relationships. They too can touch a nerve or warm a heart.

Those who responded have written eloquently and thoughtfully about their choices. In some cases they hadn't thought about a particular book for years. Others have copies dog-eared from constant thumbing. All have generously agreed to share their memories, many revealing the telling context of their selections.

Some of the books recalled in these pages are adventure stories, fairy tales, history or romance. Others are poetry, picture books, books about science, nature books and encyclopedias. Some are popular books, series books, science fiction, comics. Some choices are eclectic, obscure, difficult to find, out of print. A surprising number helped pave the reader's way from childhood to adulthood, and the transition to "adult" literature. Many were inspirational, leading towards specific careers or personal choices. A number of writers reveal the initial and lasting excitement over their personal discovery of an acknowledged classic—wonderful timeless books that retain their freshness and vigour, appealing to each new generation of literary explorers.

Many stories loved in childhood led their readers to a lifetime of pleasure among the pages of books, some specifically to a career in writing. For me, one of the most exciting aspects of compiling *Everybody's Favourites* was discovering the popularity of a particular series by Lucy Maud Montgomery. Not, as might be expected, *Anne of Green Gables* (and its sequels), although that book and its feisty heroine are understandably well loved both at home and internationally. The unexpected discovery was that a disproportionately large number of contributors—mostly women writers—were remarkably affected by Montgomery's Emily books, *Emily of New Moon*, *Emily Climbs* and *Emily's Quest*. This series is far less well known outside

Canada than the Anne books, but within our borders its importance to a particular creative community is huge. Its impact is worthy of further analysis and study. The Emily books, although I discovered them later, are without question among my own personal favourites.

Since beginning this project, I have frequently been asked, "What is *your* favourite children's book?" Perhaps now is the time to answer. From the outset, I knew I would have no trouble responding. When I was about four or five, I persuaded my parents and sister to read and reread *The Story of Ferdinand*, by Munro Leaf, so often that its bright red cover fell off. Years later, I shared it with my own young family. We all still love this funny and entrancing story and the wonderful pictures by Robert Lawson.

Ferdinand is a large, gentle bull who doesn't want to fight. Through a terrible misunderstanding he is thought to be a ferocious charger and carted off to a major bullfight. At the arena there is great pomp—a proud matador, elaborate costumes, a huge and excited crowd. Ferdinand resists. No amount of prodding, taunting or teasing will change his nature. He is a mild creature, attracted only by the lovely aroma wafting from the fresh flowers in the ladies' hats. He enjoys smelling them and, it seems, will not do anything else. Ferdinand will not fight. Eventually the humans in the story get the message. The sweet-natured bull is allowed to return to his beloved home and the grass, trees and fragrant flowers he loves so well.

I cheerfully immersed myself in this touching story as do generations of children still. Sometimes I acted out the parts, including costumes and a red hand-towel to tease the bull. When friends were unavailable, stuffed animals stood in. In season, fragrant lilacs were plucked from my mother's garden.

At the time, I had no idea of the shocking commotion this little book had caused soon after its publication by Viking in 1936. *The Story of Ferdinand* was the first modern children's book deemed to be truly controversial. Some called it subversive and the meaning of its text was widely debated in the media. For differing reasons it was banned in war-torn Spain (pacifism!), burned by Hitler in Germany (propaganda!), denigrated by some in the U.S. (communism!, anarchy!). Leaf insisted he created the amiable Ferdinand and his comic predicament "simply to amuse young children." Well, of course he did, and it does.

Perhaps it is only coincidental that after Ferdinand's impact I came to love gardening and especially flowers—roses, gardenias, lilies of all description. To study drama at university. To love the private pleasure afforded by reading as well as the somewhat less predictable and far more public play of politics. To hang out, as much as possible in this frantic, urban chaos, in my favourite places and with favourite people, especially close friends and family. On the other hand, I truly can't stand pomposity and loathe the very concept of a bullfight. Have I unconsciously absorbed a deeper message from *The Story of Ferdinand*—to simply stop in your tracks every once in a while to smell the flowers? I hope so.

Not long ago I stumbled upon another deceptively simple picture book. It's called *Busy, Busy, Busy* by Jonathan Shipton, illustrated by Michael Foreman.

As with Ferdinand, the text is spare, the plot uncomplicated. A woman is trying to do housework and care for her child simultaneously. In one drawing she is literally chained to the sink, tied in knots to the cascading laundry. In another, she is caught in the tangled cords of an iron, vacuum cleaner and falling radio. The child senses his mother's frustration—she is at the point of tears—and yearns to lure her away from the apparently never-ending parade of chores. He innocently and sweetly attempts to cheer her up.

Eventually, and just in the nick of time, the child succeeds. The final panorama shows the two of them together, gazing skyward. A flock of Canada geese swoops overhead in a V formation. Mother and child are entranced, hugging, rapturously watching. A moment later would have been too late.

What this mother and child need, what they may, through the child's persistence, have fortuitously found just in time, is fifteen minutes for sniffing flowers with Ferdinand. The same happy time could be enjoyed reading a book or playing together.

Kindred spirits with my beloved Ferdinand, kids are like the little boy in *Busy, Busy, Busy*. They want to drink in the magic and variety of the world around them. They are in no particular hurry to rush off to the next event. They wear no watch. They aren't being stubborn and certainly in no way intend to offend anyone. They are merely being themselves.

"A Cow Story" is a short tale by Mariam Habib from a collection with the alluring title *How I Learned to Speak Dog and Other Animal Stories*. The narrator is driving to a conference, barrelling along, oblivious to the passing scenery. On a narrow country road she is forced to stop because of an obstacle, an intransigent cow. It offers a bland, brown-eyed stare—massive, carefree immovability. The driver pauses too, looks around, begins to notice her surroundings. Because of that cow, Habib's narrator must temporarily stop "driving."

A busy adult, she is inspired to break the journey, to take a few precious minutes to feed her senses and admire the landscape.

What is it about these bulls and cows and kids? What I have determined from Ferdinand, the stand-still cow and kids in general is this: children are children only fleetingly. The time we spend truly *with* them—reading, talking, playing, watching, sharing stories, hanging out—is extremely valuable. It is of the same nature and quality as stopping for a cow, catching a glimpse of those remarkable, noisy geese, smelling the flowers.

In my case, and that of many contributors to *Everybody's Favourites*, literature had just that sort of enormous and valuable impact on our young lives. Reading made us stop and reflect. Because of books, we came to observe, understand and appreciate the world with fresh insight.

I hope *Everybody's Favourites* leads readers of all ages to more and more stories, to some of the timeless old ones, and to many wonderful and exciting new ones as well.

·1· Early Memories

"Give us wings"
—Paul Hazard

Why do so many adults retain powerful memories of stories they heard or read when they were very young? Perhaps it is because storytime, for fortunate children, is linked like lullabies, nonsense games, baths or bedtime with intimate contact with mom or dad. Certain story memories may be inseparably blended with the pleasant recollection of a cozy cuddle on a parent's lap. Adding to the pleasure, these oft-repeated tales are customarily told or read in combination with soft pillows, warm blankets and a familiar bed or comfy couch. For young children, the magic of books becomes happily associated with good feelings, security and pleasant sensations.

When young children first make contact with books themselves, it tends to be a tactile or physical experience. They stare at the pictures, touch or taste brightly coloured objects, chew covers and corners. First books are generally board books, puffy bath books, sunny ABCs and attractive counting books.

Small children love all kinds of picture books as well as gentle gimmicks like pages with texture or surprises. They respond to clear, vibrant images, pictures and stories about animals, other children, the world around them. Magic and fantasy mingle easily with the real and may be incorporated into imaginative play. Before long, most kids can explore a book all by themselves, turn the pages, contemplate the drawings. Some make up original stories to explain the pictures.

Long before they actually read, eager youngsters may be familiar with dozens, even hundreds of stories. They respond to their favourites as warmly as they do to a familiar adult smiling above them. It is a special and enlightening milestone when a youngster realizes that the urge for more stories can be satisfied independently, through books.

It is remarkable how the memory of a simple story encountered many years ago may linger with an adult. Nostalgia, yes, but a reflection, too, of the deep significance and essential quality of the best of these books.

What are generally referred to as "fairy tales" are a typical example of these unforgettable stories. For many adults, these familiar—though in many cases very old and often rather strange—stories provide the earliest literary memories. A great many survived for centuries (in various versions through the oral tradition) before Perrault, Andersen or the brothers Grimm gathered and published them in their notable collections.

Charles Perrault wrote his *Tales of Mother Goose* (including "Little Red Riding Hood," "Cinderella," "The Sleeping Beauty," "Puss in Boots" and several others) three hundred years ago, publishing a number together in 1697. Mme. de Beaumont created *Beauty and the Beast* around 1750. The brothers Grimm's collection *German Popular Stories* (1812) appeared with little fanfare. It was not originally intended for children but compiled as an academic exercise—a history of the oral tradition in Germany. A beautifully illustrated English edition (published in 1823, with exceptional pictures by George Cruikshank) inspired the Grimms to compile a more ambitious second volume containing over two hundred folk-tales (including "Hansel and Gretel," "The Shoemaker and the Elves," "Rumpelstiltskin," "Rapunzel," "Snow White and the Seven Dwarfs," "The Frog Prince" and "The Twelve Dancing Princesses"), as well as German versions of Perrault's tales. Children ever since have remained spellbound by these timeless stories of ancient kingdoms, magic spells, good and evil. They continue to be so well known, so firmly established in collective memory that many adults, decades after hearing them, can recount quite a few without text or hesitation.

Hans Christian Andersen's *Fairy Tales Told for Children* was published in his native Danish in 1835. The first English translation appeared in 1846. Andersen continued to compose stories—adapting folk-tales and creating original work—for more than forty years. His fairy tales are among the best known in the world, translated into dozens of languages, constantly retold, reillustrated and anthologized. Andersen himself, a sometime actor, loved to read them aloud to audiences. Some of his characters experience the sting of isolation, loneliness or persecution and must struggle valiantly against oppressive forces. His stories reveal that stunning blend of the fantastic and the real that makes fairy tales both memorable and enchanting. Among the best loved are "The Princess and the Pea," "The Little Mermaid," "The Ugly Duckling," "The Emperor's New Clothes," "Thumbelina," "The Little Match Girl," "The Snow Queen" and "The Steadfast Tin Soldier."

Today these classic rhymes and stories for the very young have been joined by hundreds of newer stories and picture books, folk-tales from all cultures, retellings and adaptations. Among the most popular of these newer fairy tales is *The Story about Ping,* a book perpetually reprinted since its first edition in 1933. Its author, accomplished storyteller and artist Marjorie Flack, was able to give her little Peking duck a charming and endearing personality—one that has clearly affected generations of children. Kurt Wiese was invited to illustrate Ping because he was familiar with China and his expressive lithographs are integral to the overall effect.

But there are lots of other early memories—stories and characters that have brought young listeners and readers enormous pleasure over many years. First encounters with *Winnie-the-Pooh*, *The Arabian Nights*, *Peter Rabbit* and Dr. Seuss. There are understandably ardent fans of *Babar*, *Curious George*, *The Velveteen Rabbit* and *Goodnight Moon.* Personally, along with Ferdinand, I have a special affection for the tender bear Corduroy, forever missing his button, and for the mischievous Madeline. There are, it seems, dozens of other stories and picture books that remain special to individual readers.

Some early memories recall an exotic locale, an emerging sense of a wider world out there somewhere. Others introduce a new skill or insight, an appreciation of differences, the spark of recognition. Those recollected here seem to have stimulated the imaginations of the young children who first discovered them and they remain vivid in their adult counterparts who enjoy them still.

Sandra Gwyn (writer)

In St. John's in the early 1940s, when I was very young, the book I loved best was this irresistible tale about the adventures of a mischievous yellow duckling who lived with his "mother and father and two sisters and three brothers and eleven aunts and seven uncles and forty-two cousins" in a boat with two wise eyes on the Yangtze River. I found it, appropriately enough, in the children's department of the Gosling Memorial Library on Duckworth Street. I can see myself now—pigtails and scabby knees—trudging up the stone stairs to check it out yet again, even though I already knew it by heart.

Looking back, I think what entranced me was the mix of familiar and exotic: I knew all about ducks, and in that era St. John's harbour was full of wooden sailing boats. But "wise-eyed junks" swept me into another world entirely.

The Story about Ping is still in print and I keep on giving it to all my four- to seven-year-old acquaintances. Kurt Wiese's wonderful illustrations continue to enchant; even for kids who know all about computers, Marjorie Flack's text is a voyage of discovery. Indeed for me, it was a voyage of discovery that led to my future husband. That is to say, when Richard and I first met, circa 1955, one of the first things we found out about each other was a shared passion for Ping.

Richard Gwyn (writer)

In *The Story about Ping* (by Marjorie Flack) Ping, who at one stop along the Yangtze fails to get back aboard his junk before it and his family sail on down the river, speaks to the primal fear all children have of being left behind. It spoke directly to me, at the age of seven, because the Yangtze itself, with its thousands of junks, was just down the road from the house in Shanghai's International Concession where I lived with my sister, Susanna, and mother and father and a Chinese-American nanny named Jessie.

It spoke to me with the chilling tones of terror, though, because the Japanese—this was 1941—occupied all of Shanghai but for the British and American and French Concessions. I knew they were bad because Jessie told me so. Sometimes we heard the gunfire between them and Chinese troops. My father, an intelligence officer with the British legation, told me the Japanese had no quarrel with us.

Ping, though, was too much like me, definitely naughty and a bit bold. Once, I got Jessie to take me to a park she'd talked about and show me the Chinese babies there, swaddled in old clothes and left by their parents to die. My parents were furious with Jessie. But when I read, and reread, how Ping, because of his naughtiness and boldness, had gotten left behind, having all kinds of adventures before finding his own "wise-eyed" junk again, I thought I might be left behind if the Japanese ever picked a quarrel with us.

They did not quarrel with us. But when they did, my father and mother were clever enough to know how to escape, as I always knew they would be. And they took Susanna and me with them, as I always knew they would. And Jessie came too, to India.

Jim Cameron (geographer and friend of Castor canadensis)

The story of a little yellow Duck named Ping on a river boat "with two wise eyes" on the Yangtze River made a lasting impression on my young imagination. In the 1940s before television, children's perceptions of the rest of the world were derived from such simple images.

Ping's adventure began when he became separated from his mother, father and his extended family of sixty other ducks. He was helped by a boy to find his way home. The story, of course, has a happy ending. I was and continue to be addicted to happy endings. Yet what was of particular interest to me at the time was that the boy and his family had different faces with different shaped eyes and wore a special kind of clothing. It was perhaps my first glimpse of the world beyond Southern Ontario.

As with all small boys who liked animals, I could easily relate to Ping and the boy who helped him. The fact that this event happened far away (my parents told me it was a country called China) meant that I could identify with a larger world, even though I had never seen a real person from China.

The illustrations in *The Story about Ping* are still so clear and striking that when I saw them again recently, they brought back my first impression of this far-away place with people who looked so different from my family, yet were not so very different after all.

Sonja Smits (actor)

When my sister and I were very young, our mother bought a set of books that were our introduction to the beauty of books. They are so beautiful that I recently had them rebound as a gift to my children and my sister's daughter. They were large, white hardcovered books, filled with magnificent illustrations. Each chapter started with an elaborately decorated letter, sometimes jewel encrusted or in the shape of a sword. The words, literally, a thing of beauty. Tales of Hans Christian Andersen, *Pinocchio*, *Alice in Wonderland*, *The Arabian Nights*. These books given to us at three and five years of age spanned our childhood. When I was very young there was "Little Red Riding Hood" with its frightening illustrations of a very wicked looking wolf. "The Ugly Duckling," a story I secretly related to, thinking one day I too would grow up and discover who I truly was. "The Wild Swans" and the brave princess, knitting with stinging needles as she is being carted off to be burned as a witch. I hoped some day to be as brave.

My recurring dreams of flying were inspired by her brothers who had been transformed into wild swans by day, princes by night.

And, as I got a bit older, the mysterious world of Ali Baba in *Arabian Nights* was revealed with its bejewelled curved swords and magic lamps.

Years later, I travelled to Morocco, walking through the souks and going to the desert and having mint tea with Bedouin traders.

The desire to see other people and other worlds was fuelled, I am sure, by those childhood tales. They showed me the power and magic in storytelling; I knew it was a place I wanted to be. So I became an actress, which is my way of telling stories.

Sarah Ellis (writer)

James James Morrison Morrison Weatherby George Dupree; Jonathan Jo with his "mouth like an 'O' and a wheelbarrow full of surprises"; The King with his modest desire of "a little bit of butter to my bread"—I met these folk at an early age when my mother read us the poems in A.A. Milne's *When We Were Very Young*, and they are there in my head still. When I look back at the poems, opening my well-worn childhood copy of the book, I am surprised to see not only these old friends but myself on almost every page. The pleasures of sitting halfway up the stairs, I enjoy this still. The second chair in the poem "Nursery Chairs," the one that is a lion's cage, I have one just like it. A passion for bread and butter, a loathing for rice pudding, the pleasures of walking in the rain wearing a Great Big Waterproof Mackintosh, taking care not to walk on the cracks in the sidewalk, the secret conviction that there are other secret worlds just out of sight, between the two trees at the end of the garden, under the lily pads. Was I really so influenced by *When We Were Very Young*? Or was I just lucky in an early encounter with a book so suited to my sort and condition? Likely a bit of both.

Andy Barrie (broadcaster)

At the age of seven my hobby, passion, my obsession, was puppets. This was probably provoked by the recent arrival of our first TV which fed fifties kids a constant diet of puppet shows like "Howdy Doody," "Uncle Chichimus" and "Kukla, Fran and Ollie." I was the only kid on the block and, I thought, the planet who was into puppetry. This might explain why my local library had only two books on the subject: one about Punch and Judy, which seemed beneath my seven-year-old's sophistication; the other a beautifully written and illustrated little volume called *Marionettes—A Hobby for Everyone.*

Mable and Les Beaton, whose little boy I dearly wished to be, had built a complete marionette theatre in their basement, where they invited friends to see their productions, starring magnificently life-like marionettes. The book gave detailed instructions on how to create the puppets, props, stages and sets, even supplying tissue-paper patterns for the marionettes' cloth bodies. My mother was put to work at the sewing machine, which she eventually taught me to use. A year later, I was inviting friends over to our basement to see my puppet shows.

I strongly believe that grownups who love their work can trace their career choice back to an epiphany they had as children. I had mine between the covers of the Beatons' book. I'm a radio broadcaster today, a performer who is heard but not seen, just as I was when I spoke for the marionettes dangling from my hidden hands onto the pool of light below. That's where I learned about showmanship, poise and projection. It was the Beatons' book that taught me about applause, and how to earn it.

When my childhood hobby disappeared, the book did, too. But a few months ago I visited a puppetry festival and learned that the book had been a bible to budding puppeteers all over the world. After being out of print for forty years, it had just been republished. I sent away for it, and checked the mail every day for weeks, the way I once did for my Snap, Crackle and Pop hand-puppets (twenty-five cents and one Rice Krispies boxtop). When I finally saw it again, I almost swooned from the pure pleasure of holding my childhood in my hands.

Diane Francis (writer)

I loved Dr. Seuss books. They were funny and off-the-wall and colourful and instructive. They were like comic books with cartoon characters between hardcovers. They were big. They were beautiful.

My favourites were *Horton Hatches the Egg*, *How the Grinch Stole Christmas*, *The Cat in the Hat* and *Green Eggs and Ham*. My Seuss books occupied a special place in the little bedroom I shared with my sister. They were kept on a shelf between our twin beds back in Skokie, Illinois.

Unlike any other books I read as a child, my small Dr. Seuss collection was something that I read and reread. Needless to say, I bought them for my two children and will buy them again if I have grandchildren.

Mark Tewksbury (Olympic gold medallist, swimming)

When I was a child I was fascinated by the Dr. Seuss collection of books. Many stand out, but one in particular, *Oh, the Thinks You Can Think!*, reminds me of my childhood. One of my aunts gave the book to me when I was five years old and it made a lasting impression on me. Obviously, the book is not a literary classic, but the story and the pictures taught me at a very young age about the power of dreams and imagination. Dr. Seuss, perhaps better than any other children's author, creates not only fantastic stories that capture a child's imagination, he also illustrates his stories with characters and images that are colourful and original. Beginning a Dr. Seuss book for me as a child was like entering a far-away land of fantasy and excitement. I could never predict where the next page would take me, but somehow it always seemed to be even more outrageous and fun than the previous one.

What did this teach me? The closing page of *Oh, the Thinks You Can Think!* best summarizes the lesson: "Think left and think right and think low and think high. Oh, the THINKS you can think if you only try!" The last four words stuck with me for a long time. If you only try! Perhaps subconsciously I learned that anything is possible. But you have to think about it, try, create the impossible and make it possible. This would eventually take me to the heights of Olympic champion, but it all started as a child in the world of the Rink-Rinker-Rink, by spending a night in Na-Nupp, and by thinking about why a Beft will always go left. By using my imagination early in life I was able to continue to dream as I grew older. The world of Dr. Seuss ignited that ability in me.

Sheila Copps (Minister of Canadian Heritage)

I have always loved reading, and I am delighted my daughter, Danelle, derives the same enjoyment from curling up with a book as I did at her age.

It's tough to pick just one favourite book, so I have chosen two—one as a daughter and one as a mother!

Temagami Guide, by Jack Hambleton, is a story of life in Northern Ontario, near my father's home town. This book fascinated me and made my imagination race. And now, each time I visit Canada's wondrous northern regions, I think back fondly about that time and, most of all, about my dad.

As a mother, I have read one particular book to Danelle so many times, she and I both know it by heart! The book is *Love You Forever*, by Robert Munsch, and it is a wonderful way for both children and adults to understand the circle of life. Not very often does a book produce both a smile and a tear, but this one certainly does.

Roy Romanow (Premier of Saskatchewan)

My parents, Mike and Tekla Romanow, came to Canada from Ukraine where there is a rich tradition of oral literature for children. And so, my fondest memories are of the lyrical Ukrainian folk-stories that are passed on from generation to generation. Most of these are tales of mystery and magic that end with the victory of good over evil.

Ukrainian folklore for children has a strong educational purpose, but what I remember best is the sound of my mother's voice, warm and confident, as she brought the vivid images and playful language of these tales to life. Storytime not only connected my sister, Ann, and me with our heritage, it drew us together as a family, and inspired us with the strong belief that good always triumphs over evil.

Mark Thurman (writer/illustrator)

As an adult I love reading books—books on all sorts of subjects. I didn't always like reading, partly because I was a slow reader, and because reading and sharing books wasn't part of my family life.

As a kid I drew characters and stories constantly. Reading and writing words seemed so slow and complicated, especially compared to drawing. I read books only when I had to—at school.

Our public school didn't have a library, but fortunately we were within walking distance of the Parliament Street public library. There a wonderful librarian, Helen Stubbs, read to us. Some of the stories became my favourites, and I took them out of the library to read at home: Dr. Seuss's *The 500 Hats of Bartholomew Cubbins*, Wanda Gág's *Millions of Cats*, H.A. Rey's Curious George books, and Virginia Lee Burton's *The Little House*.

In grade 7 our home-room teacher, Alan Gordon, told us stories. In the morning he told part of a story, and if we worked hard, he would finish the story before we went home. He was an excellent storyteller, because most days the work was done, even by the worst students.

Just how important these two people were in my life only became apparent years later, when I started writing and illustrating picture books.

Thank you, Helen Stubbs! Thank you, Alan Gordon!

Maryann Kovalski (writer/illustrator)

There was a book that's probably no longer in print that stays with me still and creeps into my mind often at the oddest times. It was one of those thousands of children's books that gets printed and forgotten, considered a disappointment by those who published it because it didn't become a classic. I'm ashamed to admit this, but as a child I didn't pay attention to titles or authors' names. I'd just meander through the shelves at the library. If I liked a book's cover and the way it felt in my hands, I'd open it. If the illustrations captivated me (I'd flip through chapter books searching for the lovely moment when I'd find a black-and-white line drawing) and if the typeface was satisfying (big fat serif type with little cartouche drawings at the chapter heads) and the feel of the paper (I preferred thick newsprint) and the smell of the binding, I'd take it out.

When I was nine, I found the book that was all of the above. It was about three little girls whose parents went out for the evening (to the theatre, I think) and allowed them to be alone without a babysitter. They made spaghetti with meatballs. All the lights went out and they ate their meal in the dark by candlelight. I checked the book out often and stared at the illustration of the three of them sitting around a checkered tablecloth with a candle stuck in a wine bottle, behind them darkness all around. I wanted to do that so much. I wanted so to be in the illustration. My parents never went anywhere, much less to the theatre. But more than that, I wanted to be in that atmosphere, away from adults and the pressure of school.

It's funny the way that image has stayed with me and how I long to be there still. To this day, whenever I feel life to be too much or need comfort, I search out the simplest Italian restaurants with those checkered tablecloths that every stylish foodie would sneer at and order spaghetti, and always it works—I'm comforted and I feel myself to be as close to being in that picture as I'll ever get.

It's not profound. I wasn't politicized. I wasn't changed from Saul to Paul. But I wouldn't be surprised if I became a children's book illustrator because of it. And it may be why I've so stubbornly retained my parochial palate, to my husband's despair.

Nino Ricci (writer)

The first book I ever owned, and perhaps the seminal one of my life, was a rather hefty text called *The Guiding Light* that told the story of the Catholic Bible in pictures and captions. It was presented to me at my birth by a group of merchants in my home town, no doubt anxious for my future patronage (though most of them have since either died or gone under); and it has accompanied me on my life journey ever since.

In my early years, the book's primary usefulness was in its providing a few blank pages here and there for me to execute, in crayon and magic marker, various failed attempts at artistic expression. But I eventually came to the point where I was able to read the thing, and its stories and images, for good or ill, became the backdrop against which all my future experience was set. It was from *The Guiding Light*, for instance, that I got my first notion of female nakedness, through the depiction of Eve in the story of Eden (though the lushness of the garden, what with its waist-high flowers and breast-high tree limbs, unfortunately obscured some of the more interesting aspects of Eve's anatomy); and it was here also that I learned of the chastisements of hell, of the gruesome martyrdoms of the apostles and saints, and of the great love that God showed in allowing his only son to be nailed to a cross and left to hang there till he was dead. The images I was left with were ones that in later life frequently served as inspiration for my own writing, and also often recurred to me in the many years I subsequently spent in therapy.

I am not aware if *The Guiding Light*, which was published in 1955 by Greystone Press in New York and was edited by the Right Reverend Monsignor Dante del Fiorentino, is still in print; I fear it might not have survived the reforming influences of the Second Vatican Council. But for terror, sexual intrigue and sheer adventure, parents could do worse for their children than to offer them, in some form, the stories of the Bible.

Bronwyn Drainie (writer/broadcaster)

I must have read *Ballet Shoes* (by Noel Streatfeild) at least a dozen times between the ages of eight and ten. I remember reaching the end of the book and turning back to page one without so much as a bathroom break. I remember my mother pulling the book out of my hands the summer of my ninth year, saying, "Read something else, for heaven's sake!"

Why such passion and obsession? First of all, the story was English and full of exotic details like gasfires and tram conductors and high tea. American books always felt flat and familiar, while English ones were incredibly romantic. But *Ballet Shoes* was also about child performers and since I was already a star-struck little creature (my parents were both actors) it was the perfect book to fuel my fantasies.

It was the story of three orphans, Pauline, Petrova and Posy, who were collected and brought home by an eccentric paleontologist who lived in the Cromwell Road in London. (See what I mean by exotic? These girls lived *in the Cromwell Road* whereas I lived *on Harper Avenue* in Toronto.) Their orphan status alone was enough to set my imagination in motion, but their devotion to the life of the stage was what made them heroines. You see, after dumping the girls back at his London house, which was being maintained by a bevy of nieces and cooks and nannies, the paleontologist conveniently disappeared again for years on his travels and forgot to send money. So the big old Victorian house soon filled up with boarders, and the three little girls had to help out with the household expenses by joining the Children's Academy of Dancing and Stage Training.

Imagine their lives, as I did over and over. First of all, no parents to boss them about. Second of all, no school! Instead they did lessons at home in the morning with two of the boarders, who were retired university professors. Third, they had dancing classes every day and acting classes on Saturday mornings. And once they were trained, there were plays and pantomimes and even film work, for which they received pounds and shillings and guineas that got deposited in the post office, not the bank.

The dilemma for me was always which of the three girls to identify with. Posy was the youngest and a born dancer, so that let her out. Pauline was the eldest and destined to be a great actress, so she was naturally my idol, but she was too beautiful and self-assured to be a role model. I was astonished by her arrogant behaviour, for example, when she was playing *Alice in Wonderland* one Christmas season, and refused to wear her dressing-gown over her costume backstage, a hard and fast theatrical rule. She was chastised first by the stage manager and then by the producer, but she wouldn't back down until they yanked her out of the show and put in her understudy for the next performance. Pride certainly went before a fall in *Ballet Shoes*, but I was more impressed by the amount of self-confidence it took to indulge in that kind of pride in the first place. I knew I could never manage it.

That's where Petrova came in. Instead of being blonde and beautiful like Pauline, she was dark and serious and of Russian extraction, and she had no desire and no particular ability to be on the stage at all. She only did it to help out with her share of the household bills.

She lost more auditions than she ever won and always ended up with thankless non-speaking roles, like cats and moonbeams, that bored her to tears. And she was eaten up with self-doubt about her ability to cope in a world of talent when she appeared to have none. (Of course she did have a talent, for all things mechanical, especially motor-cars, which didn't interest me in the slightest.)

So I identified with a combination of Pauline's dreams and Petrova's doubts, and I have continued to do so to this day. I realize now, as I didn't then, that the author was conveying to her young readers the struggle between ambition and limitations that human life is subject to, and that the important thing was to be sensible and English about it all, not to let the ambition carry you hopelessly high (like Icarus) nor to let the limitations drag you hopelessly low (like Sartre and Baudelaire and all those other, mostly French, philosophical stick-in-the-muds). Cheerful determination in the face of adversity, that was the message of *Ballet Shoes*: a worthy life attitude but trickier to maintain than I could have possibly imagined at age nine.

Joy Kogawa (writer)

It would be hard to pick which of the three books I remember from Slocan that I loved the most. I cherished each one: *Heidi* by Johanna Spyri, *Little Men* by Louisa May Alcott and the blue hardcover *Highroads to Reading Book Two*. I was six years old in 1942 when our family, along with the rest of our community in British Columbia, were shipped inland to an internment centre. We were limited in what we could take. How or why my parents chose those three books for me out of my vast library of picture books and story books, I do not know. But I believe they chose wisely and well. We had no school that first year and the books became my dearest treasures. I read them over and over and over. I loved the mountains and the whispering of the pines because Heidi did. I had the companionship and shared the adventures of the boys in *Little Men*. Kindness and happiness and wonder came to me in the books and my hungry heart was filled.

But apart from those three, there is an earlier memory that speaks to me of another book. It would have been 1939 or 1940. I was four years old. We lived in Marpole, Vancouver. There was a Gospel Hall down the street that I went to on Sunday afternoons, after attending Sunday School at our Japanese Anglican church in Kitsilano.

On this particular afternoon a man, a stranger, lifted me up and placed me just to the left of centre stage. It was too weird for words.

For one thing, I wasn't used to being picked up. I could walk perfectly well. For another thing, I'd never before stood alone on a stage and faced a crowd.

I knew what I was supposed to do and I did it. The meaningless sounds came out of my mouth, one word at a time, until it was done: "John 3:16—For God so loved the world that He gave His only begotten Son that whosoever believeth in Him should not perish but have everlasting life."

I was lifted down from the place of torment when the ordeal was over. Later, outside, one of the Steeves boys said, "I saw you crying up there," and I knew it wasn't true. I may have trembled and quaked, but I didn't cry.

And so the earliest book was probably the Bible and there were Bible stories—Noah's ark, Adam and Eve, Jacob and Esau, Joseph, Abraham, Moses and Jesus, of course, and Zacchaeus up the tree and Paul, Peter, James and John. This cloud community lived in a country to which I was granted the kind of passport that cannot be lost. It's tattooed in my heart. I'm grateful for it. It has given me the keys to English literature. It has also shown me the complex human face that wears good and evil.

Today, thanks to feminism, I can question that mental edifice constructed by men. I can also grapple with the roots of anti-Semitism in the early Christian writings. At the same time, I acknowledge the call to journey and the cry for freedom that informs so many of the stories. Perhaps for me, the first step of my freedom-hungry journey began with the Bible, which, among other things, is a book of stories that talks about journeying.

Douglas Fisher (journalist)

Easy—the two books were Ontario "readers" which my father had kept from his early 1890 school days near Grand Valley. He would read the poems and stories to me in the evening while also teaching me to read: I could read every one of the second and third book contents well before I went to school at age six. Above all, I treasured the poems of action like "Young Lochinvar" or of tragic events like "The White Ship" or the "Inchcape Rock" or the short story of the brave serf who threw himself into a pack of pursuing wolves, enabling his mistress and her child to reach safety in their horse-drawn sleigh.

The most pathetic piece, the one that still starts tears in my eyes at remembrance, is about the tracks in the snow which lead to the creek where little Lucie Gray drowned. For humour I recall the *One Horse Shay* and *Grandfather's Clock*.

They were dull books in externals but wings of imagination within.

Katherine Govier (writer)

My mother read to all three of us when we were children. I loved A.A. Milne's Winnie-the-Pooh stories, mostly because it fascinated me to see my mother tied up in paroxysms of laughter over words on a page. In particular I adored the bit when Piglet fell down the hole and was so terrified he mixed up his words, and cried out "Help help a Herrible Hoffalump," etc.

My older sister had German measles and scarlet fever when I was perhaps seven, and I was supposed to sit in the room with her so I would catch it, and therefore have *had* it, so I wouldn't catch it later (this was the logic of the fifties). During that time my mother read aloud to us a novel set in Scotland called *Lad with a Whistle*, and we all wept copious tears. It was a wonderful book, and has now disappeared entirely from circulation. I did not catch scarlet fever or German measles.

After I could write my name in cursive, I was allowed to search out my own books in the adult section of the library. One of my first discoveries was Victor Hugo's *Les Misérables* in English translation. I read it, gripped in horror at the life of persecution which followed Jean Valjean's theft of a loaf of bread. It certainly turned me off any thoughts I might have had of pursuing a life of petty crime.

Judy Stoffman (journalist)

When I was a child in Hungary, before the Hungarian uprising of 1956 caused my family to immigrate to Canada, books were few and precious. We had a volume of *Grimm's Fairy Tales*, Kipling's *Jungle Book* and *Just So Stories*, and a book of Hungarian folk-tales. The folk-tales usually involved brave and clever Magyar peasant boys outwitting the infidel Turks. Hungary had been conquered by the Ottoman Turks in the sixteenth century and the iniquity of this is inculcated in children through storytelling practically from birth.

These choice volumes were kept in my parents' apartment in Budapest, while I lived for the most part in the village of Gyömrö with my maternal grandmother and grandfather, since my mother did not trust the state-run day-care system in the city to look after her only child while she worked.

Life in the village was in some ways idyllic, yet all week, until it was time to take the train to the city, I hungered for stories as much as I hungered for the embrace of my mother and father waiting for me at the Keleti station on Saturday.

When I was seven or eight I heard a story on a children's program on the radio in Gyömrö, unlike any I had read or had read to me before. It was about a beautiful little mermaid who could sing like an angel. She falls in love with a human prince when she saves him from drowning after his ship is wrecked. To be with him, she makes a Faustian bargain with the wicked Sea Witch: she will give her enchanting voice to the witch in return for a pair of legs.

Now mute, she leaves her ocean home to find her Prince. The Prince takes her into his castle, telling her she looks a lot like the girl who saved his life. She dances for him, though every step feels as if she is dancing on knives, but she is unable to tell him of her love or of her true identity.

When the Prince tells her he will soon marry another, she returns, heartbroken, to the ocean and is transformed into foam.

This story, "The Little Mermaid," was my introduction to the world of complex adult emotions. It showed me the meaning of love, of self-sacrifice, of tragedy—of the power of narrative to shake the soul. I cried for an entire day. Every word of it seared itself into my brain. I did not know, then, that it had been written by Hans Christian Andersen, or that it was one of the most famous children's stories in the world.

It also filled me with rage and frustration. Why, tell me why, I shouted at my grandmother, did the Mermaid not write down for the Prince on a piece of paper who she was? She couldn't speak, but she could have explained it in writing, couldn't she?

I rejected the idea, and still do, that we each have an inescapable fate.

It's an outrage that many children today only know this story in the Disney version, which I understand has a sugar-coated happy ending. Never would I take my son and daughter to see it.

The little mermaid taught me that love involves pain and requires heroism. She also taught me that being a good writer could save your life.

Fred Penner (family singer, songwriter)

I believe we have children for many different reasons, perhaps as a need to share our lives and pass on our perspectives and inspirations, and perhaps even for a moment to relive our own childhood.

Often my children say or do something...and I twinge...and recall that same something. There is a reassurance that comes from that feeling. It doesn't always happen, because my busyness as an adult and parent can block the easy entry into that innocent world. But the connection happens more frequently when I hear music or read books that prod my recollections.

I think of Hans Christian Andersen and nursery rhymes, Danny Kaye and Disney, but the classic tale of *The Velveteen Rabbit*, by Margery Williams Bianco, gets as close to the animistic world of the child as it is possible to do. The reading and rereading of this book instantly sparks that youthful joy and sensitivity.

The Velveteen Rabbit is fun to read, has exciting story development and I particularly like the "life lessons" and "real" meaning and insights that are implied throughout.

I am a musician, and I relate much of what I read to music. A melody can come off a written page for me, just from the sounds of the words. *The Velveteen Rabbit* makes the warmest of chords.

Sara Botsford (actor)

Every morning after my brother and sister had gone off to school, my mother and I had our "ringlet session." I would stand in the bathroom, facing the mirror, and my mother would stand behind me, first brushing my hair into a big topknot, then wrapping the hair around her finger to create a ringlet. She would then work her way around the rest of my head making smaller ringlets around her finger, and would finish off the entire "do" with an enormous ribbon around the topknot. The entire procedure took about twenty minutes to complete, and in order to keep me still, she would read to me.

Each day, I chose the book and placed it, open, on the sink so that she could see it over my head.

Each day, I chose the same book.

Each day, I chose *L'il Hannibal.*

L'il Hannibal was a young African-American boy who lived with his grandparents in the deep South, and feeling over-burdened and under-appreciated because of his endless chores, he ran away to spend the day in the forest with the local talking animals. All day long he watched as they gathered food and prepared an enormous feast, of which they all partook. Since he had not taken part in the preparation, he was not invited to share their food, and so, tired and hungry, he made his way home through the darkened forest, and was greatly relieved to see his grandpappy on the porch, calling him to supper, and asking him if he had fed the chickens.

Now, I was a girl from Northern Ontario, who had probably never seen an African-American, was the spoiled baby of three and so had no chores to speak of, and had never, at that point in my life, had even the vaguest impulse to run away. I have no idea why this book spoke to me as it did. Could it have been the wonderfully imaginative bickering of the animals as they created their feast, or the vivid, tantalizing descriptions of the food? I'm not sure. I only know that my poor mother was required to read that book long after its every word was indelibly printed in her memory, and that I, to this day, search for a copy of this book in every city I go to; in every rare-book store I see, in the hopes of finding it, and sharing it with my children.

I can no longer remember the details of the story, but I can remember the feelings of being inside L'il Hannibal's life as if it were my own.

Ian Wallace (writer/illustrator)

Over the past two decades I have spoken to young people and adults of my fondness for *The Wind in the Willows* by Kenneth Grahame. The characters who inhabit that memorable tale lie at the heart of my earliest and most potent reading experience in the comfort and security of my family. As I ventured beyond the pages of that classic book, and began the rewarding adventure of choosing books to read on my own, I felt great affection for *Little Black Sambo* by Helen Bannerman, a book that has fallen from grace with a realm of concerned critics, educators, librarians and parents. As a novice reader I never picked up on the racist undertones that are now felt to haunt its pages. I embraced the protagonist and his magical adventure with the wonder, enthusiasm and purity enjoyed only by the young.

Little Black Sambo was the *Where the Wild Things Are* of my youth. The brave protagonist, Sambo, lived in an exotic place far beyond the ends of my own maple-lined street. He dressed in clothes more brilliantly coloured than my own, or my two brothers', or our friends', and he wore mysterious shoes with crimson soles and crimson linings. He carried a grand umbrella to keep the Indian sun, not Canadian rain, off his head. Most importantly, Sambo followed in the literary tradition of the universal character who makes an emotional link to his reader. I empathized with Sambo's fear of the tigers who threatened to eat him up, and admired his bravery when confronting them. I was in awe of the magic powers of the tiger's anger that could whirl and whip flesh and blood and bone into warm yellow butter or ghee. I was delighted by the gift Sambo's father was able to present to his family at the tale's end. I could almost taste the sweet melting butter on the stack of warm pancakes that "were just as yellow and brown as little tigers."

That simple tale opened the cultural door in my life just a crack. My experience with people of colour was extremely narrow as a boy growing up in Niagara Falls in the 1950s. Only one Black family lived relatively near my home, and East Indians had not yet arrived in my community. That lone family was exotic and foreign in the same distinctive sense of other families who lived in my neighbourhood—Italians, Ukrainians, Germans—except that the Black family had skin that was far richer and darker compared to all the others and to my own. I was intrigued by how all those people lived, worked and played. How they loved and what made them laugh. I was fascinated by the language they spoke among themselves that kept countless secrets and stories beyond my comprehension. I was delighted by the aromatic foods they ate and, if I was lucky, would share with me.

In the years that followed there were other books that supplemented the treasured reading experience of *Little Black Sambo*. They, too, were significant books that added to the rich cultural mosaic of my reading youth, and young adulthood. Over time those books brought about an understanding of the universalities and the differences among us that mark us as human. Sadly others would infect the world I was entering with echoes of the racism inherent in many societies.

Today *Little Black Sambo* still burns fondly in my memory. And each time that I revisit that exotic place, I approach it with much the same wonder, enthusiasm and purity, but tempered by time and history.

·2· Adventure Stories

"The bright face of danger"
—Robert Louis Stevenson

One theory of childhood suggests that growing up is a process of overcoming obstacles. No sooner is one challenge overcome than the next appears. Perhaps that begins to explain the enormous and enduring popularity of dramatic stories of adventure and survival.

Youngsters too young to cross the street by themselves may, safe between the covers of a book, vicariously travel the high seas, explore far-away lands and brave great danger. Michele Landsberg calls adventure tales "surrogate journeys into the wonderful world." Although both children and grownups tend to respond positively to dashing heroes and exciting plots, for young imaginations the suspension of disbelief is frequently more pure and effortless. Unsuspicious and accepting of the far-fetched and fantasic, children eagerly transport themselves into the story. Thus liberated from fear and restriction, they easily identify with stimulating characters who remarkably endure all manner of hardship and turmoil.

It is quite possible that no book has provided a more lasting or thoroughly satisfying adventure than Daniel Defoe's *Robinson Crusoe* (1719). This famous survival story offers a panorama of spine-tingling episodes. (Defoe's was not, of course, the first adventure/survival story. Noah endures and overcomes a flood in the Bible. *The Iliad* and *The Odyssey* are spectacular adventures—incorporating danger, ingenuity, heroism, spectacular enemies, threatening battles and much more.

Robin Hood and King Arthur, among other heroes, share a good deal of excitement with their loyal followers including noble crusades, high drama and romantic ideals.)

But *Robinson Crusoe* is the quintessential adventure story. Not originally intended for children, the suffering Crusoe may have partially sown the seeds of his own misfortunes—shipwreck, storms, illness, invaders, etc.—as punishment for disobeying the career wishes of his father. Young readers care not at all for the reasons, and embrace each breathtaking event not as a difficulty but as an exciting new challenge. The novel's realistic framework blends convincingly with its unceasing conflict and tension. There are charts and records, even a map! For kids, the danger and struggles are the very centre of it all, the best part, the heart of the story.

The capacity to engage the reader is the critical ingredient of the successful adventure story. Charged readers become ardent supporters and covert companions of, in this case, Crusoe, on his deserted island. Although in reality they are secure in their homes with a book on their lap, in their mind's eye, they are struggling and winning in harmony with their hero, simultaneously overcoming each hardship along with him.

Children instinctively concede the practical obstacles and day-to-day problems of the protagonist's situation. They are familiar with constant surprises and daily challenges all their own. They grasp the need for resourcefulness—imagination being the most helpful response in such extraordinary circumstances. They understand and empathize with, for instance, Crusoe's sense of inadequacy. Budding artists, builders and sculptors themselves, children identify with his primitive but gradually improving attempts to make furniture, tools, pottery, art.

Fulfilling basic needs—shelter, food gathering and preparation, as well as bravely coping with threatening situations and seemingly never-ending crises—has been the bread and butter of adventure stories ever since. Whatever complex theories might explain the attraction, the bottom line is that kids continue to love them.

Adventure stories tend to be fast-paced, full of conflict and action. Most are plot rather than character driven, but there are notable exceptions. Ingenuous protagonists, both adults and children, may be pitted against the elements, other people or a combination of both. Jonathan Swift's *Gulliver's Travels* (1726) is an early example of a humorous and fantastic adventure. While kids identify quite easily with Crusoe, they are also, as observed by Paul Hazard, very much like Gulliver. They tumble clumsily from event to event, sometimes as little people (to towering adults, the complex world of grownup words and concepts, the great outdoors) and sometimes as giants (to their toys, pets, flowers and insects). Kids are bigger than a book, but smaller than the story within its pages.

Johann Wyss's *The Swiss Family Robinson*, patterned after Robinson Crusoe, was published in 1812. Although now sorely dated in tone and style, it exhibits many elements of the traditional adventure story: close-calls, strange meetings, difficult situations in need of rapid solution.

Realistic at their core, adventure stories tend to blend believable people and places with extraordinary events. Like fairy tales or folktales, they often begin with a young man in search of his fortune; there may be a quest, sometimes a guide or talisman. There are inevitably tests along the way, and to the reader's relief, a triumphant conclusion.

The hero is almost always a young man, but more recent heroines such as Karana in Scott O'Dell's *Island of the Blue Dolphin* (1960) or the young Inuit heroine of Jean Craighead George's *Julie of the Wolves* (1972) are memorable exceptions. *Island of the Blue Dolphin* may be the best-known American twentieth-century survival story. It is based on the true story of an Indian girl who survived alone, for eighteen years, on an island near California. *Julie of the Wolves* is also well on its way to becoming a classic. George eloquently expresses the inner struggle of a young girl pitted between her native heritage and the beckoning ways and attractions of the white people's world.

Adventure stories are frequently set in exotic, foreign locations—at sea, at war, in far-away lands. This adds the romance of distance to the drama and excitement. Many were written in the nineteenth century, a time of imperial expansion, patriotism and noble ideals. There is often a sense of freedom—a deliberate loosening of the strict rules of the civilized behaviour, dress and manners expected in, for example, Victorian England.

There are, of course, many variations. A few, like Edith Nesbit's *The Story of the Treasure Seekers*, allow enterprising Victorian children to participate in milder escapades closer to home. The French author Jules Verne introduced science-based adventure fiction, successfully blending geography and natural science with exploration and compelling fantasy. His *Journey to the Centre of the Earth* (1864) and *20,000 Leagues under the Sea* (1869) have enormously affected the diverse realms of science fiction, conservation and film-making. His richly satisfying books continue to delight generations of adults and children.

Contemporary readers gobbled up Howard Pyle's swashbuckling, romanticized (and beautifully self-illustrated) *The Merry Adventures of Robin Hood* (1883) as well as his four volumes of chivalrous and inspiring Arthurian legends. American Mark Twain's *The Adventures of Tom Sawyer* (1876) and *The Adventures of Huckleberry Finn* (1884) took dramatic fiction peppered with adventure to new heights (and mass popularity) through narrative power, literary craftsmanship and memorable characters.

One of the best known late-nineteenth-century writers of breath-taking adventure fiction is Robert Louis Stevenson, whose *Treasure Island* (1883) and *Kidnapped* (1886) are acknowledged classics of great scope. *Treasure Island*'s hero, Jim, is on a dangerous quest for buried treasure. He must overcome a variety of villains (including the still infamous Long John Silver) as well as contend with relentless adversity. In both novels, along with dazzling narrative, Stevenson has imbued his characters with depth and complexity. This helps explain the longevity and enduring appeal of his remarkable stories.

Because of its large and overwhelming landscape, Canada has long been a popular setting for sagas of adventure, escape and survival. The opportunity suggested by our mighty rivers, huge mountains, wild animals, stunning landscape and extreme weather suggested Canada as a natural location for stories of perseverance and battling the elements. The first gripping tales were by British authors, some of whom never set foot on Canadian soil.

While few have historically met the standards of the great classic adventure novels, it is especially stirring for Canadian kids to read exciting stories set in our own "exotic" wilderness or far north. American Gary Paulsen gave two stirring survival stories, *The Hatchet* and its sequel, *The River*, Canadian settings. The backwoods are sometimes not very far from familiar towns and cities. Tim Wynne-Jones's *The Maestro* (1996) is a modern example that works splendidly. It begins with a young man's personal struggle with his violent and abusive father, building to a heart-stopping conclusion that adeptly incorporates elements (danger, escape and survival) of the traditional adventure story.

Writers like R.M. Ballantyne and G.A. Henty were extremely popular in their day but are read far less frequently now. They each composed numerous adventure stories incorporating idealism and lofty values, including courage, decisive action and respect for the land and native peoples. Ballantyne spent six years (1841–1847) working for the Hudson's Bay Company. His enthusiasm for this country is evident in the first two of his many books, both set in Canada: *The Young Fur Traders* (1856) and *Ungava: A Tale of Esquimaux-Land*

(1858). Henty, also British, was a vigorous and prolific writer. His *With Wolfe in Canada* (1887), which reflects the viewpoint of American historian Francis Parkman, is one of very few children's books about the conflict between French and English.

Captain Frederick Marryat spent a brief time in Canada in 1837. The unhappily uprooted family in his *The Settlers in Canada* (1844) hurry back as soon as possible to the civilized society and predictable comfort of their British home. One dauntless son elects to remain in Canada. He lives with native and other friends, acquiring important survival skills that assist him in coping with the great outdoors.

The early Canadian adventure story often featured a white boy and his native friend. Characters are frequently idealized and stereotyped. The native child, for example, is almost always wise in the ways of the forest and more "centred" than the impulsive and less thoughtful other child. Both characters struggle to get along, to appreciate each other's talents and to adapt to their surroundings. These stories represent the beginnings of a focus on environmental issues using positive role models. Sadly, there are few girls along for the fun. Stevenson wrote *Treasure Island* for one particular child, his stepson. He exclusively promised "a story for boys, no need of psychology or fine writing... [and] Women were to be excluded"!

Similar stereotyping is evident in the swashbuckling novels of popular American writer James Fenimore Cooper—noble heroes, stoic Indians, women (when they appear at all) almost invariably in need of rescue. These stories set a pattern endlessly repeated in many a Hollywood western—wild-frontier movies made over a century later. Cooper is best known for *The Last of the Mohicans* (1826).

Catharine Parr Traill wrote the first Canadian children's novel and it is, not surprisingly, an adventure story. *Canadian Crusoes* (1852), in more than its title, pays tribute to Defoe's seminal classic. But *Canadian Crusoes* (although set around Cobourg, Ontario, a locale somewhat less exotic than a deserted island) shares with *Robinson Crusoe* what Sheila Egoff describes as "the irresistible stuff of the isolation story: the procuring of food, shelter and clothing and the need for protection against the elements, wild animals and unfriendly natives." The young protagonists, two fourteen-year-old boys and a twelve-year-old girl (!) show gritty determination and great courage. Unfortunately, the dialogue is rather stiff and the language too lush for current taste.

James De Mille was the first major writer for children actually born in Canada. He wrote a series of adventure stories beginning with *The B.O.W.C. (Brethren of the White Cross)* (1869), followed by several others including *Lost in the Fog* (1870), *Fire in the Woods* (1871) and *The Treasure of the Seas* (1873). Egoff describes his books as "insouciant stories of boy life, carefree and amusing as opposed to the cult of 'manliness,' and noticeably free from didacticism, both religious and instructional."

Despite their quality, Defoe's *Robinson Crusoe* and Swift's *Gulliver's Travels* inspired many pretenders but few successful imitations. Sir Walter Scott was one writer who successfully kept the genre alive and extremely popular. His *Ivanhoe* (1820) was an acclaimed romantic adventure, once again written for adults but eagerly adopted by children.

Around the middle and later half of the nineteenth century, children's literature in general—including adventure fiction—definitely began to pick up. (Charles Dickens published his momentous *Great Expectations* in 1861.) While not technically adventure stories, his tales of hardship such as *Hard Times* and *Oliver Twist* exposed the plight of poor urban children exploited yet resilient in their exciting and sympathetic quest for survival.

By the time Twain's *Tom Sawyer* and *Huckleberry Finn* took the literary world by storm, the dry spell was definitely over. Not long after, Rudyard Kipling's atmospheric adventure/fantasies about Mowgli, a "wild" child raised by wolves and trained by a bear and a panther, enthralled wide-eyed readers of *The Jungle Book* (1894) and *The Second Jungle Book* (1895). They have continued to fascinate and impress for more than a century.

The exotic orphan adventurer *Kim* (1901) was adopted by a Tibetan lama, prowled Indian bazaars, wore numerous disguises and spied on the Russians. Infinite mystery is combined with adventure in this heroic quest. These books are, in my opinion, stunning classics, works of literature that delight readers of all ages.

In Canada, adventure persisted as a popular form for fiction for children, though never on so high a plane. In 1890 and 1891 respectively, James MacDonald Oxley (from Halifax) wrote two rollicking adventure stories with no higher purpose than escape and entertainment (*Up among the Ice Floes* and *The Wreckers of Sable Island*). C. Phillipps-Wolley's *Gold, Gold in the Caribou: A Story of Adventure in British Columbia* (1894) sounds good but was apparently predictable and short on characterization. Also considered dull were Marjorie Pickthall's attempts at adventure stories such as *Dick's Desertion* (1905). More successful was Egerton Ryerson Young's *Three Boys in the Wild North Land Summer* (1896), a winter sequel in 1899, and *Children of the Forest: A Story of Indian Love* (1904).

One of the best Canadian adventure stories of the period was Ernest Thompson Seton's *Two Little Savages* (1903), a book that has suffered from its unfortunate title. Two boys pretending to be "Indians" learn valuable skills without didactic overload. The narrative is lively and entertaining. In this turn-of-the-century novel of happy pretending, Seton foreshadows Arthur Ransome and his warm and distinctive Swallows and Amazons series.

Ransome's twelve wonderfully detailed books are grounded in the security of a stable Edwardian family on summer vacation in England's Lake District. They have been chosen as favourites by several contributors to this book. Ransome breaks the traditional children's book code by dauntlessly mixing classes, age-groups and genders, and creating a distinctive and enchanting combination of reality and fantasy. The results are spectacular. His books feature resourceful, imaginative boys and girls who share their talents. Ransome strategically introduces practical tips about sailing and camping. All the while, the children are exploring, fantasizing and participating in endless and elaborate group games. They convincingly court and accidentally fall into occasional danger, pretend piracy, high-seas and other adventures. The books remain popular because of their well-drawn and sympathetic personalities, emotional realism, lucid prose, good humour and interesting plots. Problems are almost always resolved with spirit, creativity and, best of all, minimum intervention from the grownups.

Ralph Connor is the pseudonym for Reverend Charles William Gordon. His *Glengarry School Days* (1902) is still relished by children and teachers despite (or perhaps because of) its description of everyday exploits anchored in school experience while growing up in rural Ontario in the 1860s. Canada is credited with founding the "school adventure" story, a genre currently manifested in many school-centred stories, from the hilarious, reader-friendly novels of Gordon Korman or Mary Blakeslee to the gritty and stimulating Ran-Van trilogy by Diana Wieler.

Canadian adventure stories in the early twentieth century included novels like *The Adventures of Billy Topsail* (1906), a fast-paced Newfoundland sea story about a boy and his dog that is well remembered because it was often reprinted in school readers. British adventure stories took an historic turn with a number of wonderful books set largely in Roman and Saxon times by Rosemary Suttcliff. The dramatic and realistically detailed *Eagle of the Ninth* (also a school text) startlingly brought to life the people and predicaments of a far-away era. Suttcliff's many novels are, like Ransome's, still cherished for their convincing characters and emotional truth.

On this side of the Atlantic, character development and coming to grips with internal as well as external hardship gained ground in the stories of Canadian Roderick Haig-Brown. *Starbuck Valley Winter* (1943) and *Saltwater Summer* (1948) are two relatively modern and very readable Canadian young-adult novels set on the west coast.

Farley Mowat's fast-paced tales of heart-thumping suspense, survival in extreme conditions and respect for the northern Canadian landscape—its climate, the power of the land, its animals and its people—are classic adventures as stirring today as when they were written. *Lost in the Barrens* (1956), a northern survival story, and *The Black Joke* (1962) are typical examples.

Canada's most famous Arctic adventure writer is James Houston and his best-known survival story is *Tikta'liktak* (1965). It is about a young and determined Inuit boy who gets stuck on an ice floe. Based on an ancient legend, the story reflects the value and immediacy of the oral tradition. *The White Archer* (1967), *River Runners* (1979) and *Whiteout* (1988) are further examples of intensive spiritual journeys as well as powerful tales of survival and courage. Houston seamlessly combines the action and excitement of the traditional adventure motif with modern psychology, character development and introspection. His impressive canon includes numerous books immediately identified as adventures by their titles: *Frozen Fire: A Tale of Courage* (1977), *Black Diamonds: A Search for Arctic Treasure* (1982) and *Ice Swords: An Undersea Adventure* (1985). Houston's career has spanned over thirty years and he has illustrated most of his own books.

Among the first Canadian Inuit-written adventure stories published in English is the tragic but evocative *Harpoon of the Hunter* by Markoosie (1970). Immediate and straightforward in style, it is the antithesis of the traditional survival story. Undeniably moving and powerful, it is rather bleak in outcome and not for the faint-hearted. It breathes authenticity with resonant and symbolic undertones.

Today many stories for children and young adults incorporate elements of the classic adventure story. While incessant action is no longer typical, there are frequently formidable obstacles for the protagonist to overcome. Also, along with external challenges, numerous internal struggles—of will, confidence, identity and so on—are frequently incorporated into the plot.

Graham Fraser (writer, journalist)

I have a very vivid childhood memory. I was five, and my father was carrying me up to bed. He stopped at the bottom of the stairs and asked my brother, who was sixteen, "Do you think Graham is old enough for *Swallows and Amazons*?" Like all "is-he-old-enough" questions, this one was fraught with expectations, and my brother, who was already generous in spirit, apparently advised that I was. It was the beginning of an enchantment: my entry into the world of four Walker and two Blackett children that was as vivid and important a part of my childhood as bicycles or summer camp.

The magic in these books lies less in the genuine excitement than in the characters Arthur Ransome created, and the seriousness and respect with which he treats them. The first book was published in 1930, and they continued through the 1930s. They have been in print ever since.

There are two keys, I think, to the enchantment each book offers, beyond the traditional pleasures of reading an author so comfortable with the plot conventions of suspense. The first is Ransome's total lack of condescension to his characters or his readers. This emerges in his patience. Details matter. He describes the sailboats so carefully that it is possible to learn how to rig one, just by following his description. He is equally patient in describing how the tents were pitched, fires laid and meals cooked. He does not make fun of the imaginative games these children play, in the way that Mark Twain teases Tom Sawyer. He understood the rigour that was required in creating a shared world of the imagination; he was an heir to the same set of imaginative conventions that Baden-Powell used when he created the scouting movement.

The second striking thing is the respect that Ransome clearly had for girls. Boys, in fact, remain in the minority in the adventures. It is an asexual world; in twelve books, the children move into adolescence but remain as engaged in their adventure as they did in the first one. It is a reminder of how sexualized late childhood and adolescence have become, seven decades on; the unembarrassed, unchaperoned camaraderie of these young people seems almost other-worldly.

There were other books of my childhood that captured me and took me prisoner again and again; still others resonate as much from having read them aloud to my own sons as having had them read aloud to me. But few, if any, sustained me through the years of my childhood like the Ransome books. There was a constant interplay of lore and logic, imagination and practicality, storytelling and instruction. After reading them again and again, I felt I had learned the words to sea shanties, how to tie a bowline and how to treat people with respect.

Silver Donald Cameron (writer, broadcaster)

I'm probably best known for my books on the sea, ships, fishing and sailing, and I've often thought with amusement that my interest in the sea comes largely from the books I read as a child. Two authors stand out: Roderick Haig-Brown and Arthur Ransome.

Ransome was a fascinating man, I learned much later. He seems to have been something of a gentle naif, but an extremely gifted one—folklorist, foreign correspondent, café companion of the restless young Russians who ultimately formed the first Soviet government. In fact Ransome himself married Trotsky's secretary. He also wrote some good books for adults, including a couple of sailing books.

But I knew nothing of that when the librarian at Lord Kitchener Elementary School suggested that I might like to look at "the Ransome books." Ah yes, Lord Kitchener. We were a very British country in those days and Ransome's books were also very British. But I fell in love with the Swallows and Amazons series (so named for the title of the first book) and indeed I love them still.

Written in the 1930s, Ransome's books focus on several groups of English children who are passionately involved with boats and sailing. The Walker children have a dinghy named *Swallow*; the two Blackett girls have one called *Amazon*. Other children come and go in the series: Dick and Dorothea (fledgling scientist and writer, respectively), three working-class boys in *The Big Six*, and so on. And then there is Captain Flint, a.k.a. the Blacketts' Uncle Jim, every kid's dream uncle, who lives on a houseboat, joins the kids in their games, and later takes them with him on sailing voyages which reach as far as China.

Those books—there must be a dozen—are as vivid to me now as they were fifty years ago, even the few (like *Peter Duck*) which I have not reread. Returning to them in later life, I am struck by their innocence, which gives them a dated feel; child abuse, drugs, pornography and profanity were not then in the mainstream of polite literary conversation. But I am also struck by Ransome's narrative skill and literary quality. Not only does he manage the stories themselves with aplomb—though some of the plots are wildly implausible, he almost always achieves the necessary suspension of disbelief—but he also has a sure feel for the social milieu, a firm grasp of the characters, and an economical, clear and literate style.

Of them all, my favourite is probably *We Didn't Mean to Go to Sea*, in which the four Walker children, weekending aboard a friend's red-sailed cutter, find themselves swept out of Harwich by the tide while the owner is ashore. A gale arises, calling up all their reserves of skill and knowledge and courage, and in the morning, when the gale has cleared, they find they have saved the ship and themselves—and crossed the North Sea to Holland.

Astute readers will see some resemblance to my own young-adult novel, *The Baitchopper*, where two young boys in a fishing village are carried out to sea overnight aboard an inshore fishing boat, and in the morning, after a gale, make a landfall in a French-speaking Acadian village across the bay. And it might just occur to some clever sleuth that I cruise the Maritimes in a little red-sailed cutter myself, and that my first cruising boat was a schooner called *Hirondelle*, which is the French word for "swallow." Yes indeed: there is a large debt, and I am happy to acknowledge it.

In the still-raw frontier province of B.C., Roderick Haig-Brown was the only writer I knew who wrote for me—for a teenager growing up on the west coast of Canada. It did not occur to me for some years that possibly I myself could aspire to be a writer; writers, I had deduced from my schooling, were by definition British and dead. Even Haig-Brown was British, but he was not dead. He was living in Campbell River, not far from my home in Vancouver, and he was writing about my territory, a reality I knew and recognized.

Haig-Brown wrote two books for teens, and they too remain vivid in memory. The young hero of *Starbuck Valley Winter*, Don Morgan, drops out of school to run a trapline on Vancouver Island. He experiences not only the rigours of a winter in the Canadian woods, but also some of the complexities of the human heart, which force him to make difficult moral choices, and to do a lot of growing up in a short time.

Don succeeds, and in *Saltwater Summer* he uses the profits from the winter to buy a small trawler and go salmon fishing. I knew nothing about trapping, and didn't especially care for the woods—but I knew something about salmon fishing, and I loved fishing boats and fishermen. It was *Saltwater Summer* that really captivated me.

Saltwater Summer has plenty of adventure—storms, accidents, rescues at sea. I loved all that action, and I loved the boat-handling, the navigation, the mavericks and eccentrics holed up logging and fishing along the coast. But I particularly loved *Saltwater Summer* for its deep decency—its portrayal of a boy not yet seventeen, trying his strength in the adult world. Don's boat is mortgaged, and he has to learn to deal with drink and bullies, with politics and racism, with friendships broken and repaired. He's hot-tempered, moody, prone to discouragement—as I was. He fails as a man, and fails again, just as he fails as a fisherman. But he eventually succeeds, emerging tempered by the experience. He becomes a man like the men he admires, a man who deserved—and got—my admiration.

To look back on these books after almost half a century is to realize how deeply I was marked by my early reading. Ransome and Haig-Brown (and others) drew me deep into their worlds and out of my own. I was, almost literally, transported, changed, challenged to think and to grow. It seemed like magic. It still does. I can conceive of no finer calling.

And if, in my own work, I have managed to transport one or two readers myself, I am only passing on what I was given.

A.J. (Jack) Diamond (architect)

Swallows and Amazons, by Arthur Ransome, created a whole world in which children were trusted and treated as responsible beings.

It was also a self-contained world of ineffable satisfaction. Although far removed from the world in which I lived, I could imagine the sublime experience of being in a barge, sleeping on a bunk, and hearing the waters of the canal lapping against the hull, of travelling through peaceful countryside and passing through the locks.

Children feel powerless and puny, and hence their attraction to Superman, in many manifestations. The lives that children led in *Swallows and Amazons*, and other Arthur Ransome books, were more credible, and therefore utterly desirable, empowered lives. I envied them, dreamed of being with them on their adventures. Even when they took their parents along, the parents were like friends and treated the children as equals.

From these books I realized that I could live in many worlds through reading. It became a ritual to take a book out of the library every Saturday morning. I can still feel the atmosphere of the children's library in the old Durban city hall—a heavy, masonry Edwardian building of mannered, classical detailing and interiors of dark mahogany.

Mostly I remember the wholesome odour of the books and the anticipation of stepping through the covers of the book, like Alice through the looking glass, into gratifying worlds of the author's and my imagination. It would be hard to measure the accumulated pleasure derived from reading since those childhood days. I now cannot imagine being without a book and the anticipated pleasure of books yet to be read.

Welwyn Wilton Katz (writer)

I was nine years old, and I was sitting alone, pencil and paper in hand, making a list. Kettle, saucepan, tea, matches, I wrote; tent, blankets, pillow. At the bottom of the bluff on whose wooded summit I sat, the Medway River snaked its way from Dead Horse Canyon toward the Thames.

There was no lake here, and no island. Even a very small sailboat would quickly go aground in the beaver-dammed shallows below me. But it was water, and there was a wilderness of sorts around it. It was the closest I could get to the English Lake District, and to the sailing, camping, child-affirming world of the Swallows and Amazons books I adored.

It is now sixty-seven years since literary critic and journalist Arthur Ransome began publishing his famous series of children's books. He wrote twelve Swallows and Amazons books.

The Swallows were the four Walker children, John, Susan, Titty and Roger. They named themselves for their little sailboat, *Swallow,* with her brown sail and her deep keel. The Amazons were the Swallows' allies, Nancy and Peggy Blackett. I liked their boat *Amazon* a lot, and in later books, I liked other ships: *Titmouse* and *Scarab* and *Wild Cat* and *Goblin.* But it was *Swallow* that I loved.

Although the self-styled Amazon pirates, Nancy and Peggy, were exciting and attractive, as were the two Callum children—clever, absent-minded Dick and his "writerly" sister Dorothea—they didn't quite reach me the way the four Swallows did. Titty was my special favourite. She was my age, nine, and was passionately imaginative. Among the Swallows, she was the most articulate. John was my second favourite—silent, capable and deeply honourable. Of the many children Ransome invented, those two could make me cry.

Why were these twelve novels so good? They were wonderful stories, of course. But their endurance is, I think, based on the way they truly access the world of childhood. "So long as a child is a child," Ransome said once, "it lives in a world of its own, more beautiful and free than any we can make for it."

Ransome finds his own way into that world, calmly, intelligently and honestly. The honesty shines on, long after the book is finished.

I learned to sail on *Swallow* when I was nine years old. When I finally managed, in my mid-twenties, to wangle my way onto a real-life sailboat and took a course in real-life sailing, it was like meeting an old friend.

Camping, too, occupied a big part in my dream world because it was so integral to *Swallows and Amazons*. I made my first camping list at age nine, looking down on Dead Horse Canyon; it didn't change very much when, as an adult, I pitched my first real-life tent. Banking a night fire so it would last till breakfast, as the charcoal burners in *Swallows and Amazons* had taught Susan and me, or shivering to a loon call while reading about Dick's loon in *Great Northern* were affirmations to me.

And when I visited for the first time Coniston Water in the Lake District, the place where Ransome wrote and set his *Swallows and Amazons*, I felt I had really come home.

Though it has been a long time since I was nine, I have never stopped reading those twelve novels. My two favourites, *Pigeon Post* and *Peter Duck*, are now dog-eared and spine-cracked.

Ken Danby (artist)

I love books. I've always loved books. As a child, I required little encouragement to become totally immersed in the joys of reading—and completely absorbed by the tales that I read. It allowed me to become a "time traveller," to experience high adventure "first hand," and explore the drama of life that ignited my imagination.

Great writers are capable of such inspiration and I am especially grateful for the introduction to the "classics" that I so enjoyed as a young boy. So many come to mind that it's difficult to identify one as being more special than the others. Writers such as Longfellow, Stevenson, Defoe, Cooper, Clemens and Doyle were all particular favourites, and of these, I expect that Robert Louis Stevenson could be singled out for *Treasure Island*. This was certainly a book that consumed and inspired me in my youth.

However, it was not only Stevenson's descriptive words that riveted my attention. They were greatly assisted by the masterful paintings of N.C. Wyeth that accompanied the original Scribner's publication of 1911 (which became the "classic," and remains so today). Wyeth created fabulous images that so perfectly captured the spirit and the setting of the characters that they became "etched in my mind" as the action unfolded.

I'm sure that it's not a coincidence that all of the other authors I mentioned also had books illustrated by Wyeth. Obviously, for me, his was a profound contribution to their storytelling; he provided the "visuals that inspired." He brought *Treasure Island* to another level of fascination and enjoyment, and certainly helped to propel my imagination.

As a young boy, it was the visual experience that I loved to explore, from my earliest memories. It became "the flesh on the bones" of the story. Wyeth gave this to *Treasure Island*, and countless other classics, in spades. (I vividly recall Robert Newton's marvellous portrayal of Long John Silver in Hollywood's classic *Treasure Island*, and I suspect that he, too, was inspired by the images created by Wyeth.) Ironically, as a young artist, I once again experienced a Wyeth influence, only it wasn't from N.C., but his son Andrew, who was achieving considerable renown as a painter of life, rather than as an "illustrator."

In 1962, I visited a major exhibition of Andrew's work in Buffalo, N.Y., which reinforced my previously made decision (of the year before) to return to representational image making (after dropping out of art school in 1960 in frustration at the narrowness of the focus). Here was an artist who was working in a realistic direction and still generated great respect, which, as I had been told at art school, was not possible.

I was perhaps ten years old when I was profoundly influenced by N.C. Wyeth's illustrations on behalf of such classics as *Treasure Island*. Twelve years later, his son's work influenced the direction of my art.

Brian Doyle (writer)

Two very different books, when I was young, influenced me to pursue a career as a writer.

The Coral Island, by R.M. Ballantyne (1858), featured hero Ralph Rover. But it wasn't Ralph who excited me, it was the vocabulary Ballantyne used in those old-fashioned chapter synopses the nineteenth-century novelist often employed. One early chapter synopsis read: "The Coral Island—Our first cogitations after landing, and the result of them."

I remember feeling the guilty pleasure of "stealing" Ballantyne's, or, as I thought, Ralph Rover's word "cogitations" and taking it all around with me, using it with my friends and slipping it in at school when the teacher was listening. What power! To know a word nobody else seemed to know.

The experience opened up a language hoard for me. Very exciting.

The other book, *Freckles*, by Gene Stratton Porter (1940), affected me through method rather than vocabulary. Freckles, an abandoned Irish orphan, is given a job guarding valuable trees in the wild limberlost swamp of Indiana. One day, on his rounds, he stumbles upon a lost girl and is struck dumb by her delicate beauty.

Here's the passage that made me want to be a writer: "The wildly leaping heart of Freckles burst from his body and fell in the black swamp muck at her feet with such a thud that he did not understand how she could avoid hearing it. He really felt that if she looked down she would see it."

Imagine! An Irish boy's heart surrealistically falls with a thud in the mud at the feet of a girl-angel. I wanted then to be able to write like that. I was ten.

Pierre Berton (writer)

I will always remember the electric thrill that ran through me when a wild, human figure leaped unexpectedly from a pine tree on that apparently deserted island which Robert Louis Stevenson created so many years ago. My heart thumped, like Jim Hawkins's, for this was one of several unexpected surprises in *Treasure Island*, in my opinion the best boy's book ever written.

It has everything: adventure, mystery and unforgettable characters such as Long John Silver, and that haunting piece of doggerel about fifteen men on a dead man's chest. It gripped me as no other book had. Blind Pew, the Admiral Benbow Inn, Cap'n Flint and parrot, the dreaded Black Spot, and the good ship *Hispaniola* form part of the cultural baggage I still carry with me. I wish I could find another tale half as good.

Monty Hall (television host)

All books stirred my soul when I was young. Booth Tarkington's *Penrod* and *Penrod and Sam* captivated me. *Tom Swift* amused me, the Horatio Alger series of books gave me hope that I too would rise from poverty to become the boss. But *Tom Sawyer* and *Huckleberry Finn* far outshone the others, perhaps because they were written for a more mature adolescent.

My mother plied me with *National Geographic*, my father with sports books. I was bedridden for a year, and books transported me from my bed to wonderful adventure.

Monica Hughes (writer)

Over and over again I return to my favourite author, E. Nesbit, whose books I discovered in the classroom library of my first school in West Ealing, a suburb of London. Among these wonder-filled novels was one called *The Story of the Amulet*, first published in 1903.

Time travel! I had never heard of such a device before. To find a broken amulet in a second-hand store and to be able to search through time for the missing half and so find one's heart's desire. What a magical premise that was.

Life in the 1930s was, for our family, very ordinary, indeed boring. We had just returned from living in Cairo to a home in a new London suburb, a place without glamour, colour or adventure. For the first time I realized that adventure was to be had between the covers of a book. I had only to read, with a receptive mind and imagination working at full steam, and the miracle happened. I was back in ancient Egypt or witnessing the destruction of Atlantis.

Not long after I discovered this book we moved to Edinburgh, a city with many antique and second-hand shops. Was I very naive? I know that I was impelled by Nesbit's story to spend considerable time turning over the trays of bric-a-brac that were enticingly left in the entrances to these shops, hoping that one day I might find such an amulet—or, failing that, a magic ring (which is another Nesbit story).

I no longer believe absolutely in amulets and magic rings, but I do passionately believe in the power of good fiction to engage the reader in a happy "suspension of disbelief." As a writer of imaginative fiction for young readers, I truly believe, for the time it takes to write a book, in whatever I am writing about.

Ramsay Cook (writer, historian)

It had a black binding with faded silver lettering on the spine. It was very thick—perhaps three hundred pages. I know it was written by Richard Halliburton but I am unsure of the title, though *The Royal Road to Romance* is how I have always remembered it. It was a book of astonishing adventures experienced by the hero who travelled to the most exotic places—at least to me, who thought that the annual Regina Fair was exotic and Saskatoon a very long way away. What sticks most in my mind and imagination was his swimming feats. (I already loved, and still do, Johnny Weissmuller, better known as Tarzan). He crossed the Hellespont (this was in the "Byronic Tradition," I recently learned from Charles Sprawson's *Haunts of the Black Masseur* which doesn't mention Halliburton). But best of all he plunged into the pool in front of the Taj Mahal in the moonlight. I have never forgotten that—nor lost the ambition to copy my hero.

George Bain (journalist)

Something is wrong. Here I am poised to write about the favourite book of my youth having just discovered that, except in bits and pieces, I don't like it. I don't really care much for its author, my hero; I find him too intent on playing the part. But do I blame him? Or me? He wrote the thing in 1925 and I read it in the early thirties. From then, I went on thinking, without ever having reread it, that I would never forget it. Which, as this testifies, I never have. Up to a point.

Some of the blame for my being in this equivocal position must go to Arlene Perly Rae for inviting me to join this throng in identifying youthful reading enthusiasms. Without that, it is unlikely I ever would have sought out the old favourite again. Had I not done that, I never would have thought that perhaps I was misled in allowing it to encourage me to be a journalist instead of, say, a banker—which, come to think of it, may be true.

My favourite was *The Royal Road to Romance*. It was the first-person story of a young man, immediately on graduating from Princeton, having set off on a foot-free ramble around the world. He was going to climb mountains, swim rivers, get to know cities, not just look at but examine, inside and out, famous buildings and other man-made structures—the Taj Mahal, the pyramids of Egypt, the fortifications at Gibraltar—and observe the ways of people around the world.

Wow, that was for me! Already, to see the world was a tantalizing thought and here was a young guy telling how he did it, on his own, partly with money earned from writing about it as he went, recounting in dramatic terms some of the wonders there were to be seen. That sort of thing can lead to thoughts of a compatible career, of which journalism clearly might be one.

But reminiscences about the memorable influences of one's most susceptible years can be tricky. Can I say that anything—a book in particular—was the most memorable of its kind at the time without my being sure how well I remember it? Obviously I would have to reread it. When eventually I found it in the second of two libraries, and then with the help of a librarian, a book by a Richard Halliburton with two "l"s, not one as I'd been looking for, I clearly was in not position to be dogmatic about the reliability of my memory.

Also, at the time, had I been asked, I would have said the author's account of swimming the Hellespont was one of the high points of the book, along with his climb to the top of the Matterhorn, and his penetration to Leh, the capital of Ladakh, 14,000 feet up in the Himalayas. In my rereading, I found no mention of the Hellespont, except for a couple of lines when he tossed a coin to see if his next direction would be north from Egypt to Greece or east to India: "For years my secret passion had been to swim the Hellespont, yet no less consuming was my adoration of the Taj Mahal." India had won. So where did I get that graphic memory of the swim? Did he, in another book, which I had forgotten, go back on a subsequent tour to satisfy his passion for the Hellespont?

But can it be that, along with my memory having become less than the steel trap it never was, cynicism has set in? In the rereading I found myself occasionally muttering that this guy was not altogether the free spirit I admired at eleven or twelve, but a well-off young guy with connections.

When he and a mate from Princeton set sail for New York, having been hired by the ship's captain as crew aboard his American cargo vessel, they went "assisted by a peremptory letter... from the president of the shipping company instructing him to do so." That later jump from Egypt to India aboard an American tanker was assisted by the author's "carrying an omnipotent personal letter from the American military attaché to the consul at Port Said."

He was very much aware of his own importance, was not one to underplay his endless acts of daring, and was something of a bully to the menials he encountered along the way. His attitudes in general to natives and women were of a sort to get him hung up by the thumbs at any university in his own country in the politically correct eighties and nineties. Nothing of that other side of my hero struck me until I reread the book that had so impressed me sixty or so years earlier. It's not just true that you can't go back. It's disturbing to try.

Peter Kent (broadcaster, journalist)

I stumbled upon the book by accident.

I remember being dispatched from Miss Stubbe's grade 8 English class at Calgary's Viscount Bennett Junior High School. A woman of diminutive stature—her name pronounced Stubby—she endured with good humour the "size" jokes of successive waves of oafish thirteen-year-old boys.

On this particular day, Miss Stubbe was determined to get a passable book report out of one of her most uninspired students. I was told to go to the library, to scan the shelves, and to return only when I had a book—of at least two hundred pages, she insisted—that interested me.

An unlikely goal, I thought, meandering through the aisles farthest away from the authority figures behind the library counter. The shelves of well-handled volumes—most re-bound in the dreary blues, greens and purples favoured by school boards in the early fifties—seemed to hold nothing of great interest.

And, then, a new addition to the shelves—still wearing its original cover—caught my eye.

Reach for the Sky, the black block letters of the title proclaimed, over an artist's depiction of a banking Spitfire. The subtitle, in bright yellow, explained that this was *The Story of Douglas Bader—Hero of the Battle of Britain.* On the first page, promotional paragraphs gave a hint of the stirring contents of Paul Brickhill's biography of the wartime ace.

I was hooked. I devoured the book, marvelling at Bader's lonely childhood, the pre-war accident that claimed both of his legs, his uphill battle to get back into the Royal Air Force, his amazing accomplishments in the Battle of Britain, the dozens of enemy aircraft he shot down, the ultimate downing of Bader himself...and his unlikely escape from the notorious German prisoner-of-war facility Kolditz Castle.

My parents were pleasantly surprised... although I'm sure they would have preferred a Waugh or Fitzgerald or Hemingway for my reading breakthrough.

Miss Stubbe was satisfied, if not with my book report, with the simple fact that she'd won yet another young dolt to the world of books.

A few years later, by then a Sea Cadet, intent on a flying future with the Canadian Navy, I had the great honour of actually meeting Douglas Bader—Sir Douglas Bader by then.

The conversation was all too brief. I remember blurting out how much his story had meant to me, while trying without success to determine whether he was still using the much-repaired pair of prosthetic legs that had carried him through such heroic adventures during the war years.

Decades later, Bader was interviewed by a young South African journalist. She was enchanted by the seventy-year-old's engaging "bulldog ferocity," his description of "fright—not terror" when there were "a few bullets in the cockpit" and by his humility.

Bader revealed that he only viewed the film *Reach for the Sky* eleven years after its release.

"Saw it at home on a Battle of Britain Sunday. On television. Could've gone to the premiere, but didn't want to steal Kenneth More's thunder. It was his night, y'know. Thoroughly enjoyed it."

The yellowed clipping of the interview was placed before me when I sat down at the kitchen table with the Toronto Public Library's well-handled Fontana paperback edition of *Reach for the Sky* to compose this piece.

Rereading the article by the young journalist—now my wife—made for a serendipitous moment. Cilla's column, from a 1980 edition of the *Johannesburg Star*, also provides a much better read than my original, long-lost book report.

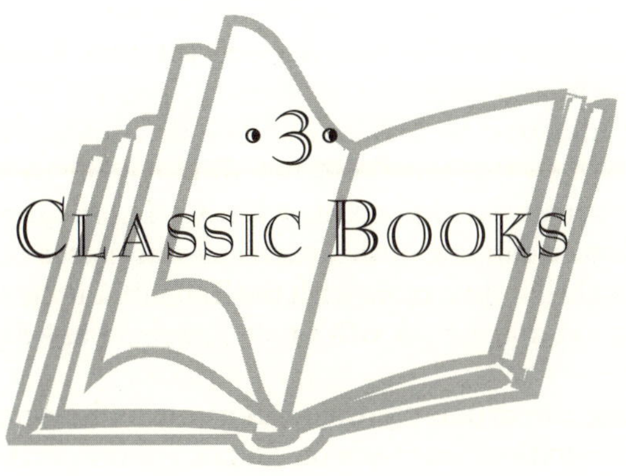

·3· Classic Books

"Books of all time"
—John Ruskin

What are the classics? It is almost impossible to identify specific qualities that allow certain books to transcend their own generation and offer lasting and universal appeal, but there do tend to be a few common chracteristics. There is enormous variety in the books that have survived. They seem to be not solely books for children, but because of their lasting literary value, they are acknowledged and esteemed by readers of all ages. It is impossible to accurately predict those stories that will prevail from today's wide selection, but it is fun to try.

Many traditional classics for children are remembered for their immortal characters. Among them are Robinson Crusoe, Gulliver, Tom Sawyer, Huck Finn, Jim Hawkins and Long John Silver, Alice, Charlotte and Wilbur, Kim, Jo March, Anne Shirley, Emily Byrd Starr and Mary Lennox. Young children discover their own favourite book personalities, both real and imaginary, animal or human, whom they often know as well as their playmates or siblings: Winnie-the-Pooh, Babar, Corduroy, Madeline, Curious George, Cinderella, Jacob-Two-Two, Peter Rabbit, Peter Pan (to name just a few).

Classics cross all categories and genres. They may be poetry, adventure, fantasy or family stories. There are classic fairy tales, legends, books of history, knowledge and natural science. Although there are a (loosely acknowledged) group of books that are (semi-officially) deemed to be classics, in a very real sense, each story chosen by a contributor to this book is a classic to the one who treasures it.

A classic is not always recognized in its own time. Several contributors wrote about Frances Hodgson Burnett's *The Secret Garden*. This novel and *Sara Crewe* (later retitled *A Little Princess*) are far more popular and highly regarded now than when they were first published. *Little Lord Fauntleroy* (which was more of a hit originally) has faded in comparison. *The Secret Garden* is a spellbinding tale with both Gothic elements and Edwardian sensibilities. It is a story largely about two spoiled and difficult children. But it is also about the redemptive power of love—and gardening, magic, friendship, persistence and the complexities of human nature.

There really was a garden behind Burnett's home in Manchester, England, and poor children played in the streets just outside it. Burnett drew on her own experience and memories and with her vivid imagination she was able to spin those meagre facts into a gripping and unforgettable story.

Great books are rediscovered, reread, prized and enjoyed by countless generations of adults and children because of universal truths, memorable characters and literary quality. They continue to speak to us because what they say is eternally relevant and well expressed. (Aesop's fables offer insight and common sense.) They free the imagination, are beautiful—often deceptively simple—in their style, and generally beguile both heart and mind. They reveal authors unafraid to tackle eternal themes and deep emotions. Classics are rarely sentimental. This does not mean they are apprehensive of pulling on the heartstrings. Far from it. But they tend to do so with a certain dignity and a respect for life that includes the natural world of plants and animals.

C.S. Lewis's *Chronicles of Narnia* and J.R.R. Tolkien's *The Hobbit* and *The Lord of the Rings* are acknowledged twentieth-century classics. Fantasy novels combine realistic detail (in *Narnia*, for instance, a real wardrobe, four seemingly normal children, a recognizable setting) with imaginative elements such as talking animals, witches, enchanted forests and so on. Tolkien had extensive and well-researched knowledge of myth, history and ancient lore. He combined his studies with his love of fairy tales and spectacular attention to detail to create a "secondary world" in his complex and revolutionary works.

In *Books, Children and Men* Paul Hazard lists several characteristics he considers essential for a book to be considered very good. His list is a helpful standard by which to evaluate both classic and modern literature for children. Hazard insists that great books remain faithful to the very essence of art, that they offer children "an intuitive and direct way of knowledge, a simple beauty capable of being perceived immediately." For younger children he prizes books that "provide them with pictures...pictures chosen from the riches of the whole world; enchanting pictures that bring release and joy." He values those books that "awaken not maudlin sentimentality but sensibility; that enable them to share in great human emotions; that give them respect for universal life." He relishes books that "respect the valour and eminent dignity of play; which understand that the training of intelligence and of reason cannot, and must not, always have the immediately useful and practical as its goal."

He likes books of knowledge "when they have tact and moderation; when instead of pouring out so much material on a child's soul that it is crushed, they plant in it a seed that will develop from the inside." He especially likes books that "distil from all the different kinds of knowledge the most difficult and the most necessary—that of the human heart."

Hazard's qualifications set a high and challenging standard. Which of today's stories will make the cut? Are there any contemporary picture books or novels that will have the power and resonance of *Robinson Crusoe*, *Alice in Wonderland*, Aesop's fables or *Peter Pan*? Who knows? No doubt dedicated and insightful authors and illustrators, both now and in the future, will do their best to create great literature. It is up to readers and posterity to decide which book or books, of the vast quantity being published for children today, are worthy of carry-over to the twenty-first and subsequent centuries.

Nazneen Sheikh (Sadiq) (writer)

Alice's Adventures in Wonderland, by Lewis Carroll, was a book I stole from my elder sister's closely guarded bookshelf. Instead of taking the dread afternoon nap, as per my mother's stern injunctions, I crawled under the dining-room table and entered the world of Alice.

Forty-two years later I may not have emerged.

My identification with Alice's perception of a largely irrational and contradictory world was acute. I was a highly imaginative child, encouraged to be both independent and at times rebellious. Her adventures were the ones that often appeared in my make-believe play world. The bottle which said "Drink Me" or the cake which said "Eat Me" haunted me for months. The notion of magical elixirs which permitted one to instigate change was pure enchantment. I remember feeling curiously empathetic to the Queen of Hearts, whose bark was worse than her bite. There were people in my childhood who displayed the same brand of mock ferocity.

Finally, what the book did was to celebrate both adventure and the concept of dreaming. These are things that happen to everyone anywhere and at any time. To casually manipulate the norms of imagery and present them as fantastical scenarios ensnares both the child and the adult. The same freedom results in the composition of "Jabberwocky." There is a great deal of evidence in contemporary literature which reveals that some work, if largely misunderstood, could be jabberwocky of sorts.

I think Lewis Carroll was quite brilliant, because he inventively teaches children how language can be both flexible and ambiguous. I don't think my love of the English language could have been nurtured without reading this book as a child.

Joan Clark (writer)

When I was ten and eleven years old and living in Sydney Mines, Cape Breton, I became enchanted with a book now largely unknown. It was entitled *The Five Little Peppers and How They Grew* by Margaret Sidney. The story was about a poor family of five, two girls and three boys, who brought themselves up while their widowed mother scraped together a living as a tailor. "Poor things!" the stout-hearted and cheery Mrs. Pepper would say of her flock, "they're just scrambled up!" Were the children unhappy? Not a bit. They struggled through good days and bad with determined vigour and cheerful accord.

As the younger of two sisters, I was impressed by the children's goodness and cooperative spirit. My sister and I shoved and scratched one another at the slightest provocation. Punishment for avoiding the dirty supper dishes was being dragged to the sink by the hair. I was fascinated by the way the five little Peppers thrived on adversity, pitching into tasks I avoided. When Polly told her younger sister, Phronsie, to sit at the table, Phronsie sat, whereas in her place I would have flounced out of the room. Thinking about the difference between the Pepper family and mine, I had the idea that the numbers of children made the difference. The more children in a family, the better they got along. I told myself that when I grew up, I would have at least four children.

After reading *The Five Little Peppers and How They Grew*, I adopted a train family. This was an imaginary family of four (two boys and two girls), who lived in a caboose whose interior I furnished with items from Eaton's Catalogue. I made numerous lists, agonizing over decisions about what to buy. A sofa for $99.95 or a velour chesterfield for $119.50? I bought the family's clothes, winter and summer, organized their blissful lives. My imaginary family was poor but happy.

Though the writing in *The Five Little Peppers and How They Grew* is clumsy and mannered (overwritten we would say now), I was impressed by its values, which were the importance of caring for one another and facing adversity with courage and optimism. Though I read this book as a child, its influence followed me into adulthood. When I became a mother of three and a family of eight children moved into our neighbourhood, I was unprepared for the bitterness of the children's fights, how the sisters claimed they hated each other. "I wish you were dead!" they would scream at one another. I was unprepared because I had persisted in thinking that the more children in a family, the merrier. Though I have since dispelled this notion, I continue to hold *The Five Little Peppers and How They Grew* with fond regard. Its aura of self-sufficiency and good cheer was genuine, based on children who held a profound and, I like to think, lasting affection for one another.

Sylvie Fréchette (Olympic gold medallist, swimming) (translated from French)

The book that I read at the beginning of my adolescence that really touched me was *The Diary of Anne Frank*. My mother strongly recommended it, and since I was leaving to spend part of the summer out of the city, I wanted to take some good books with me.

I had always adored reading, but to read about the life of a young girl close to my age, a girl with a life and concerns so different from mine, certainly made me think. While I thought only of spending beautiful summer vacations with my family by the lake, elsewhere on this planet there had been a young girl who fought for her life and that of her family, who lived in fear, hiding without enough food or heating... It was then that I realized how spoiled and lucky I was to have grown up in a beautiful country, a land without war, surrounded by people I love and who love me. It was then I decided that I must get the most I can out of life, and make the most of what life brings me. If, one day, I have children of my own, I will certainly urge them to read this book, exactly as my mother did.

Steve Podborski (World Cup skiing champion)

In many ways the story of my skiing career and the fairy tale of the Crazy Canucks' rise from nowhere to the toast of the skiing world is a parallel of sorts to the book that hooked me in my high-school days, *The Lord of the Rings*, by J.R.R. Tolkien.

The story of how little people can come to affect the counsels of the great and wise is a story of how I often felt as we, a tiny ski nation, competed with the rest of the world, and, in the end, triumphed.

My small injuries along the way (three knee surgeries, separated shoulder, concussion, etc.) and constant focus on one goal for years at a time seemed to pale beside Frodo's challenge. In a small way my small burden was easier to bear.

The price paid for glory and freedom is clear in the book. I rejoiced and grieved along with the different characters, as I rejoiced and grieved with my team-mates in our adventure.

I believe that these are both wonderful stories. Tolkien has written a classic that I will continue to enjoy every few years for the rest of my days.

Barbara Smucker (writer)

I read my first real book at age eight. I had mastered the Mother Goose rhymes and shorter tales in the first-grade reader, but never a whole book. Fortunately there was a public library near my home and I chose this special book there with a feeling of importance and almost reverence. The book was *Heidi* by Johanna Spyri.

I carried *Heidi* home and secluded myself from three noisy younger brothers in a corner of our wide front porch and began: "The pleasant old village of Meyenfeld lies at the foot of a lofty mountain."

I was enchanted. I lived on the prairies. There wasn't even a hill in sight. As I continued I was taken to another country, Switzerland! I immediately identified with Heidi, a little orphan girl, just my age. She loved the mountains, the goats, and even the grouchy old grandfather called "Alm Uncle" who was forced to take her in. He wasn't grouchy at all. He loved Heidi.

Heidi also found friends in Peter, the goatherd, in Peter's blind grandmother and in Clara, the invalid daughter of a wealthy man in the city of Frankfurt. I wiped tears from my eyes when Heidi was taken from Alm Uncle and her beloved mountains and sent to live in the city. But in the end all was well.

I closed *Heidi*, held her story lovingly against me and immediately started back to the library for another book.

Margaret Buffie (writer)

I was one of those lucky children whose mother read to them every night before bed—all the various fairy tales, as well as the *Bobbsey Twins*, *The Boxcar Children*, *Alice in Wonderland*, *The Wizard of Oz* and others. But curiously enough, the one book that affected me most profoundly was the simple tale of *Heidi,* by Johanna Spyri. I still have the battered hardcover on my shelves. I looked at it again the other day and found that both my sister and I had signed our names inside it—each claiming it as her own personal property. I think I ended up with it because I was on the spot when my mother moved and I shamelessly begged for it.

Why am I so attached to this book? For a number of reasons. As a child I suffered from excruciating homesickness. Heidi also suffered from a debilitating form of homesickness and I really understood what she was going through—and, of course, it was also a relief to know that another little girl had those same feelings. Also, Heidi was independent and free-spirited—something I definitely was not—and because I admired her terribly, I tried to emulate her and that helped me through awkward days at school. But the thing that affected me most was that, in an odd sort of way, Heidi taught me how to see—how to look at the world outside of my own worries and feelings—and to find joy in it. Heidi examined everything around her with such relish—the snow as it fell over her beloved mountains, the way the light fell over her loft bed in the morning, the beauty of the skies. Heidi took such pleasure in the sights and sounds around her that I started to look at my own world in the same way.

I think this book was just one of the many things that helped me develop as an artist and as a writer, but it definitely has its own unique place in that development.

Michael Ignatieff (writer, broadcaster)

I must have been eleven or twelve when I first read *Paddle-to-the-Sea* (by Holling C. Holling), but it's still with me: the little canoe, carved and painted by a Native elder somewhere above Lake Superior and set on a hill in mid-winter to await the spring run off. I remember the canoe slithering down the icy creeks, slipping past the log booms on the rivers and then past the red ore boats on the Great

Lakes. I seem to remember it going over Niagara Falls at one point, and then making its passage, increasingly worn and battered, up the St. Lawrence, until it is washed ashore in Newfoundland. I loved the book—and passed it on to my own children—because of its essential hopefulness. The little canoe does reach its destination, thanks to the people along the way.

Alison Gordon (writer)

There was an Australian book I remember fondly called *The Magic Pudding* by Norman Lindsay, about the eponymous sweet that walked with the protagonists, a bowl with little legs, and could be anything they wanted to eat, endlessly renewable. I also recall a serialized adventure story my father told us each night, about Tad and Joe, two Indian boys who got into (and out of) no end of difficulties. There was also Holling C. Holling's *Paddle-to-the-Sea*, another exploration of my Canadian roots. But the memorable book, for me, was *Stuart Little*, E.B. White's charming tale of a mouse born into a New York family of humans. Because I was a little girl born in New York, I could identify with his adventure in Central Park. Its author has continued to delight me, as an adult, with his essays and letters. And the connection has happily continued with my friendship with his stepson, Roger Angell, who is the best baseball writer on the planet, and an inspiration to all of us who love the game.

Priscilla Galloway (writer)

Among all the books that have helped to form me, Homer's *Odyssey* has a special place, although its most significant early impact has little to do with the story.

At the age of eight, I attended the two-room Model School in Victoria, B.C. Marion James taught grades 1 to 3, and Isobel Bescoby, grades 4 to 6. Miss James was my beloved teacher for only one year, since I transferred after a wretched grade 2 at my neighbourhood school. Neither teacher discouraged me from reading books not usually considered suitable for my age.

Did I always lose myself in literature? I have never quite understood how anyone can do otherwise. I suffered if I had to put down the *Odyssey*, perhaps while Odysseus, chained to the mast, was beguiled by the sirens' song. It was agony to close the *Iliad*, perhaps while Achilles still sulked in his tent, or while Hector put on his great war helmet and frightened his little son. I might not know what would become of these heroes, but I knew it would be terrible and wonderful: "awesome," in an earlier sense of that now-trivialized word.

On one soon-to-be-memorable afternoon, I opened the *Odyssey* as soon as school was out, reading as usual while I walked down the hill to the bus stop. The Mt. Toimie bus would come soon, from which I would transfer to a streetcar which would take me most of the way home. Luckily for me, there were no school buses in those days. I think even I would have found it difficult to read in the noisy babble of a modern school bus. As usual, I had taken out my ticket and tucked it between two fingers of my left hand, the one that held the book.

Bliss. The tale of tales wove its spell. I was vaguely aware when the bus arrived and the short line-up moved. I moved automatically, book still open, up the steps. I felt for my ticket. Nothing. I looked. *Nada.*

It was my last ticket, and I had no money to buy more. Frantically I stared at the floor, at the steps, then pushed my way out of the bus, kneeling to look on the ground by the big tires. The driver waited, muttering under his breath.

"Priscilla," came Miss James's quiet voice, "is this what you're looking for?" She stood inside the bus, looking down at me. She held a ticket, green, child-coloured, in her hand. Did she say she was glad I loved wonderful books? She may have, but I don't recall. Her lesson has been unforgettable, however. I was entranced, so much so that she took the ticket from my fingers and I felt nothing, noticed nothing. Two or three of my classmates, also waiting for the bus, watched her do it. It was hilarious; they were still laughing at me the next day, and I was teased for weeks. I had turned two or three pages after the ticket was gone and the others were giggling, and I'd never looked up from my book.

Sometimes I meet another book junkie, though mostly we closet ourselves alone with our habit. Ours is a righteous passion. Who shall dare to flourish a bus ticket in our faces? Let Zeus pick up a thunderbolt; let Athene raise her spear!

Charlotte Gray (writer)

I think our family copy of *The Water-Babies*, by Charles Kingsley, must have come from my Hampstead grandfather, who was an avid book-buyer and reader. Books were a sensuous as well as an imaginative experience for him. He stroked their covers respectfully, and if interrupted while reading he would clutch the volume (usually Dickens) to his heart. He is the only relation I can imagine buying a beautiful leather-bound early edition of a children's book, complete with extraordinary illustrations by someone with the wonderful name Warwick Goble.

It was the illustrations that drew me to the book. All those naked infants, with strange gills on their shoulders, gliding through the water. Seaweed and sea anemones gently undulating in the current. Schools of tiny fish, perfectly aligned, poised to shoot across the page. Jellyfish, swollen and semi-circular, tentacles streaming behind them, floating through the ocean like balloons across the sky.

From the illustrations, I moved into the text. I needed to find out who the mysterious ladies in diaphanous gowns were, and why Tom, the hero, was accompanied by a dog. And I discovered Kingsley's extraordinary knowledge of and sympathy for aquatic life. His descriptions of the dragon-fly emerging from its nymph, and of a family of otters playing in the river shallows, owe their strength to the careful observation in which Victorian naturalists specialized. Kingsley combined it with the kind of anthropomorphism on which Lewis Carroll made his reputation. "A very distinguished lobster he was: for he had live barnacles on his claws, which is a great mark of distinction in lobsterdom, and no more to be bought for money than a good conscience or the Victoria Cross."

So as a child, whenever I was asked to name my favourite book, I always said *The Water-Babies*. I loved Tom's mischievous spirit. I loved the contrast between his wretched "real life," as a chimney sweep, and the weightless liberty of his underwater existence. I loved the drama of the moment when Tom liberates the lobster from a lobster pot.

But as I grew up, the lure of a book first published in 1863 faded; by the age of ten I was inhaling Enid Blyton.

Alas! The other day, I picked up a copy of *The Water-Babies* to try and rediscover its magic. I was appalled. Where once I lapped up descriptions of caddis flies building their shells and salmon-running rivers, now I see absurd moralizing and heavy-handed Christian metaphors. Where I was captivated, as a child, by the simple logic of those diaphanous ladies, now I am repulsed by the didactic smugness of Mrs. Bedonebyasyoudid and her sister Mrs. Doasyouwouldbedoneby. And, of course, I am mortified to confess that I identified with a naked little boy rather than some gutsy girl who took on the world.

Yet I am still disarmed by the descriptions of the underwater world, avidly watch Jacques Cousteau documentaries, and swim every day so I too can relish the weightless liberty Tom enjoyed.

Rosemary Brown (writer, activist)

I grew up in Jamaica, a British colony. My education was very colonial, and to my horror, when I tried to think of the books of my youth, they revealed the true extent of that colonialization. Indeed the only authors that came to mind were virtually all British or American—Louisa May Alcott, all the Brontës, John Galsworthy, P.G. Wodehouse. I remember a smattering of special books—Lucy Maud Montgomery's *Anne of Green Gables*, Astrid Lindgren's *Pippi Longstocking*, *A Girl of the Limberlost*, *Rebecca of Sunnybrook Farm* and the Jalna series.

For some reason, one book that seems to have lodged itself in the deepest recesses of my consciousness is *The Water-Babies* by Charles Kingsley. I have no idea why I have always considered it to be my favourite book, especially since, when I suggested it as interesting reading to my daughter, she almost died of boredom.

I secured a copy from the library and read it again. Sitting there on the beach, under an umbrella, it came alive for me. Once again it left me with a smile. This time, however, I understood why. It was because, throughout the reading, I could hear the voice of my Aunt Leila. She was the scholar, the first woman in Jamaica to win a scholarship to the University of London, and the person who developed in my brother and in me a passion for literature. She used to read with us. We learned to read with her, and she always managed to infuse any book we shared with enthusiasm and joy.

She loved explaining to me all the hidden nuances in Kingsley's text, so despite being a fantasy, *The Water-Babies* also became, for me, a mystery and a morality play. On this reading I loved it even more, although I wonder that as a child I could have survived some of the longer passages with their preachy tone.

I am not sure what impact, if any, this book had on me except to remind me of the pleasure that reading has always been to me, and to remind me of the person who first exposed me to such pleasure.

Thank you for the opportunity to examine one more thing about my peculiar upbringing. It even now amazes me that all the books and stories written by the early Caribbean writers were dismissed as folklore and not fit for educational curriculums. The only Jamaican writers we did learn about were people like Hugh Sherlock, who was in fact an Englishman who had chosen to make Jamaica his home, and who wrote some truly beautiful poems about the island.

Today, of course, if I were still a child, I would be reading —much sooner—V.S. Naipaul, Sam Selvon, Austin Clarke, Louise

Bennett, Dionne Brand, Olive Senior, Cecil Foster and a raft of others, but back then my entire fantasy life was peopled with repressed English gentry.

Gail Bowen (writer)

It was the morning of December 25, 1949, I was seven years old and down to my last and best present. My grandmother and I were both serious readers, and her Christmas gift to me was as invariable as the three tissue-wrapped undershirts (girl's sleeveless flannel) that my Aunt Edna unfailingly left under the tree. Always before, Nana had chosen a book that radiated promise from the moment I tore off the wrappings, but this year she'd come up short. The book in my hands was heart-plummetingly plain: a dull blue-green cover and inside, nothing but words—no pictures of elephants in crowns and ermine; no governess flying over London clutching her magic carpetbag; not even a drawing of twelve little girls in two straight lines.

"Read me the first few sentences," my grandmother said. "Give it a chance." And because I loved her, I read. "'Christmas won't be Christmas without any presents,' grumbled Jo, lying on the rug. 'It's so dreadful to be poor,' sighed Meg, looking down at her old dress. 'I don't think it's fair for some girls to have plenty of pretty things, and other girls nothing at all,' added little Amy with an injured sniff. 'We've got father and mother and each other,' said Beth contentedly from her corner."

I read *Little Women* all that day and into the night. I was in another time, in another house, with another family. From the moment Louisa May Alcott's little women packed up their one holiday treat, a special breakfast, and carried it through the snow to the poor, I gave them my heart. There were four of them: Meg, the oldest, was warm and maternal with a gift for smoothing ruffled feathers and rough edges; Amy, the prettiest, had a talent for art and slept with a clothespin on her nose to give it a French tilt; Beth, the youngest, was so selfless I knew instinctively she was destined for a sad end; Jo, my soul-mate, strode through life with hair flying, fingers ink-stained and eyes fierce with the determination you see only in the eyes of a girl who knows that someday she will be a writer.

Almost fifty years later, the March sisters are with me still, and so are the lessons I learned from them. As different as they were in talent and in temperament, these young women valued and supported one another. They celebrated one another's triumphs, shared one another's sorrow and enhanced one another's lives. I might have learned about sisterhood without reading Louisa May Alcott, but I count myself lucky that on Christmas Day, 1949, I had a grandmother who believed it was important for me to know that the lives of all Little Women have worth and dignity.

Janet Lunn (writer)

I still remember coming to the end of *The Secret Garden* for the first time. I was in the little summer house my father had built beside our brook (we lived on a farm in Vermont in those days). At once I wanted to run and tell everyone about it and, at the same time, hide the book so no one could ever find it. It was my secret garden and it was much too personal to share. It is still so important to me that I read it at least once a year. It still enchants me, it still touches me deeply.

Over the sixty years since sitting by our brook with Mary and Colin and Dickon, I've thought a lot about why this book is so important, not only to me but to so many people. I've discussed it in lectures about children's reading. I've written about it. I've even given it as her favourite book to the heroine in one of my own books in order to acknowledge my debt to it. What Frances Hodgson Burnett was saying in *The Secret Garden* has informed my whole life.

From the first sentence of the book in which Mary Lennox is described as "the most disagreeable child ever seen," I was Mary. When she found an old garden as neglected and unwanted as herself and determined to make it live, it was my garden, too. As Mary brought that garden to life with the help of the moor boy Dickon, the most engaging character I've ever met (even at the age of eight I was in love with Dickon), Mary, herself, found new life. So did her cousin Colin, as disagreeable as she, the crotchety old gardener Ben Weatherstaff and, at last, Mary's uncle, the unhappy, widowed Archibald Craven. I loved them all.

Like all church-going Christians, I learned the story of Christ's passion in early childhood. The image of Jesus, meek and mild, nailed by his hands and feet to the cross filled me with horror; the image of the risen Christ meant nothing, Easter was Easter eggs and new clothes. No, the deep understanding of redemption and resurrection came to me from *The Secret Garden*.

I was not particularly unlovely nor certainly unwanted but I often felt that way. It is, after all, one of the fears intrinsic to the human condition. The story of a child who personifies those fears and finds a way through them is a treasure beyond price.

And, at the core, there is the garden, that small, contained space, magical, peaceful, beautiful, intaken from the wild, far from "the madding crowd," a place at the heart's core where there is always peace—and sometimes joy—to be found.

When I read the book that first time, I could not have articulated why I knew it had become so vital to my life. But I knew. Now, when I talk to children about books and they ask—as they always do—"What is your favourite?" I always reply, *The Secret Garden*. I see sudden answering smiles on many faces and then there is that look in those eyes that says, "But this is my private garden," and, at the same time, "Oh, do you love it so much, too?" We know we have shared something deeply important.

P.K. Page (writer)

I think my favourite of many favourite books in my childhood must have to be Frances Hodgson Burnett's *Sara Crewe or What Happened at Miss Minchin's*, later to be expanded and renamed *A Little Princess*. I also loved her *The Secret Garden*. She seemed to have perfect pitch for little girls.

I remember reading *The Secret Garden* when I was ill in bed with an earache and being so drawn into the enchantment of the book that the pain became secondary. But for all the curative powers the book clearly contained, my number-one, all-time favourite was, nevertheless, *A Little Princess*.

For a prairie child, which I was, it created a totally foreign world. That is not quite true. I had one point of reference: Sara's father, Captain Crewe, was a soldier, whom I loved extravagantly. My father, too, was a soldier, whom I loved extravagantly. Otherwise the book was beyond all my small experience—a boarding school in England, a French maid, expensive clothes and dolls, but more wonderful and exotic still, India.

When Sara's fortunes were reversed and she became a charity child, deprived of all her privileges, and moved up into an unheated garret, my heart broke. But I was learning about reverses. And when, pinched with cold and hungry after a bleak day of running errands for Miss Minchin, Sara found her garret magically transformed into a haven of warmth and plenty, my heart was healed again. This, perhaps, was my first intimation of that transformative opening of the heart which has since occurred on rare occasions, usually unexpectedly. As a child I remember feeling I had been given all the riches of India.

Susan Swan (writer)

I turned down the *Bobbsey Twins* (too sappy) and read *Little Women* out of a sense of duty, but when my mother handed me a copy of *The Secret Garden*, I read it without resisting.

And that was all I did. I read it before breakfast. I read it during school recess. I read it in the bathroom late at night after my parents were asleep. My mother seemed to understand my addictive behaviour. She'd gone through it herself when she first discovered *The Secret Garden* tucked away in my Aunt Louise's china cupboard, misplaced and forgotten.

I was the third generation in my family to be swept away by Frances Hodgson Burnett's 1911 story that celebrates the efforts of an orphan girl, Mary Lennox, to solve the mystery of a secret garden on her uncle's Yorkshire estate.

Would rereading it be like returning to one of those houses I thought was imposing when I was small, but look cramped and dingy to adult eyes? Would I find my beloved story hackneyed and stereotyped? I didn't expect to enjoy *The Secret Garden*, but its simple, well-crafted style and idiosyncratic characters won me over a second time. And once again, I found myself lost in the atmosphere of childhood, experiencing its straightforward pleasures and its full-blown adult feelings of sadness, despair and powerlessness.

I was nine when I first read *The Secret Garden*, only a year younger than Mary Lennox. (Lucky for me Mary was ten, because I considered books with heroines younger than I was too babyish to read.) Mary was like a big sister, a role model I could pity and envy at the same time because her orphan state meant she could be unrepentantly selfish and more rude than I thought possible in my family, where civility was a household god.

Mary had lost both parents, a British army officer and his wife, to cholera in India and, with her thin little body and contrary little yellow face, she was a most disagreeable-looking child. Everybody finds her hard to handle and Mary dislikes everybody in return. Everybody, that is, except for the young housemaid Martha, and her brother Dickon, who introduces Mary to the animals of the Yorkshire moor.

Like Mary, I too was at the mercy of adult whims and schedules. Shunned by her uncle, Mary had hours and hours by herself to kill on the estate, Misselthwaite Manor. I had less freedom, but time felt interminable in that grade 4 classroom studying for spelling tests as Dickie Robitaille, the class troublemaker who sat behind me, whispered into my neck gory scene-by-scene accounts of *The Creature from the Black Lagoon.*

And like Mary and her invalid cousin, Colin, I believed in transformations; I had just traded away my case of standard HB pencils (with boring, middle-of-the-road nibs) for my friend Beth's emerald-coloured pencil with a darker, softer 2B nib. Once I owned the special 2B pencil, I knew my problems with sloppy calligraphy would be over and I'd write daintily, like Beth.

So I identified with Mary's secret struggle to reclaim the old rose garden and I admired the way her friendship inspired Colin to join her campaign. The truth no adult will tell you, Frances Hodgson Burnett seemed to be saying, is that childhood is an ordeal, but with some basic tools like fresh air, effort and encouragement, you can transform any joyless world that imprisons you.

I didn't know it at the time, but Burnett was also passing on the basis of my writerly values. Namely, that literature is a secret garden you discover in the privacy of your imagination and that healing, rebirth and the evolution of the self are the central goals of experience. How humbling and even embarrassing to discover the blueprint for much of my adult thinking inside a childhood story! And yet—why not? It could be argued that thinking can't exist without stories, no matter how simple. Just as Jesus used parables to explain his principles, we need literature to express our beliefs as well as our feelings.

And finally, in *The Secret Garden* Burnett reminded me of a problem I've never been able to solve. In the last scene of her novel, the story moves from Mary to Colin, who walks toward his father inside the luxuriant new growth of the garden "as healthy as any boy in Yorkshire."

Yes there it is—the unabashed mythologizing of the female nurturer! Mary's greatest victory, it turns out, was her ability to nourish Colin. This is the kind of mythic female stuff I swallowed rapturously as a girl, and later learned to distrust. Paeans to female caretaking have always masked the way our society takes the work of mothers for granted, sweeping out of sight the gruelling expenditure of energy and time that has been going on for centuries with the assumption that the job is, in itself, its own reward.

So I've been reticent to celebrate female nurturing in case I wind up adding to this disavowal of women's experience. For me, nurturing has been a furtive and guilty pleasure, delicious, dangerous and doubly intoxicating because the needs of a child, a friend or a lover so often seem in competition with the time required to write a book and the labour involved is never commensurate with the recognition you get for it.

Maude Barlow (chair, Council of Canadians)

The Little Prince, by Antoine de Saint-Exupéry, is perhaps my all-time favourite book, and dearly loved by my (now adult) children as well. It can best be understood by the lessons it teaches; every day they return in some new and yet mysteriously ancient way to test me.

The Little Prince visited a king who lived alone on a very small planet and who understood he had to give practical orders if he was to be obeyed. In commanding the sun to rise and set every day, he consulted an almanac and twice a day chose carefully the exact time to assert his authority. From him I learned that to do what is humanly possible under the circumstances can border on the miraculous.

The Little Prince practised a great lesson for our time of emerging ecological consciousness—that every living plant and animal is unique and precious, and must be preserved with great care. "When you've finished with your own toilet in the morning, then it is time to attend to the toilet of your planet, just so, with the greatest care."

The Little Prince met a businessman who set such great store in "matters of consequence," like counting money and adding sums in a great ledger, that he never smelled a flower, or looked upon a star, or loved anyone. The Little Prince said that the businessman was not a man at all, but a mushroom—an apt description, I believe, for more than a few CEOs I know!

The Little Prince understood what all children know—that the land of tears is a secret place and must be respected. He also knew that the smallest acts of love, like tending a small vain flower, are the greatest. This is a hard lesson, and requires great patience.

A wild fox taught the Little Prince another very great lesson: we cannot buy friendship in a shop. We must work hard at friendship and observe the proper rites. Then you become forever responsible for what you have tamed. This lesson can be very sad. "One runs the risk of weeping a little, if one lets oneself be tamed."

The Little Prince had great courage. At midnight in the desert he bravely met the yellow snake who solved all riddles and he let the snake's poison take him home. "He did not cry out. He fell as gently as a tree falls."

For, you see, the Little Prince understood the greatest lesson of all. He knew that his body was the shell of his soul and that he could still love and be loved from far away. "It is only with the heart that one can see rightly; what is essential is invisible to the eye." When I live this lesson, the world is unendingly wonderful. Thank you, small one.

The Right Honourable Roméo LeBlanc (Governor General of Canada)

I was sixteen before I discovered *The Little Prince*. I already admired Antoine de Saint-Exupéry for some other works—*Terre des hommes* and *Vol de nuit*. But I was struggling with them, finding the content sophisticated and the philosophy difficult.

At my school I came, by chance, across *Le Petit Prince*. I rejoiced to find what seemed to be a simpler work. It was a story for children about a Little Prince who came from his own planet. Right at the start the little prince knew that the narrator's boyhood drawing, which everyone else mistook for a hat, really showed an elephant inside a boa constrictor.

Later when I taught at a rural school in New Brunswick, I often used *Le Petit Prince* in class. I would ask students to read passages aloud and then write about their feelings.

I remember especially the story of the fox and the rose, when the prince learns that what makes a flower (or a friend) your own is the time you give to the flower so that it becomes more important to you than all the others.

Over the years that I taught, I suppose three or four hundred students read the book with me. Working with them, I came to believe that *Le Petit Prince* was philosophy as deep as anything Saint-Exupéry had written. When I run into my students forty years later, it is astonishing how many refer to it.

In fact, when I was called on to decorate one of my former pupils with the Order of Canada—he had become an important figure in baroque music—he later sent me a copy of *Le Petit Prince*, to thank me as his former teacher.

In those long-ago classes, my students never learned philosophy in any technical sense. But I hope that many will remember the fox, with what he called his "simple secret: It is only with the heart that one can see rightly."

Carol Matas (writer)

Ozma of Oz by L. Frank Baum could be the most perfect book ever written. I say "could" because this is a subjective conjecture, my strictly subjective conjecture. I suppose what I should say is, I loved that book when I read it and going back to it for the purpose of this piece made me love it all over again. The book thrilled me. I thought, "How could anyone think this up? Imagine this?"

Here's an example. Washed up on the shore of the magical land of Ev, Baum writes a scene in which Dorothy discovers a tree which grows lunch pails. Lunch pails!

"Inside she found, nicely wrapped in white papers, a ham sandwich, a piece of sponge-cake, a pickle, a slice of new cheese and an apple. Each thing had its own stem and had to be picked off the inside of the box."

And the characters! Strong, funny, courageous girls, like Dorothy and Ozma. Ozma who was a princess and had such dignity, and yet was always loving and considerate. And the bad guys! The nasty wheelers, the devious Nome King, and my favourite, Princess Langwidere, who changed her character every time she changed her head!

Dorothy was a wonderful character. She had a sense of humour, she was resourceful, brave, determined, and always willing to stick up for the underdog. Ozma, too, was brave. And perhaps that was the quality I admired the most—they would unflinchingly risk their lives to save the lives of their friends. And friendship ran deep in this book, in all his books. Friendship and love. And humour. Mustn't forget the humour. At one point Dorothy asks the sawhorse (which is alive) if it is intelligent. "Not very," said the creature. "It would be foolish to waste intelligence on a common sawhorse, when so many professors need it."

Frank Baum gave me an invaluable gift, the pure pleasure of reading—that moment when you encounter something completely new, like an explorer discovering a new land, when you are thrilled because what you are reading is so exciting, so new, so breathtaking in inventiveness, that you are changed forever, in some way. So my vote goes to Frank, and to *Ozma of Oz*, *The Marvellous Land of Oz*, *The Road to Oz*, and all the rest of the books in that series.

Cynthia Belliveau (actor)

I was a voracious reader and writer as a child. I loved going to the Stratford Public Library and selecting books. Each simple, rectangular block of pulp equalled some new exotic adventure, some new world or life to explore, some realm of a writer's imagination to enter into. I loved the way the library looked, especially the way the books smelled and felt in my fingers. I loved learning the Dewey Decimal System; even the way those words "Dewey Decimal System" sounded rolling off my tongue.

Today my vast collection of books is arranged according to that system. Choosing a favourite book is difficult. I read every Trixie Beldon and Nancy Drew book, and everything Enid Blyton wrote. I especially loved *The Secret Seven*. I loved *Grimm's Fairy Tales* and Aesop's fables. But the book that I still carry with me in my travels today is *Pippi Longstocking* by Astrid Lindgren. She was and is my heroine, my inspiration.

What child doesn't at one time or another dream of living without the constraints and rules and oppressiveness of parents. Pippi lived in a wonderful old house with her monkey and her horse and just a romantic notion of a parent at sea. Of course there were always complications in my fantasy, but Pippi had them all worked out. She need never be afraid, for she had the strength of ten men. And she need never go wanting, for she had a bottomless chest of jewels and gold coins. But the thing about Pippi that most affected me and still lives with me today is her passion and her spirit of fun. She made all those chores, that I felt burdened with, into fun. For example, when the kitchen floor needed scrubbing, she strapped scrub-brushes to her feet and joyously skated in the suds.

That sense of seeing things through different eyes still inspires me. My philosophy of living is very much based upon Pippi's ability to make work fun, to listen to those inner voices that tell when to eat or sleep or dance or play rather than waiting for the parental voice, that ability to transform the mundane into the extraordinary. Today, whenever I feel a little lost, I pull out my ragged copy. Before long I'm seeing the world through Pippi's eyes. I'm back in the joy and the passion of life and the delight in everyday things.

Howard Engel (writer)

For as long as I can remember, I have known the stories of King Arthur's Court, all the way from Merlin and Uther Pendragon down to Sir Galahad and the achievement of the Holy Grail. My mother, Lollie Engel, read these stories to me using the version of the Malory tales as told in his "forsoothly" style by Howard Pyle. These stories pulled me out of my own pre-war life and tumbled me into a world of knightly quests and noble deeds.

Pyle also illustrated the stories. I loved his velvety black-and-white pictures of the knights, their caparisoned horses and their ladies in distress. He had a wonderful way with the textures of cloth, whether it was white samite on the sleeve of the Lady of the Lake or the covering Lancelot hastily pulled over himself when interrupted from his couch.

My mother and Pyle opened the door into the mythic British past and awakened in me a love of English history that is still very much with me. For one thing, Camelot was different from our view of the CNR tracks at the end of our backyard in St. Catharines. I once tried to save tin cans with the idea of making a suit of armour from them. For the body, I used a carton discarded from Carroll's Red and White Store on Western Hill, not far from Edith Cavell School where I was struggling with grade 3. I managed to make a fair piece of work of the body, legs and arms. If you ignored the word "KOTEX" on the carton, I could easily pass for a "ver-ray, parfit gentil knyght."

I was thinking about my mother's reading to me this week. Whenever I came down with measles, mumps, chicken pox or whooping cough, she was always there ready to read to me. It wasn't always King Arthur; she led me into Ellery Queen, Nathaniel Hawthorne, Thomas Bailey Aldrich, Rex Stout, Robert Louis Stevenson and Mark Twain as well. She had a way of reading the text that wasn't overly dramatic—she never "took the parts" of the characters—but she read with intensity, entering into the stories so fully that the bedroom was transformed into Camelot or the Mississippi or the Isle of Mull in a moment. She brought Kipling's Grand Trunk Road in India as alive as she did Nero Wolfe's Manhattan brownstone. I don't want to forget that, and all the other things she introduced me to between the covers of a book.

Frank McKenna (Premier of New Brunswick)

I have had the chance to experience many excellent books and was an avid reader even before I started school. However, one of the books that has given me the greatest joy is *The Story of King Arthur and His Knights*.

When I was growing up, the story of King Arthur touched so many emotional hot buttons for me that I have read and reread it many times. It is the story of the constant battle of good versus evil, with good invariably prevailing. It includes the indomitable and uncompromising quest for the Holy Grail. It outlines stirring tales of courage and élan. The stories of Sir Tristan, Sir Lancelot and Sir Gawain, who fought the gigantic green knight, have always inspired me.

My imagination was gripped by the story of the magical sword

Excalibur, the alchemy of Merlin and the dazzling centre of all that was good and inspiring—Camelot. The story of King Arthur was not always uplifting, however. The treachery of Sir Lancelot and Queen Guinevere always touched my soul with sadness. The wide range of emotions, the fanciful flights of imagination and stirring characterization left an indelible mark on my memory.

Clyde Gilmour (broadcaster)

My father, John Milton Gilmour, grew up in Ottawa. He was already a great book-lover before he and my mother, the former Olive McCabe of Arthur, Ontario, were married in Calgary in 1910. She, too, was an avid reader. One of Dad's prize possessions was a complete set of Mark Twain's books. I began browsing in them when I was maybe seven or eight. By a wide margin, the one I enjoyed the most was neither *Tom Sawyer* nor *Huckleberry Finn*, but *A Connecticut Yankee in King Arthur's Court.* No doubt some of Twain's mockery of ancient chivalry and religiosity was wasted on me at this early age. But the book gave me an enduring fascination with Arthurian mythology and the hushed timelessness of the English countryside. I was lucky enough to marry a lovely woman named Barbara Donald, who was an authority on books (chief of sales at the Hudson's Bay book department in Vancouver) long before I ever met her. My father died in 1951, my mother in 1960, my wife in 1995. Their faces and their voices were as alive as ever in my mind just recently when I started a nostalgic browse through *A Connecticut Yankee in King Arthur's Court.* Three hours later I turned out my bedlamp. The book holds up wonderfully well.

Twain's *Yankee* was portrayed in Hollywood by Will Rogers in 1931 and by Bing Crosby in 1949. Both movies had some good moments, but they barely hinted at the magic on Mark Twain's pages.

My lifelong obsession with this story has also helped me, I feel sure, to respond fully to the mysticism and polyphonic grandeur of such music as *Fantasia on a Theme by Thomas Tallis*, composed by Ralph Vaughan Williams in 1910. If Hollywood ever does yet another remake of Twain's sad and funny Arthurian fable, the producer should insist on putting the *Tallis Fantasia* on the soundtrack.

Patrick Watson (journalist, former CBC Chairman)

My father came into my room and handed me a new selection from the Book of the Month Club. "I think you might like this," he said. He was usually right; so I opened the blue linen covers and savoured the smell as I always loved to do with a new book, and plunged right in. I was nine years old.

It was *The Sword in the Stone* by T.H. White, the first volume of what would become the trilogy *The Once and Future King.*

I was rapt, enchanted, swept away. I read it through in a whoosh. Then I started at the beginning and read it through again. Before long I could quote parts of it, and still can. I bet I have read it twenty times. I still pick it up with delight. It is about a boy ill-thought-of by his powerful half-brother and serious elders, but beloved of animals and—oh wonderful!—also of the great magician Merlin, who recognizes in him a great spirit to be cultivated. It is a fable about loyalty and steadfastness, about the love of the texture of things and the beauty instinct in nature, and about the wonder of creation.

There were obvious enchantments for a ten-year-old in a family of five siblings, given to fantasizing his specialness. But there was rich eccentric humour and there was a poetry in the language that the boy somehow responded to with curiosity and delight, piecing together from context the meaning of obsolete medieval words like Austringer and Complines, Coneys and Mews. And thinking how fine it was that Merlin and his coterie of magical animals would say elegant and mysterious things like "I feel eternal longings in me," or "Oh, for quietus with a bare bodkin."

Years later I would be amazed to find, as I made my way delightedly into Shakespeare for the first time, how very often Shakespeare (and many other great English poets) quote lines they must have got from my favourite book, *The Sword in the Stone*, a form of plagiarism that bespoke the magician Merlin, who lived backwards in time, remembered everything that was going to happen but had a hard time recalling what he had eaten for breakfast.

"The bell invites me," said the mad Goshawk, Colonel Cully, as he murderously approached the boy called The Wart (who will become King Arthur); "Hear it not...for it is a knell that summons thee to heaven or to hell." It was wonderful to discover—six or seven years later—Macbeth speaking the same words, Shakespeare obviously having admired T.H. White as much as I did.

Now that I am turning my hand to fables for adults, disguised as children's novels (*Admek, A Beaver Odyssey* is in the works and looking for a publisher), I find that the model to which I turn with affection more than any other source of influence is *The Sword in the Stone*, counting on the delight that captured me to have the same spell-casting power as I rework it in more modern guise (though still antique, as befits my respectable years, and eccentric as befits...well).

I still have that same old blue-covered, much-thumbed and loved and worn, hardbound copy my father handed me almost sixty years ago. It still smells good.

Michael Coren (writer)

I think I was five years old but I'm not exactly sure. That very ambiguity, of course, is one of the joys of remembering childhood. My teacher, Miss Powers, began reading us a story about magic lions, of adventures in a distant land that was in fact very near, of battles with darkness and even of meeting Santa Claus. I thought then that Miss Powers had the most lovely voice that I had ever heard. More than three decades later only the voices of my wife and children are more sweet.

The story was C.S. Lewis's *The Lion, the Witch and the Wardrobe,* and before my teacher had finished the first chapter I made my mother go out and buy me a copy. I began reading it at 4:00 on a Monday, after school, and finished it the following morning. I didn't sleep that night. But the magnificent paradox of the book, and of all the Narnia stories and most of C.S. Lewis's work, is that by not sleeping for a few hours I was awakened for the rest of my life. The moral, intellectual and spiritual message of the book was superbly implicit, and indelibly profound, and it led me not only to joy and peace but, many years later, to writing a short biography of Lewis.

More important, it enabled me to pass on the intense and fulfilling excitement of *The Lion, the Witch and the Wardrobe* to my children, as I know they will to my grandchildren. Like all of the best children's tales, it ends nothing but begins everything. I wish I could read it again for the first time every day of my life.

Wendy Mesley (broadcaster)

Once there was a little girl named Wendy. She had been raised in a family that wasn't quite like the ones most of her friends grew up in. And this made her look at things differently. She was very imaginative and enjoyed spending time by herself. But some of the other kids thought she was a bit odd. And this sometimes made her feel lonely.

But then she discovered a book called *The Lion, the Witch and the Wardrobe*, by C.S. Lewis. And slowly she came to see that it didn't matter so much what the other children thought. That she could be proud of being different. That she didn't have to change what she believed in just so the other kids would stop making fun of her.

If she wanted, she could even go out and find another land to play in. And maybe, the other kids might even want to come play with her there. In this world, girls got to do or be anything they wanted... just like the boys. They got to have adventures and big dreams. It was okay to be a tomboy, okay to be a leader (even if you still got scared sometimes).

It's still one of her all-time favourite books!!

Patrick Lane (poet)

The book that I read and reread as a boy was *Swiss Family Robinson* by Johann Wyss. Between the ages of nine and eleven years I read the book a hundred times and think now it was because of my imagining a perfect family. I identified with the boys in the book, their perfect father and mother, their time on a tropical island, and must have wished it my own family. I held it to me like a bible, a talisman of what life could be like. The most important book of my boyhood.

The next book to change my life was James Frazer's *The Golden Bough,* which I bought in a used-book store in Kelowna, B.C. I read its myths and texts all through my sixteenth and seventeenth years. More than any other book, it affirmed my vision of one world of ritual, religion and harmony and shaped much of my thought from 1955 to the present. I still have the copy in my library, one of the few books that have survived my tumultuous life.

Bill Cameron (broadcaster)

The Wind in the Willows (by Kenneth Grahame) must have had a cover once, but I don't remember it—only the smooth blue binding with the gold print. Inside, heavy creamy paper, rough and smooth at the same time, slightly ragged on the long edge of the page. In sunlight the paper glowed and the sketches—etchings? or woodcuts?—of the animals and the river-bank world floated into the air.

At the age of seven I had no idea what or where England was, but the book taught me what the best of Englishness might be. It was different from any Englishness I discovered later. Class didn't matter.

Mole, a burrowing short-sighted creature, could chuck his life over his shoulder and run away to join the Water Rat, a rodent of a completely different kind, a canny wet capable fellow who could operate a rowboat and a can opener. Toad the toff, the mansion-inhabiting trust-fund Toad who fell into manias for cars, caravans, locomotives, was well-loved and often forgiven by his sensible friends. Badger, the rough king of the deep caves, turned out to be quite a fine and warm-hearted fellow after all. And the sneering hordes of stoats (Bolsheviks, probably) were easily beaten by a small group of good fellows.

You can escape. You can take up a completely different life. You can be an ass and be forgiven. If you are right, you will win.

The world of the river was more real to me than the wet streets of Vancouver and as real as the desert and orchards of the Okanagan Valley where we spent our summers. It was green and well-mannered with quiet water but it was broken by dark woods that held all kinds of cruel beasts. That is more or less a reliable map of the world if you are seven. And there were touches of my life in the book. When Otter's son went missing in the woods, the frantic sound of Otter's voice must have been like my father's when I decided to walk home from kindergarten. My father found me on the side of the highway, and Otter found his son curled between the hooves of a massive Pan figure playing a pipe, while the world shook with wonder, but otherwise it was pretty close.

A critic I read recently holds that the Pan passage is a flaw in an otherwise lovely book, a sentimental over-the-top rhapsody and an excursion into literature. But I like it better even than the slapstick of the Mole learning to row and the rumpus of the great final fight with cudgels and cutlasses in the Great Hall. I like it best of all. A small boy lost and found and forgiven.

Joyce Fairbairn (Minister Responsible for Literacy)

One of my all-time favourite books is *The Wind in the Willows*, by Kenneth Grahame. I remember quite clearly reading this wonderful story when I was very young. The world of Ratty and Mole and Badger and Mr. Toad opened my young mind to a world of adventure through the magic of imagination. It offered lessons on friendship, generosity, courage, laughter and tears.

This book taught me about the variety of personalities which make our world interesting, exciting and challenging. It uncovered a lifelong love of animals—particularly towards those who have been abused or mistreated. Our home is alive with rescued dogs and cats.

And most importantly, to paraphrase the self-absorbed but unintentionally wise Mr. Toad, the written word brought "the whole world before me and a horizon that is always changing." Books in general encouraged me, at a young age, to explore the rhythm of life beyond my own river-bank in Lethbridge, Alberta, but always to return to its comfort and reassurance.

It is hard to imagine, in this great and caring land, that there are those in our society who have great difficulty entering the world of reading and writing. As Federal Minister of Literacy I see examples of this everywhere in Canada and I also see the great need to ensure that all Canadians have opportunities to read and write and develop to their full potential. Simply put, there is almost nothing as important as this ability that has such a profound effect on our daily lives and our future.

·4· Books about Nature

"The vast unconsciousness of nature"
—Northrop Frye

Part One: Animals

"To err is human, not to, animal"—Robert Frost

In virtually every culture the oldest stories are about animals. From the earliest cave drawings to the fables of Aesop, Odysseus's Argus, and Noah's well-populated ark, animals have figured prominently in illustration and in literature. Folk-tales and native storytelling reveal, through animal characters, much about human nature and the workings of the world.

Children seem to have a natural affinity with animals. We surround our babies with a great menagerie of stuffed toys and animal images. Most toddlers are fascinated with bugs and insects—butterflies, ants and anything else readily available. Rural children are familiar with farm animals and many urban families harbour a variety of pets. Children are encouraged to tend and nurture, to feed, walk and cuddle, much as their own parents and caregivers take care of them. Hundreds of picture books are teeming with dogs, cats, bunnies, mice and other adorable creatures. Books about the world around us, particularly the animal kingdom, continue to form a fundamental and extremely popular component of children's literature.

In much of the eighteenth and nineteenth centuries, many now-forgotten authors tried to teach kids about nature through dry treatises and moral tales. These lifeless books focused on tedious explanations of outdoor skills and plant identification. They often included cautionary advice about coping with dangerous animals and earnestly promoted kindness for their domestic cousins. At least their teachings may have saved some animals from abuse at human hands. Today the abuse is more likely to be found in animal fiction—stories that are overly cute, dripping with sugary sentiment and interestingly, once again, often too blatant in their edifying implications.

But animals have featured in other ways too. Folk-tales and modern stories with talking animals, animal fantasy and books highlighting similarities in animal and human behaviour have remained understandably popular. Consider the parallel between animal and human behaviour in Homer's *Odyssey*. When the hero, Odysseus, returns home in disguise after a twenty-year absence, he happily encounters his old dog, Argus, who recognizes him instantly. The dog has waited with steadfast allegiance and tremendous patience for his beloved master's promised return. Their reunion must be one of the first great written records of animal loyalty. The episode also dramatically foreshadows Odysseus's more cautious but equally ardent reception from his devoted wife, Penelope.

Aesop's durable fables, like many folk legends, cleverly reveal human nature by using entertaining animal players. Kipling's fanciful *Just So Stories* are similar to native legends that explore how animals and people came to behave the way they do. The Bible, particularly the Old Testament, includes numerous references to animals. The admonition, for example, to feed one's animals and children before oneself—because they are unable to do so on their own—is observed daily on farms and in kitchens around the world. Animals and young children are alike in their affectionate nature, their inability to express themselves fully through language, and of course, their almost total dependence on others for care and nourishment.

The numerous fairy tales, nursery rhymes, folk-tales and myths involving animals also reflect a more rural society. Native stories are hugely populated with animals, both real and imaginary. They are used to explain everything from the Creation to weather conditions, the change of seasons, animal and human behaviour and other mysterious elements of nature.

Many enduring literary classics use animals to tell a story with wider implications. Classic examples of books with talking, humanized animals are Kipling's *The Jungle Book*, Grahame's *The Wind in the Willows* and Beatrix Potter's gentle, illustrated fantasies. In these books the animals are charmingly and effectively anthropomorphized.

Potter, for example, imbues her rabbits, mice and other characters with an appealing mixture of animal and human characteristics. A.A. Milne's Winnie-the-Pooh has childlike friends and adventures, but loves honey and lolling about outdoors. Toad, Mole, Rat and the other humanized animals in *The Wind in the Willows* behave like recognizable adults, complete with personality quirks, conversation and hilarious comic predicament.

With its female protagonist and unusual premise, the touching and resonant *Sajo and Her Beaver People* by Grey Owl (1935) masterfully links human behaviour to the survival of animals. Grey Owl was the *nom de plume* of Archibald Stansfeld Belaney, a fascinating Englishman who lived in Canada for thirty-two years. He assumed the identity of a full-blooded Indian and wrote and lived among his adopted people. He also sympathetically extended the naturalist and conservationist elements of Canadian children's fiction.

E.B. White's *Charlotte's Web* (1952) is my personal and all-time favourite among the many books with animal heroes. I clearly recall my first encounter with the story. I hear it in my father's voice. In my mind's eye I can see my mother and older sister sitting at the end of the bed, all transfixed as this elegant, funny and beautiful tribute to friendship brilliantly played itself out. Struck by the tragedy and its telling, tears fell freely. It was the mid-fifties and new to all of us. (I did not realize until years later that the book had not been around for eons.) I continue to feel an enormous affection for the book and especially, of course, for Wilbur and for Charlotte (a pig and a spider, no less!). My husband and I could hardly wait to share the story, years later, with our own three daughters. Quite naturally, it prompted the same emotional response. *Charlotte's Web* is, apparently, the most popular children's book in North America, and rightly so.

Moralistic animal stories—the best surviving example is Anna Sewell's *Black Beauty* (1877)—continued to express the laudable goal of teaching kindness to animals and condemning cruelty. Canadian Margaret Marshall Saunders's *Beautiful Joe* (1894) is a similar tale. In Saunders's version it is a dog rather than a horse that experiences both cruel and kind treatment over the course of its lifetime. Joe and the loving children who rescue and care for him enjoy exciting adventures and (deliberately illustrative) teaching experiences. Both books are idealized, the language, human characters and instructive tone rather forced by today's standards. They survive and are still well loved by many readers because of their emotional appeal and engaging animals.

From Marguerite Henry's *Misty of Chincoteague* (1947) (another story I loved as a young girl) to Bernice Thurman Hunter's Margaret trilogy released through the 1980s, stories about kids and horses have retained an enormous popularity. Other notable examples are Mary O'Hara's *My Friend Flicka* and Edith Bagnold's *National Velvet*. Similarly, Albert Payson Terhune's *Lad: A Dog* (1919), Eric Knight's *Lassie-Come-Home* (1940) and Canada's Sheila Burnford's *The Incredible Journey* (1960) keep the loyal, innovative, devoted dog alive in many hearts. In Burnford's animal adventure three pets daringly brave all sorts of difficulty and obstacles in their determined quest to return to their family. Illustrious literary cats range from Lewis Carroll's famous Cheshire in *Alice in Wonderland* through Dr. Seuss's *The Cat in the Hat*, Mog, Zoom and many others.

Richard Adams's adventure/fantasy *Watership Down* (1972), an "epic novel about rabbits," has remained popular with children and adults alike. Dodie Smith's perennial favourite, *Hundred and One Dalmatians* (1956), offered (well before Disney's sentimentalized movie) the thrill of villainy and a stimulating chase to a story of animal–human bonding and tender relationships.

Canada is credited with making a major contribution to the genre of animal literature, the realistic animal story. Both Charles G.D. Roberts and Ernest Thompson Seton composed fictionalized but believable tales about real animals in their natural habitat around the turn of the century.

Roberts may have been the first to apply psychology to animal behaviour, in his words to "get under the skin" of his subjects. But it was Seton and his *Wild Animals I Have Known* that popularized this new and original genre. Seton was a naturalist, gifted illustrator and terrific speaker. He could enthral large audiences of adults and children alike with his tales of wildlife—revealing in his "animal biographies" how a variety of real creatures spent their days, nourished and protected their young and how they died. He carefully observed animals both in the wild and around the Don River Valley near his home in Toronto. Seton presented animals in their natural setting whether that meant adjacent city yards, ravines, farms or out in the wild. He carefully ascribed to them thoughts and language (communication among themselves), which, while slightly romanticized, is never inconsistent with their actual behaviour.

Charles G.D. Roberts is as celebrated today for his suspenseful but realistic animal stories as for the significant novels and poetry he also created. Among his more lasting tales are *The Kindred of the Wild* and *Red Fox*. A contemporary and friend of Seton, Roberts frequently wrote nostalgically about growing up in New Brunswick.

He especially loved bears and his *Thirteen Bears* (a selection of stories gathered and published posthumously) reveals his pleasure in both words and wild beasts.

Seton and Roberts use a combination of dramatized fiction and carefully observed actual behaviour to highlight the typically courageous, even heroic, instinctive ways animals behave in their daily lives. Sadly most wild animals die prematurely from natural hazards or predators such as other animals (wolves, owls, foxes). Many succumb to a cruel death at the hands of human hunters.

Canadians continue to be very active, even paramount, in writing groundbreaking and memorable animal fiction. Farley Mowat, in hilarious stories like *Owls in the Family* and *The Dog Who Wouldn't Be,* added humour, vivid incident and family context to animal stories. For the humour alone he deserves the eternal gratitude of generations of children and adult readers.

In *Never Cry Wolf* Mowat reinforces Seton's and Roberts's evidence about wolves' natural behaviour (as well as acutely drawing attention to the need for conservation of Canadian arctic animals). Fred Bodsworth's *The Last of the Curlews* juxtaposes dramatic loss—of a single bird, but also of an endangered species—in a haunting and unforgettable story remembered fondly by contributors to this collection.

Contemporary North American animal stories include many ancient Native legends adapted to the written format and often beautifully illustrated. Native tales sometimes involve creatures that can change their form through trickery, causing enormous mischief. They may also include a wide variety of real animals. Some of these stories offer a brilliant combination of both traditions, the anthropomorphic and the realistic. Frequently added to this are tribe-specific or spiritual components all their own.

One fascinating early Canadian collection of Native animal stories is Pauline Johnson's *Legends of Vancouver* (1911). These are tales she personally heard from Chief Joe Capilano and then adapted into everyday English. Cyrus Macmillan's *Canadian Wonder Tales* (1918) and *Canadian Fairy Tales* (1922) are two important collections that include many animal stories. Further Native retellings by writer/collectors Christie Harris, Robert Ayre (among the first of the great Raven stories) and others kept these stories (historically passed down through the oral tradition) alive and accessible in a printed English format. For the first time they became available to a wider audience. In 1967 a Nootka chief, George Clutesi, published *Son of Raven, Son of Deer*, moral tales that had been retold in families for centuries. Designed to teach and delight young Native children, these are thought to be very old stories. In them, perhaps not surprisingly, lessons are taught through illustrative animal experience much the same way as they are in the centuries-old fables of Aesop or relatively recent (only three-hundred-year-old) stories of Lafontaine. Today many more Native and Inuit stories are being published. Storytellers like Ricardo Keens-Douglas both tell them and write them down. Although they display wide variety, a common theme is the crucial connection people must have (or make) with animals and the natural world.

Although several animal stories are collected in this chapter, others are sprinkled throughout the book. It is notable how many reminiscences involve endangered species, conserving wildlife and protecting their environment.

Timothy Findley (writer)

I first encountered *Wild Animals I Have Known* when I was a boy growing up in Toronto. It was read to me by my father, for whom it had also been one of childhood's literary centrepieces. Part of its magic comes from the fact that the author, Ernest Thompson Seton, began his professional life as an artist and this book, like most of his others, is enhanced by a profusion of charming and informative drawings. As a complement to all the full-sized illustrations, almost every page of *Wild Animals I Have Known* has some detail of animal life set out in pen-and-ink sketches in the margins. For these alone, the book is guaranteed to enchant any child.

Adding to my early fascination with these narratives was the fact that each time my father read one of them to my brother and me, he would take us down into the Don Valley and show us where the story had taken place. Saturday afternoons in spring and fall were often spent seeking out a likely location for Raggylug the Rabbit's confrontation with the snake—or the spot near the river where Redruff the Partridge had saved one of his chicks from a marauding squirrel.

The Don Valley could then be traversed only by horse trails and a train track that followed the course of the river. It has since been scarred by a great roaring highway that cuts against the natural flow of the land. But the ravines remain a blessing and a haven for beasts whose lives are the echoes of those who appear in *Wild Animals I Have Known*—the rabbits, crows and foxes of another time.

The tales are certainly romantic enough to qualify as authentic adventure stories with dashing heroes, alarming escapades and narrow escapes. But Seton himself gives warning in his preface that "the life of a wild animal always has a tragic end." This, I think, is what ultimately gives *Wild Animals I Have Known* its staying power—namely, its unbending honesty about the facts of life and death. There is not a single sentimental thought put forward in the book—no deliberate pulling at the heartstrings—nothing manufactured—nothing falsified. Seton's purpose was to reveal the passionate pursuit of survival that lies at the heart of every animal life—a pursuit for which, it seems, much of humankind has lost its passion.

Anyone who can read this book and set it down without gaining a sense of compassion for the animals with whom we share this planet is clearly doomed to lack a sense of compassion for fellow human beings. And surely it is never too soon to encourage that sense of compassion in any child who can read.

There are also enchanting encounters in all these stories with the sheer charm of Ernest Thompson Seton's imagination. As when, for instance, he sets out the seasons of the moon as perceived by Redruff the Partridge: the drumming moon—the berry moon—the moulting moon—the snow moon—et cetera. Or when he draws a map, showing how Raggylug outwits the hound who is chasing him by circling around him so many times, in so many directions that the poor dog is dizzy and fails even to see the rabbit when, at last, Rag "freezes" practically under the dog's nose. The reader—of whatever age—will also be able to learn the various tunes of crow-music—set out on five-line staves and even given key signatures by the author.

I cannot recommend this book highly enough. It is a classic, yes—but there are better reasons than that to have it in your library and to make it available to children—and to adults. We live in a time when nature is increasingly being placed in hazard—not only by what we do out of ignorance, but by what we fail to do because we have ceased to pay attention. This book's best gift—from the moment of contact—is the dedication to life that is implicit in its title. The word "known" says it all—because to be known is to survive, at least for as long as it takes to be seen.

Robert Bateman (wildlife artist)

As a young teenager in the 1940s I would head off on my bicycle every two weeks and fill my carrier with books from the St. Clements Public Library in North Toronto. I would borrow all of the books by all the nature writers represented in the library at that time. The ones I read over and over again were by Sir Charles G.D. Roberts and Ernest Thompson Seton. It was, therefore, a great event for me to receive for my eighteenth birthday Seton's autobiography *The Trail of an Artist-Naturalist*. There is something about a real life lived that has a stronger ring to it than any made-up stories. Seton's life certainly did have a strong ring for me. In 1866 the Seton family came to Toronto, where young Ernest spent every spare minute prowling and exploring the natural world of the Don Valley.

He explored the details of the lives of animals and plants, and dabbled in the traditional ways of the original Native tribes of the area. In doing so he was also exploring *himself*. Two of his most famous books, *Wild Animals I Have Known* and *Two Little Savages*, came out of this period. These are illustrated with his lively and vivid drawings of details of those lives. His talent with a pen and brush matched his inquisitive eye. Nothing escaped his notice.

Seton went on to become a national and even international figure whose life was a vital mixture of adventures in nature, renderings in words and drawings, and public appearances as a great communicator. Like Charles Dickens a few years earlier, Seton was much in demand as a speaker. He consistently packed lecture halls in North America and abroad.

Since my teenage years, my main goal in life has been to have adventures in nature and to put them down in paint. In the past few decades I have also wanted to communicate not only the beauties of nature but the perils it faces. I am sure that the life of Ernest Thompson Seton has played an important part in the person I have become.

Freeman Patterson (photographer)

For several years back in the forties, I was the only student in my grade in the Long Reach (New Brunswick) School. But there were always fifteen to eighteen others unevenly clumped in the remaining seven grades—friends, foes or mere acquaintances, depending on the season, our moods and a code of behaviour too complex for any of us to fathom.

There was one teacher. Different teachers in different years, but always only one. Some ran a very "tight ship," some maintained reasonable control simply because we "liked" them, and one or two utterly lost control of the boisterous throng. But all of them, without exception, had our undivided attention for a few minutes after lunch. This was the time when the teacher read to us.

All of the teachers were "she," and when she read, we eagerly anticipated every twist of plot and sighed very audibly over every favourable denouement. Usually, she read from two books, first from one for the younger children, and then from one for the older students. It never seemed to matter that the students in the upper grades had heard the younger children's stories before. In fact, to hear a tale for the second or third time was to have an enhanced experience. Besides, it proved that you had been around for a while, and knew more than those who were hearing it for the first time.

The books that the teachers read were often brought to school by children whose families valued reading. Many that I carted in (all of which I'd read myself and wanted to experience again) were animal adventure stories written by Thornton W. Burgess around 1914–17, and published in six series by Little, Brown and Company in the late twenties and early thirties. The titles of all my books began "*The Adventures of* ..." and detailed the daily exploits of such characters as Paddy The Beaver, Peter Cottontail, Danny Meadow Mouse, Jerry Muskrat and Grandfather Frog, who inhabited the Green Meadows and the Green Forest this side of the Purple Hills. All the characters turned up in the same general habitat in every book, so we children could easily imagine the smiling Pool, the Lone Little Path and the Old Briar-patch. In fact, these were places that, in a very real sense, we also lived, places where we fled from danger, played jokes on each other, and became a community with all its checks and balances.

My sister inherited the books and read them to her three children, but at my request she brought me several the other day, and I relived the adventures of Peter Cottontail. Fifty summers and winters have passed since I first met Peter, but I love him and the book as much as ever.

Buffy Sainte-Marie (singer, songwriter)

When I was a little girl, my favourite story was *The Tale of Peter Rabbit* by Beatrix Potter, which my mother would read to me, usually at bedtime. I can remember the feeling of being inside the story, surrounded by the wonderful words, and imagining the characters wrapped in the wonderful sounds of my mother's naturally dramatic voice.

Reading or hearing a story has always been to me quite different from seeing a movie. Listening to *Peter Rabbit*, I could smell the summer and feel the weather. Summer has a certain sound too, and I can still hear the crickets and the cicadas singing under the weeds just beyond Mr. McGregor's garden.

I think I owe some of my love of performing to the experience of being inside *Peter Rabbit*, courtesy of my mother's love of reading aloud. She was never self-conscious about enjoying the sound of the words. She'd break up laughing when she found something funny, and react naturally to whatever was going on in the story, oblivious to herself as "actress," and totally immersed in the story itself, which then could fill my entire world with its magic.

I think also that as a songwriter who enjoys the playfulness of words, their rhythm and their bounce and their shapes and their rhyme—which can greatly lighten and add charm to even the most serious of songs—I owe a debt of gratitude to Beatrix Potter. Imagine Mr. McGregor with a flower pot in his hand which he intends to "pop upon the top of Peter." I only wish I could come up with something like that!

Recently while waiting for a flight from Vancouver to Winnipeg, I went into the airport book store. There was a pocket-sized edition of my favourite story. I purchased it and soon put it in the hands of another little girl. She read it sitting in a pool of sunshine next to my living-room window. Her eyes opened wide, and I could tell by the expression on her face that in her own world she could hear a certain sound that is still familiar to me. It's Mr. McGregor's hoe, and it's going "scr-r-ritch, scratch, scratch, scritch." I sure like that sound.

Susan Musgrave (writer)

From as far back as I can remember, my father read me a story every night before I went to sleep. The one book that I asked for, night after night, was *Pookie* by Ivy Lillian Wallace, about a rabbit with wings. His mother could never keep his wings tied back properly and because he was "different" he was eventually forced out of the burrow to "seek his fortune." There was a series of Pookie books wherein he had many adventures, such as deciding to put the world right by making Winter go away, and everything went wrong and of course I knew how he felt. The thought of one illustration can still induce a thrill, and a shudder: Pookie on a frozen ledge, his worldly goods tied in a red-and-white hanky on the end of a stick, facing Winter, a hideous icy apparition with icicles for fingers and a wicked icy face. Pookie had been sent by all the woodland animals to beg Winter to come back. There is talk of Instinct, and I remember asking my father what that word meant because it was probably the biggest, strangest word I'd heard in any story up until then. Pookie prepares to freeze to death, but just then a gust of icy wind blows him into Belinda's window. (Belinda is a kind girl who lives alone in the forest, and is lonely herself.) Belinda lays him in her workbasket to thaw, and he stays on to live with her.

I think I grew up wanting to be different from everyone else, because I identified so much with the underdog—in this case, a rabbit with wings. I also respect (and love) Winter and I live by my Instinct—still one of the strangest-sounding words I know.

Stan Klees (co-founder, the Juno Awards)

I think it was just before World War Two when a teacher at King Edward Public School in Brantford, Ontario, gave me a hardcover copy of Marshall Saunders's *Beautiful Joe*. I took it home to read.

I think it was the first time I ever had a hardcover book that wasn't a textbook and I was thrilled. It was also a great book and I think it may have been the catalyst that led me to writing. Today I find myself writing a great deal and working in a business where writing is of great importance. I still read a great deal, although much of my reading is done with the television set on. Now if the truth were known, the book that really had the biggest effect on my life was *Forever Amber* by Kathleen Winsor. It was a racy book for its time and I read all five hundred pages without putting it down.

Adrienne Clarkson (broadcaster)

Higglety Pigglety Pop! Or, There Must Be More to Life, by Maurice Sendak.

Although this isn't a book I read when I was a youngster or a teenager, I realize that I should have read it then, as it would have saved me a lot of worry and heartache later. As a matter of fact, I didn't read it until I was thirty but now I reread it all the time and keep it by my bed. It's a beautifully illustrated book and it came out in the early seventies. I remember interviewing Maurice Sendak at the time it was published, without realizing, then, how important the book was going to be for me.

The story has as its heroine Jenny—a small terrier—who lives in a beautiful house with a staircase and a window on the landing and her own geranium. But one day she realizes that there must be more to life than having everything and she sets out to join the Theatre of Life. While trying to find out what the Theatre of Life is all about and what her role is going to be, she loses her good red sweater by sleeping in the woods overnight, and spends time taking care of a perfectly monstrous baby, but in the end she does play her role in the Theatre of Life and realizes that this is much more important than having everything.

It is a parable; it is a very funny story; it is TRUE! After twenty-five years or so, this book is still in print, and I think everybody aged ten and onward should read it.

By the way, when you come to the drawing of the monstrous baby, to whom Jenny becomes a nanny, you'll recognize that it's a self-portrait of the author/artist, Maurice Sendak!

Kathy Stinson (writer)

A few months ago I was going through some files and came across an essay I wrote in 1970, when I was in grade 13 at Vincent Massey Collegiate in Etobicoke. The essay explored the theme of "man and nature" in the novels of Fred Bodsworth: *The Last of the Curlews*, *The Strange One*, *The Atonement of Ashley Morden*. The experience of reading these books, as well as the spirit of the books themselves, has stuck with me.

As a teenager, most of the books I read were borrowed from the public library. I was drawn to *The Strange One* by its title. It was thrilling to discover that the book was set in my country, my city. It had never bothered me on any conscious level before that most of what I read took place elsewhere, but it was a kick to encounter the University of Toronto in this book. Even more exciting for me, however, was how the author had interwoven, through alternating chapters, the life of a young woman and the life of a bird. I knew before, intellectually, that humans were part of the animal kingdom, but I felt it in a meaningful way, as I never had before, through these interwoven stories that Fred Bodsworth told in a book I did not want to end. I did not know at that point in my life that I was becoming a writer, but it's interesting to recall how intrigued I was then with the structure of this novel.

When I finished *The Strange One*, I returned to the library to look for more books by this author. I found *The Last of the Curlews*. The senseless shooting of the birds in this book inspired in me a depth of emotional response that surprised me. I found also (perhaps a little later) *The Atonement of Ashley Morden,* which allowed me to get inside the mind of a young man participating reluctantly in war and trying desperately to atone for his acts of cruelty against other human beings. Never, since reading Fred Bodsworth's books, have I ever assumed superiority of the human species on the basis of "intelligence."

At a high-school reunion some years ago, I recalled how I had fervently urged my history teacher, Doug Parker, to read *The Atonement of Ashley Morden*. I became curious about how a book that had aroused in me such passion would strike me these years later, and I reread it. (Always a risky venture, yes? Will the magic still be there?) I must admit that the moralizing in the book seemed a little more heavy-handed than I remembered from my first reading. But what a fine story it remains.

I met Fred Bodsworth at a Writers' Union meeting once, found myself a little tongue-tied, awed even. He was, of course, a wonderfully humane person, and immediately put me at ease. As happens with good books sometimes, *The Atonement of Ashley Morden* was not a commercial success. But after our meeting, Fred was left with no doubt he had, with his writing, certainly touched this reader's heart. Some time ago, I dropped my 1970 essay in Fred Bodsworth's mailbox. (We live only streets apart.) I did not call first. I hope he is well. I hope he enjoyed reading it.

Susan Crean (writer)

There were many books I read and loved as a child. I lived and relived the adventures of Wart in *The Once and Future King*, Jo in *Little Women*, Tess in *Tess of the D'Urbervilles*, and lost my heart to *Beautiful Joe* so profoundly that the long-awaited sequel, *Beautiful Joe's Paradise*, could never make up for the dog's death in the first book.

Two books I read in my teens had an enormous impact on me, the kind that makes you see the world differently after reading them. The first was a biography of British prime minister Benjamin Disraeli, which I read when I was twelve and staying with my grandmother. For months I went around cursing my luck for having been born too late to ever meet him. (He died in 1881, which meant Gran at eighty-seven was too young to have met him too.) Disraeli, of course, was famous for having been Queen Victoria's favourite first minister, preferred over his stuffy rival Gladstone, who was leader of the Liberal opposition. Disraeli was a novelist and a man of action who became one of the most influential politicians of his time, a Jew born in very Protestant England who overcame prejudice through the force of his own intelligence and cunning. The book, written by André Maurois and published in English in 1928, was perhaps more romance than history, but it told me about something I had seen in our neighbourhood and at school but never heard adults talk about, except in connection with Germany and the war. This was anti-Semitism.

Although the elder D'Israeli had converted to Christianity when Disraeli was a boy, the accusations of foreign ancestry and suspect un-English origins were never stilled and there was no doubt that it clouded Disraeli's parliamentary career despite its brilliance. There was also no doubt that "Dizzy" triumphed in the end mainly because of the patronage and support of women. I was fascinated by the role they played in his life, and by his unbelievable good fortune in having one for a sovereign.

The other book that changed me was Fred Bodsworth's *The Last of the Curlews*, which I read a year or so later. It is the story of the tiny Eskimo curlew which migrates the full 9,000-mile length of the Americas twice each year, breeding in Canada's high Eastern Arctic and wintering in far reaches of Argentina. It had been teetering on the edge of extinction for some time when Bodsworth's novella was published in 1955. (Sightings continue to be reported occasionally. A couple of summers ago curlew eggs were thought to have been spotted.) *The Last of the Curlews* is the simple story of a young male curlew's lonely migration in search of a mate, but it was startlingly real to me, and the imagined view of the world unlike animal stories I had read before. Here was raw nature as experienced by a sentient creature other than human, the tragedy of extinction written with pathos but without sentimentality. And here too was a journey described with the authenticity of a documentary, though no writer could ever have witnessed the events described.

The human imagination, I discovered, can be inspired by facts but need not be limited to them.

In real life Fred Bodsworth is an expert birder, one of Canada's best. Years after I read his book, we became friends and he introduced me to bird-watching. One day he told me about a trip he made to Russia at the invitation of ornithologists there who were very discreet and respectful, but kept insisting he tell them about the mating habits of curlews. The description in the book, it seems, was too convincing for them to believe he hadn't seen it all for himself.

Joy Fielding (writer)

The first book that I remember affecting me as a child was something called *Leiningen versus the Ants*, by Carl Stephanson, later made into a Hollywood movie with the more intriguing title *The Naked Jungle*. It was about flesh-eating ants in Africa, although most of the plot now escapes me. Suffice it to say, once these angry ants crawled up your pant leg, you were a goner.

I was introduced to this book by my grade 3–4 teacher, Miss Knectle, at Homewood Public School in Toronto. I can't remember the precise details, whether it was once a week or every day, but I do remember that Miss Knectle would read aloud to us from this novel a little bit at a time. I loved these sessions, and the story of Dr. Leiningen completely captured my imagination in a way no book had before, and only a few have since. It is probably from here that I began my lifelong love affair with horror and suspense, both in movies and on the printed page.

Another book that affected me was the classic *Old Yeller* by Fred Gipson. I remember sobbing when Old Yeller died. I was about thirteen at the time, and again, this was a book we were reading in class. Interestingly, I read very little outside the classroom until I started university. Then suddenly I started reading everything in sight. But, like a first love, *Leiningen versus the Ants* (and to a lesser extent, *Old Yeller*) occupies a special place in my heart.

Melinda McCracken (writer)

I grew up in Winnipeg in the 1940s and 1950s surrounded by dogs, cats and horses. I read about animals in books I borrowed from the public library. My own animal companions took on the heroic qualities of the animals I read about in these books.

At thirteen, I was horse-crazy. I begged my dad for a horse, to no avail. I hung out at the stables, drew horses and devoured horse stories.

Marguerite Henry opened the door for me to the rich folklore and history of the horse world. Henry published few books. But *King of the Wind* (1948) and *Born to Trot* (1950) are classics, reprinted many times over. Children's libraries are full of animal stories, but only a few are truly well written, well loved, and endure as Henry's have. The heroes of both *King of the Wind* and *Born to Trot* are male. Since they did not do things exclusive to boys, a "tomboy" like myself had no problem identifying with them.

Of the two, I preferred *Born to Trot*. Set in Kentucky, it is the story of Benjamin Franklin White, the real-life "dean of colt trainers," his son, Gibson White, also a harness racer and trainer, and Gibson's filly, Rosalind, who has set a record for a mile.

Born to Trot gave me access to a faraway inaccessible world. It is a very exciting story, rich in racing lore. When Henry creates events you live, breathe and taste every moment of the dust, sweat and speed of those races.

When I neared the end of *Born to Trot* (by flashlight under the covers), I wished the book would never be over. For when it did, its world would end too. I came to the end, and burst into tears. When I got the books out of the library this winter, I found myself in tears again. I've worked as a writer for many years, and have learned a lot about writing. Why should these humble horse stories still move me so much?

Well, it's because I now understand what a good writer she was. Henry was a good writer in 1950, and she would still be considered good today. The real world is so violent, so disappointing. Marguerite Henry's world was exciting, rich and gentle. I need a place like that to escape to these days.

Henry wrote with an unabashedly joyful spirit that, in the Age of Irony, we might consider too over the edge, too Pollyanna. You can smell the hay, feel the wind, brush the golden flanks of Sham or Rosalind, share the horses' joy as they run free.

The kindly characters in her story prevail; the meanies are quickly vanquished. We can only hope our own children encounter such people. Henry must have been horse-crazy herself, so convincingly does she express her characters' love for the horses in their care. This bond has everything—magic, myth, trust, gentleness, kindness, understanding, faith, courage, work and dreams. Writing about horses, Henry taught her readers good values—respect, kindness, generosity, how to perceive and relate to someone we love, and how rewarding relationships can be.

Jo Ellen Bogart (writer)

In my childhood reading, I followed the pattern of many young readers, which is to find a book that pleases and then look for other books by the same author. One author I did this with was Robert A. Heinlein, prolific writer of science fiction. Though I read a number of his books, the one which stuck with me best was *The Star Beast*.

Thinking back on Heinlein's books, with the help of several Web sites dedicated to his work, I can see now that what spoke to me most was not the science, but the relationships. In *The Star Beast*, a family passed down a more-or-less dinosaur-shaped alien from generation to generation and the beast, called Lummox, was friendly and a confidante to many children. Lummie could do what many a child has dreamed of a pet doing. She could talk. As I remember that future world, the sign of being a "being," rather than an animal, was having arms. Speech was disregarded, since it could possibly be just parroting.

I remember disagreeing strongly with that reasoning, but realizing that any future contact with other worlds would be very tricky in that regard. After all, we on earth have yet to settle our relationships with the creatures we think we know well, or with other members of our own species for that matter.

I don't recall just what threat there was to the alien when she was regarded as an animal, but I do remember being outraged. The fact that her species was very long-lived and that she did, as she matured, fulfil the arm requirement, was beside the point. I guess I wanted everything to be treated well, animal or not.

There are many fine books which detail injustices practised upon people and animals, but somehow this lightweight science fiction story was the one that started me thinking about such issues as what makes us human beings and who determines who gets what rights. Being an animal lover, I enjoy having pets in the house, but still grapple with my conscience over the morality of keeping animals, and I try to do well by them.

Part Two: Science & the Natural World

"Little things are infinitely the most important"—Sir Arthur Conan Doyle

Several contributors have selected books about science and nature, despite the fact that for many years there were very few of these intended for children other than textbooks. Now there is a substantial body of readable and exciting non-fiction written and published deliberately for children. Many of these books make the natural world instantly come alive. They speak to a child's natural curiosity: What is it? How does it work? Why does it behave that way? They respond to the craving for explanations, information, facts. But to really connect, whether science, fiction or a combination of the two, winning books about nature must be presented with panache.

One of my current favourites is Canadian: *Discovering the Iceman*, by Shelley Tanaka, illustrated by Laurie McGaw. This non-fiction adventure combines mystery, historical evidence and solid scientific research. Add spectacular illustrations and photographs, a creative episode that puts meat on the bones of the story and you have a mesmerizing mix. This is all intended to reveal an enormous amount of detail about the frozen remains of a centuries-old man found amazingly well-preserved in a glacier.

Other creative non-fiction books use innovative layout, side-bars, contemporary language and child-friendly examples to illustrate their subject. Exciting new explorations of the solar system, the magical workings of plants, ventures into great shipwrecks like the *Titanic*, inventions and serendipitous discoveries, forays into the human body, atlases, encyclopedias—all, when imaginatively presented, have the potential to whet interests that may last a lifetime. Some information books about science and nature seem particularly suitable to CD-ROM and other on-line exploration. But few computer programs to date have found the key that will unleash the wonder and magic of a powerful (and portable) book.

Perhaps, given this emerging crop of remarkable books about the natural world and the expanding universe, when the next generation is asked about a special book, even more respondents will be likely to mention one about science.

It is, I believe, the great achievement of contemporary children's nature books to release science from the rather intimidating realm of "textbook" and make it genuinely accessible and pertinent to kids' lives. From the David Suzuki/Barbara Hehner *Looking at...* series (Insects, Plants etc.) to books about the environment, books of experiments, natural non-fiction, books about the body, a variety of nature-centred magazines and the hands-on and do-it-yourself book-and-toy sets, entry to the intoxicating natural world is now easier, more user-friendly and far more fun than ever before.

The following essays demonstrate that everything from butterflies to black holes may engage the inquiring mind of a curious child. These books foster a growing identification between humanity and nature, and may well lead a motivated child to a special interest in the mysteries of our planet and the orbs beyond.

Fred Bodsworth (writer, ornithologist)

The book that most influenced my childhood? A strange and offbeat one for sure. I am certain it will be nobody else's selection.

I grew up in Port Burwell, a small Lake Erie fishing and coal port. It wasn't a bookish environment. It was the hard-up 1930s, a home with few books, a small school library, no public library. What I did have in good measure was an abundant variety of wild nature, with the lake and beaches at my back door, and fields and woods across the street that seemed to stretch interminably beyond.

I spent much time just rambling, looking at everything that darted, crawled and flew, catching and examining them close up when I could, and wondering a lot of whats and whys. Mine was an insatiable curiosity. I wanted to name things, and know them—why the poplar leaves trembled in the breeze when others didn't, where butterflies went for the winter, and endlessly more.

I read the animal stories of Ernest Thompson Seton and Charles G.D. Roberts, devoured them over and over again. I loved them, but there was a deeper level to my curiosity they were not reaching. I wanted facts, not stories. There was no TV or video, so inevitably the thing that opened the door to the beginnings of the hidden, deeper explanations I was seeking was another book, but certainly, in this age of books about everything for kids, an unusual one. So unusual that a part of my memory keeps asking: "Are you sure?" And another part keeps repeating: "Yes, damn it." That little book at that time was a window to a kind of information that I hadn't realized was available outside museums and universities.

It belonged to a friend, but it had obviously had previous owners. It was a tattered little thing called *The Butterfly Guide—A Pocket Manual for the Ready Identification of the Commoner Species Found in Canada and the United States*. I cannot imagine how a book of that sort found its way to a small and isolated Depression-era Ontario village. I never dreamed there were so many kinds of butterflies and so much to know about them. It described where they lived, their life histories, what plants their caterpillars ate, the butterfly families and how and why they were related. It mesmerized me. I never coveted a book so eagerly. I had to have it, and my friend knew it, and pressed a hard bargain. I finally traded a pair of skates and a bicycle pump for it, and my parents were angry ("Good grief, even the pages are falling out!"). But it was my first nature book, the first little glimpse of the fascinating science of the world of life around me. And its major impact was not just what that book itself would tell me, it was the discovery that that kind of book existed, and the realization there must be more.

In a couple of years, by the time I entered high school, I had a respectable moth and butterfly collection and was an expert of sorts on my region's Lepidoptera. High school introduced me in a more formal way to botany and zoology. My natural science interests expanded, particularly to birds, and there were more books, many more. A few years later I was struggling with Darwin's *The Origin of Species*.

At a later time I might have become a life scientist of some kind, but it was beyond my reach then. However, journalism was not, and a journalist I became. But I never ceased being a naturalist too. In time I would own and wear out many guidebooks—bird guides, wildflower guides, tree guides—but none has the hallowed place in memory occupied by the butterfly guide which, for a pair of skates and a bicycle pump, first showed me the way.

Donn Kushner (writer, scientist)

I read *Microbe Hunters* by Paul De Kruif as a teenager. It is a history of microbiology that has formed part of my memory ever since and it probably had a greater influence than I realize on my decision to embark on a research career.

The book tells of the work of Antonie van Leeuwenhoek, who first saw and described micro-organisms, and of Spallanzani and others who showed that microbial life doesn't arise spontaneously but comes from other life. It describes the so-called "heroic age" of microbiology and the work of Robert Koch, Louis Pasteur and others who showed that micro-organisms are responsible for diseases (as well as a multitude of chemical changes) and developed ways of preventing and curing these diseases. It goes on to recount the work of Elie Metchnikoff, who discovered phagocytic cells; Paul Ehrlich, the founder of chemotherapy; and those brave scientists who studied dangerous diseases such as malaria, sleeping sickness and yellow fever which are carried by insects.

Microbe Hunters is still a very good read. I often mentioned it in class, over the thirty years during which I taught microbiology. Modern texts that deal with the history of microbiology don't disagree fundamentally with its accounts. It is much more accurate than some of the modern, very popular texts dealing with this or that plague.

As a writer as well as a scientist, I have been much concerned with ways in which science and scientists are portrayed in fiction. Usually it is difficult to interest lay readers in these strange folks' devotion to abstract and difficult concepts. De Kruif—probably using some literary licence—makes his scientists come to life. The reader feels the excitement of discovery, a subject somewhat detached from the immense practical benefits to humanity of some of these discoveries. The book also brings out the fully human sides of the great microbiologists, their failings and failures as well as their successes, and shows to what extent scientific discovery is a human activity.

Ernie Coombs (Mr. Dressup)

I was raised in a family that loved to read. There was always a weekly trip to the library in our small city and the maximum number of books allowed was borrowed on our cards.

In my pre-teen years, after graduating from the Uncle Wiggly animal series and other young kids' books, I remember voraciously going through our library's stock of African travel books written by the husband-and-wife team of Martin and Osa Johnson. They were photographers and collectors of animals, and though they were safari "B'wanas," they wrote with respect and affection of the African people and the fauna of that land.

I had always been interested in nature, and through the piles of old *National Geographics* at our cottage I was bemused with foreign lands as well. The Johnsons' books took me on fabulous trips away from my home for as many hours as I could steal from homework and chores. Sometimes I even cheated sleep, devouring a book in my bedroom for as long as my eyes would stay open, so that I could finish it before I had to take it back to the library.

There were other books and authors too, on various subjects, but to this day my favourite read is a good travel book. Failing that, almost any book will do, because, though I hate to denigrate the medium which has employed me for the past three decades, I prefer books to television by a wide margin. They're portable, available when and where you wish... and if you fall asleep while enjoying a book, it doesn't blare and flicker at you from across the room for the rest of the night!

Terence Dickinson (writer, astronomer)

When I was twelve years old I had read all the astronomy books in my school library at least twice. I think I must have been born interested in the stars. I remember as far back as age five being captivated by the sight of a brilliant meteor. There is something about the immensity and mystery of the universe that lit a fire inside me that still burns.

With the school library exhausted, I started pestering my father to take me somewhere to see something more. We ended up at the main library in Weston, Ontario, on a Saturday afternoon in the summer of 1956. One of the books had no dust cover, just its naked navy blue hardcover with the title *The Conquest of Space* down the spine. But when I opened it, I experienced one of those great moments of discovery—the ones that become etched in the brain for life. The full-colour, incredibly realistic illustrations of alien worlds had a depth and power unlike anything I had seen before.

The artist was Chesley Bonestell, an architectural illustrator who had a long-established career in Hollywood painting mattes (backgrounds) for movies such as *Citizen Kane*. He became interested in astronomy in 1944, at age fifty-six, when he did a rendering of Saturn that today hangs in the Smithsonian Air and Space Museum.

It took me more than a year of saving to get my own copy of *The Conquest of Space*. And I was not alone in wanting one. First published in 1948, it was an instant best-seller, ultimately going through fourteen printings. Today it is a prized collector's item. Bonestell's illustrations overshadowed the book's outstanding text by the German-American science writer Willy Ley.

The Conquest of Space was primarily intended for teenagers, but I loved the way it treated me as an adult, assuming that I would be able to digest the grand sweep of what future space travel might be like—could be like. It was the first book with technically accurate (for the day) colour illustrations of planetary exploration. An entire generation of young astronomy and space-exploration buffs (like me) were profoundly influenced by this work. Thousands of scientists and engineers who years later worked on the Apollo moon program, the robotic flights to Mars and other ventures into the solar system got their first look at what it might be like in the pages of Bonestell and Ley's masterwork.

For me, it also confirmed my suspicions that the books I had seen up to that point merely hinted at what could be placed between two covers. Churned out by writers with little passion for the subject and illustrated on shoestring budgets, they were perfunctory and bland. But after seeing *The Conquest of Space*, there was no doubt in my mind that the exploration of worlds beyond would become reality. And I wanted to be part of it!

Roberta Bondar (Professor of Medicine, astronaut)

One of my favourite haunts is a used-book store. There, I find treasures from the past that are no longer available in print or in a regular book store. Since my flight into space, I am intrigued by looking at all the old science fiction that was written when I was a youngster. These books fascinate me now because I had never read many of them, as few were written for children or adolescents.

In the nature section, however, I feel refreshed to find, nearly always, a copy of *Silent Spring*, by Rachel Carson. My parents gave me a hardcover edition for Christmas 1962. I cherish this book, and have covered it with a library-type plastic jacket. In fact, I am touching it now. It is such a classic that it has been reprinted recently, in a softcover edition, and is on shelves in many book stores. Carson's detailed and well-researched account of how embracing technology, unquestioned, has led to destructive effects on our environment shaped my vision of what science is all about.

Science, of course, was Rachel Carson's investigative tool. She studied it with solid scientific methods and was the first contemporary woman scientist that I knew about. I shared her love of nature and wished that I, too, could discover important things about the world around us and communicate them as beautifully. My work now is to capture the Earth with my photographic images. Maybe, some day, my books will be on a shelf near Rachel Carson's. That would be another dream come true.

·5·

Emily of New Moon, Emily Climbs, Emily's Quest

"The delightful throes of literary composition"
—L.M. Montgomery

One of the most pleasant surprises in putting together this book was discovering the enormous popularity of Lucy Maud Montgomery's Emily books. These are engrossing and beautifully written stories about growth, integrity and self-actualization whose writing, themes and captivating central character I relished when I first encountered them years ago, and still find equally illuminating. It cannot be a coincidence. So many women—most of them writers—love a particular set of books about a Canadian orphan, a gifted, stubborn, passionate, introspective and romantic heroine who is, and this is most important, determined to become a writer. Like her creator, Emily never relinquishes that dream.

These three books are far less well known in other countries (or, so far, celebrated in our own) than the legendary *Anne of Green Gables* (1908). Montgomery, gaining renown for her insightful novels and creative stories and articles, worked on the series with intensity and enthusiasm during the 1920s. *Emily of New Moon* was published in 1923, *Emily Climbs* in 1925 and *Emily's Quest* in 1927. The author felt a unique relationship to this new heroine, confessing in private that "People were never right in saying I was Anne, but in some respects, they will be right if they write me down as Emily."

There was much in common between Maud and Emily. Maud, whose widowed father moved to Saskatchewan, was also imposed upon relatives as a girl and found emotional release in a private journal. She felt the need to communicate with an adored (but deceased) relative and wrote fervent, confessional letters to her late mother on the back of old letter-bills. She conferred these habits on her new character, a ten-year-old grieving child. Emily, too, kept a precious and secret journal. She also "feverishly ... poured out ... her rapture and her pain" on rescued letter-bills in a strict household where paper was at a premium, to a father terribly missed.

Montgomery composed her early work on a finicky old typewriter, one that made only faded capitals and could not type the letter "m" at all. Emily is given a machine with precisely the same characteristics. Although the books are not autobiographical, there are other striking similarities. The most exciting revelation is that Emily is allowed to occasionally experience "the flash," that rare and exquisite moment of insight that her creator too treasured whenever it occurred.

Emily was a "kindred spirit" of her famous predecessor Anne of Green Gables. Anne is cherished for, among other things, her personality, her articulate, sensitive nature, her occasional outbursts of truth-telling (that invariably get her in hot water), her literary and dramatic talents, her loyalty and her pride. Emily is not so lighthearted or funny a heroine as Anne, but she shares the other attributes. She is more driven, her expressive and creative nature directly and specifically channelled almost entirely to writing. She explores various kinds of composition, among them poetry, prose, journalism, biography and longer fiction. Emily is more ambitious than Anne, a creature with a calling. Through her, Montgomery exposes some of the private aspects of the writer's life—the pain of rejection, the thrill of having a poem or article published, the sweet satisfaction (and amazement) of opening and savouring the thin letter of acceptance of a manuscript for publication. Emily does not emerge fully formed as an able and talented writer. She hones her craft, learns a great deal from others and even more from self-criticism and (sometimes bitter) experience.

Like all Montgomery's heroines, both Anne and Emily must cope with, and eventually triumph over, well-meaning but difficult, narrow-minded and stodgy adults. Montgomery has a telling capacity to express the isolation felt by a child or adolescent in a judgemental, often unfair world with its seemingly bizarre set of expectations and regulations.

There is much for an aspiring author to absorb from the Emily books about the process and obsession of writing. But their landscape extends to the problems and joys, the highs and the lows of all creative endeavour. Almost any reader will respond enthusiastically to these sensitively written, emotional and lyrical novels. They will identify with a young girl (later, a young woman) coming of age and into her own. Many readers will be, like the following contributors (and me), endlessly fascinated by this exceptionally sympathetic and imaginative heroine. It is profoundly satisfying to get to know Emily Byrd Starr, entirely enjoyable to watch her grow up. With each obstacle overcome, she gradually develops, like the author who created her, her own truly Canadian and engaging voice.

Alice Munro (writer)

I remember when I first read *Emily of New Moon*. I was nine or ten years old, and I was pleased and troubled by it. I decided that it was "good but different." By "good" I meant that it kept me reading at a speedy clip through a series of home-and-school adventures, provided me with a fair number of fearful thrills, and ended with upsets righted and the child-heroine vindicated after her trials, optimistically facing adolescence and a sequel. That was the kind of book I liked, and I read plenty of them. By "different" I meant that there were other things about the book that got in my way, slowed me down, even annoyed me, because I sensed a different weight about them, a demand for another kind of attention, the possibility of some new balance between myself and a book, between reader and writing, which took me, the reader, by surprise, and did not let me off so easily.

Consider the sufferings of Emily under the table, her imprisonment in the spare room, her humiliation by the poisonous teacher, Miss Brownell. This isn't the stuff of children's books, at least not of the children's books of my time. It recalls the situation of Jane Eyre or David Copperfield. The child is punished, severely and unjustly. She must bear the criticism, even the hatred of bigoted, stupid, cruel adults. And the punishment is seen to be not for misdeeds, but for existence. Emily is in trouble because she is an orphan, an outsider, and in fact because she is herself, an outlaw in her heart. This is the conflict that the author makes clear, then manages to soften a little, by putting the ladder up to the spare-room window, by making most of the tyrannical adults turn out to have a streak of decency, even to be capable and worthy of a measure of love. And so, in life, most tyrannical people are. But a feeling of menace, of dark motives in family life, never really disappears. Most of the adults in Emily's orbit are mysterious and capricious and sometimes deeply damaged; they can be black-hearted.

But what is central to the story is the development of a child—and a girl child at that—into a writer. Emily says, near the end of the book, that she has to write, she would write no matter what, and we have been shown not only how she learned to write, but how she discovered writing as a way of surviving as herself in the world. We are there as Emily gets on with this business, as she pounces on words in uncertainty and delight, takes charge and works them over and fits them dazzlingly in place, only to be bewildered and ashamed, in half a year's time, when she reads over her splendid creation. This is wonderfully done.

L.M. Montgomery makes us believe in "the flash," the moment of vision, the writing energy, the desperate commitment, of a female child living on a farm in Prince Edward Island, just as we believe in her love of ice cream and hatred of boots in summer and her desire to cut a bang (we would say "bangs") so that she will look pretty. At the very end of the book, Emily writes at the top of a blank page at the beginning of a blank notebook a statement that calmly sums up her naive egotism, cool presumption and rapturous submission to the demands of her chosen life: *I am going to write a diary, that it may be published when I die.*

One edition of *Emily of New Moon* claims on the back cover that Emily is a spirited, irrepressible girl who finds a world of family and friends after her father's death, learns a surprising lesson in growing up, and discovers that she is really not alone.

I don't like the sound of that. There's the familiar brisk assumption that books (at least books for children) are socializing agents, that it's their business to spread messages, and that the messages are cheery and confining. I don't know what sort of book L.M. Montgomery would have said that she intended to write, but the book that she did write is surely one in which Emily finds that she *is* alone, that she has chosen her life without knowing that she was choosing it, and she's exultant about the choice. She doesn't feel the shadow of a compromise, so far.

I've been trying to say what it was that the ten-year-old reader found that was "different." These are the same things the eleven—and twelve—and even the fourteen-year-old reader kept going back for. But I have a sense of things I haven't said that are perhaps the most important.

In this book, as in all the books I've loved, there's so much going on behind, or beyond, the proper story. There's life spreading out behind the story—the book's life—and we see it out of the corner of the eye. The milk pails in the dairy house. Aunt Elizabeth pouring the tallow for the candles. The slightly repulsive splendour of the parlour at Wyther Grange. The corners of the kitchen at New Moon. What mattered to me finally in this book, what was to matter most to me from then on, was knowing more about that life than I'd been told, and more than I can tell.

Kit Pearson (writer)

There are so many books that affected me when I was young, it's hard to choose just one. But there's no questioning which one had the most influence on me: *Emily of New Moon*, by Lucy Maud Montgomery.

I discovered my battered copy of this book in a trunk in my grandparents' basement just after I moved to Edmonton when I was twelve. Drawn to its cover depicting an old-fashioned girl standing with clasped hands in the dusk, I asked permission to take the book home. I was miserably lonely in my new city and school and the book was an immense solace to me; it also changed my life. Emily is an orphan who goes to live with two aunts on a Prince Edward Island farm. What saves her in her misery are her almost mystical connection to nature and her burning desire to write. I identified completely with Emily; I, too, felt most at home when outdoors and I had vague urgings to be a writer. The last sentence of the story is "I am going to write a diary, that it may be published when I die." I closed the book, rushed to the drugstore, bought a notebook, and began a diary with the same words. Later I read the sequels, *Emily Climbs* and *Emily's Quest*, which depict Emily being a writer; hence I learned all about my future career before I started it. The three books are laden with Montgomery's usual flowery language and emotions; but Emily is such a strong, passionate character (far more interesting than Anne) that these qualities don't matter. I still think that first book, especially, is the best portrayal of a creative child that I have ever read.

Budge Wilson (writer)

The book that was probably the strongest influence on my future life was, in fact, a set of books—*Emily of New Moon*, *Emily Climbs* and *Emily's Quest*. I enjoyed them much more than L.M. Montgomery's Anne of Green Gables books, probably because they spoke to me about things I wanted and perhaps needed to hear.

Although it is probably fifty-five years since I read those stories, certain things remain very vivid to me.

I remember most clearly Emily's use of "Jimmy-books"—blank books given to her by her cousin Jimmy. In these, she wrote poems and stories, and eventually an extensive diary. This must have made a strong impression on me, because at the age of fifteen, I started to write in Jimmy-books of my own. I bought large hardcovered blank books from a stationery outlet, and between the ages of fifteen and seventeen, I used them to record most of the significant things that were going on in my life. I recorded fears, awe, funny episodes, longings, exaltations, love, gratitude, earnest musings, as well as general teenaged craziness. I started each entry with the words, "Dear 41." It was my intention to leave the books unread until I reached that age. I can see now that there was a parallel there with a letter which fourteen-year-old Emily wrote to herself, to be opened when she was twenty-four. At twenty-four, she opened it and felt a mixture of depression, embarrassment and nostalgic tenderness.

Alas, I did not wait until I was forty-one. I had filled three of my books with a lot of emotional outpourings of spirit and (possibly) some intelligent comments on the customs and life of that time. Each book was close to an inch thick. A lot of my life was contained in those pages.

At the age of twenty-one, curiosity was stronger in me than caution. I reached for the first volume, and started to read. At twenty-one, you think you know everything. You feel sophisticated and complete. You are sure you know who you are. You feel disdain for anything that doesn't measure up to your own rigid standards of poise and wisdom. I read about ten pages of that first volume. That was all I could manage. I can still taste the shame and the humiliation which I felt as I read those pages. I was so overwhelmed by the fact that all that over-emotional drivel was actually recorded that I threw all three volumes into the kitchen stove, which was well stocked with wood at the time, and burning brightly.

Very recently, I was reminded that before Emily had her Jimmy-book, she wrote her thoughts in an old account book. When her Aunt Elizabeth insisted on reading what she had written, Emily tossed the whole set of writings into the kitchen stove. She did this in a state of outrage and fear. Once again I was struck by a parallel, which had not been in my mind at the time.

In my case, my feelings were directed at myself—my old self—but were strong enough to make me destroy something that had once been very precious to me.

I still grieve for those lost journals—obliterated in such a fit of pride and certainty. Now—half a century later—I am not as proud as I was at twenty-one, and not as certain about who I am. I long to read those vanished pages. Maybe I could discover a lot of things from my younger self to help explain who I am today.

However, I'm still grateful to Emily—and to L.M. Montgomery, who brought her to life. Between them, they led me in the direction of writing down the thoughts and feelings—the stories—that I find in my head. That has been no small gift to me.

Val Ross (journalist)

As kids, we read everything from Nancy Drew to *The Scarlet Pimpernel*. It was obsessive. At night, I'd crouch by the bedroom door, reading by the crack of light from the hall. A lot of what we read was junk. A few books were more special, however, and my pals and I paid them homage in rites of re-enactment.

Chief among these were C.S. Lewis's Narnia books. Despite Lewis's intended Christian subtext, there's something liberatingly pagan about his books. They are full of exuberance, talking beasts, references to classical myth. We bound willow branches around our heads in order to be dryads, and at sunset held bacchanalian romps across the lawn in the manner of the children dancing after the Messiah/Lion Aslan in Lewis's *The Lion, the Witch and the Wardrobe.*

There were two books I never discussed or re-enacted with my friends, because they were too special. One was *At the Back of the North Wind*, first published in the 1860s. It is an other-worldly, sometimes frightening story about Diamond, son of a poor London cabbie, and his friendship with the wild-haired North Wind. She variously appears to Diamond as a tiny breeze-borne fairy and a terrifying giantess who unleashes arctic storms and drowns ships. And yet Diamond trusts her. Obviously this book too had a religious subtext. It was written by an Aberdeenshire minister, George MacDonald, better known for *The Princess and the Goblin*. MacDonald is held to be a father of British fantasy writing and was admired by C.S. Lewis and J.R.R. Tolkien.

I was so impressed, I refused to cut my hair in honour of the North Wind, and vowed I would not reread the book again lest I tarnish my impression of its beauty. I have reread it, to my own daughter, and it's still beautiful, though its meandering Victorian location slows your reading speed down to a walk. But that is one of the joys of books: experiencing worlds other than your own.

The other treasured book was *Emily of New Moon*, by L.M. Montgomery. It's about a dreamy but tart-tongued orphan with literary ambitions. Darker than her Anne of Green Gables books, it is probably a child's first introduction to literary criticism, because it eavesdrops on Emily going over her bad poetry and discarding the most purply excesses.

The book was also a revelation about Canada. I started to personalize trees and listened to the wind, because that is what Emily did—she had named all the trees on her adoptive family's property at New Moon. The book celebrated the landscape of Prince Edward Island, but made me look with fresh eyes at my own favourite landscape, the family cottage at Bala, Muskoka. Years later I learned that Montgomery had corrected the last draft of *Emily* in Bala in the early 1920s.

At one point on a walk along the Prince Edward Island shore, Emily asks an adult friend why Canadian history is so boring. He replies, "The happiest women, like the happiest countries, have no history." Of course, he's right, given the history of this traumatic century. But Montgomery gives Emily a personal history that proves him happily wrong.

Goldie Semple (actor)

I was a voracious reader as a child. I still am. It helped me through many stresses and strains. Growing up—it seems to me—is difficult for everyone. And I was never without a wonderful escape or solace or a companion, when I could tuck into a good book.

I read everything, but my favourite authors were L.M. Montgomery—all of her books, not just Anne. *Emily of New Moon*, *Emily Climbs* and *Emily's Quest* were favourites—and Louisa May Alcott, of course. The Little Women series and spin-offs, but *Eight Cousins* and *Rose in Bloom* were best friends.

I know books gave me a clearer understanding of human beings and their behaviour—and high expectations of what I could ask of myself.

Anything is possible in a book. Why not in life?

Ann Shortell (writer)

"There you are, what are you doing all alone down in Ricky's room? You're so quiet I wasn't sure where I'd find you." Aunt Pauline cradles two weathered, leaf-green volumes in her ample forearms. "I've kept these books since I was a girl in New Brunswick. The boys never took much interest—but you seem to like reading."

Aunt Pauline and Uncle Charlie Stewart aren't really related, just my parents' friends. We visited, turnabout, every vacation for years. I liked it best when we travelled to them in Ottawa. With my father swapping stories and Mother making music, I could sneak off and dream for hours. Aunt Pauline's a worrier though; she always wanted to keep me busy. This time, she'd caught me on her son's bed with a magazine—no place for a nine-year-old on such a sunny day. My big-eyed stare lighted upon the top book. *Emily Climbs*, it read. L.M. Montgomery. Then Aunt Pauline handed me my future.

I fingered the rough-edged pages of the Emily book. Inside the fern border of the frontispiece, a young, dark-haired girl in a pumpkin-coloured dress and matching hair ribbon sits in a grove, surrounded by books. One lies open in her lap. Yet she's not reading; she's staring ahead, with the glimmer of a smile. As if she's seeing something wonderful, something that isn't in the picture for the rest of us. Magic in the air.

This is "the flash," Emily's creative epiphany. Nothing she writes can ever match this glimpse through the gods' curtains, but she must try. Emily Byrd Starr is already fourteen and a writer in *Climbs*, the second in Maud Montgomery's *Emily* trilogy. With the first chapter, "Writing Herself Out," I entered the sanctuary of Emily's glossy black "Jimmy-book" diary. I soon knew her much better than I could know any of the girls at school. I became fast friends with Montgomery's other heroines—Anne Shirley and the rest. But I ate Emily alive.

Emily is tall and has paper-white skin, like me. She's not really pretty, but looks much better with bangs. She's embarrassed by her slightly pointed ears, and longs for a silk dress the colour of a twilight sky. She boards with her narrow, suspicious, widowed Aunt Ruth while at school, relies on the charity of her domineering Aunt Elizabeth at New Moon. But wherever Emily rooms, she lives within herself.

My sisters laughed at my invisible friends under the stairs, but I knew Emily would understand. She had already told me so many of her secrets; surely she must know me as well. As the older girl, she had much to teach me. About rejection and pain. About not giving up. About how it's all right to be passionate and sensitive and proud. And that I, too, could believe that someday I might write something worthwhile.

Her lessons on the business of writing were practical enough: Include a stamped return envelope when mailing a manuscript to a publisher, if you hope to see it again. Find a mentor and listen to criticism—especially about the use of italics. Yet trust your own regard for your work. Emily recorded how much she was paid for her pieces, and how her family's approval of her strange obsession was gained only through public success.

Montgomery, through Emily and the other girls, introduced me to Shakespeare, Tennyson, Emerson, Kipling (all right, and Mrs. Hemans, she wasn't perfect). She showed me that the Bible is filled with poetry, and that it's fine to hold unorthodox views, whatever the neighbours say. As a teen in the seventies, I combed through used-book stores for volumes written more than half a century earlier about girls of the Edwardian era. Holding first editions brought me closer to their author. My Montgomery collection followed me to journalism school and leavened the analytical temper of my business writing years. I always assumed that Emily was Montgomery, but in writing my own novel I've learned that an author's heroine has a mind of her own. Like all imaginary friends.

I've tried to explain to sceptics that I don't reread my Emily books, I visit. Emily sat and held my hand for a few moments before I marched downstairs to be married five years ago; Emily came along to the hospital for my back surgery in the summer of '96. In case I needed her. So if I forgot my bread-and-butter note thirty years back, I'll say it now. Thank you, Aunt Pauline.

Jane Urquhart (writer)

It is curious how, at certain stages of my early reading life, I wanted to become the various children or adolescents in the literary works I admired. These fictional young people, most of whom came from another era, drifted in and out of my personality like ghosts, taking possession of my psyche and then taking leave of the murky, unformed region with equal capriciousness. When Emily took up residence, however, she was there to stay. It was as if the three books, *Emily of New Moon*, *Emily Climbs* and *Emily's Quest*, were mirrors in which I could see not only who girls such as myself had been, who we were now, but who we might eventually come to be. I could see my grandmother at fourteen polishing floors and putting up preserves in the tradition of her ancestors, my mother at twelve borrowing the village's only typewriter from the bank because she was going to write a novel, and my several aunts in their farm kitchens looking lovingly, albeit askance, at some of my more bizarre activities.

As I turned twelve, and then thirteen, I read the books again and again. I was deeply in love with Teddy, liked—for inexplicable reasons—Aunt Ruth and Aunt Elizabeth better than Aunt Laura, wished passionately to discover a Mr. Carpenter somewhere in my scholastic activities, attributed the physical and mental characteristics of Ilse to my bewildered best friend, scrutinized and then responded fiercely to beautiful landscapes, wrote sentimental poetry, and kept desperate diaries. And so it came to be that long before a single work of mine was typeset, I knew about the joy of a slim rather than a fat envelope arriving in the mail, of seeing something one has created, right there on a printed page (irrelevant that the page be part of a seed catalogue), and the absolute ecstasy of finding the right words and the right form in which to use them. Even as I write this, the child in me can hardly believe that I am writing this. I gasp in rapture and clasp the envelope with the publisher's name on it to my chest. Another step forward on the Alpine Path.

I firmly believe that Emily Starr, particularly the adolescent girl of *Emily Climbs*, is a candidate for sainthood: not, in the hackneyed sense of the term, as a distributor of goodness and mercy, but as the recipient of a "call," a "vocation." Much like two other rural and literary Emilys, Emily Brontë of Haworth and Emily Dickinson of Amherst, she is subject to the mystical "flash"—a moment of intense focus and supreme awareness—has psychic experiences, and never for one moment doubts the authenticity of her vocation. This is the force that moves her through life, the glass through which she views the world around her. It survives, in fact makes use of, rage, grief, hilarity, depression and joy. It is her companion and confidant, her dreams and consolation.

One cannot help but speculate about the autobiographical aspect of a series of Montgomery novels that deal with a young orphaned girl who is struggling to become a writer in Prince Edward Island. It is my feeling, however, that in *Emily Climbs* Montgomery is not so much attempting to re-create her own past as she is attempting to create an idealized world for a youthful creative spirit. In short, she is building the past as she would have liked to experience it: one with just the right combination of resolved and unresolved relationships, successes and failures, joys and sorrow. One in which a rural setting on a Canadian island may present some obstacles to her career but not to her vocation.

The most moving scene in *Emily Climbs* concerns this last issue. A seventeen-year-old Emily has been offered the chance by a successful editor to move to New York. Although she is initially thrilled by the idea, she cannot help listening to an older, even crankier Mr.

Carpenter, who fears she will become as "Yankeefied" as the editor who is luring her away. "Janet Royal is Yankeefied," he states, "her outlook and atmosphere and style are all U.S.—she isn't a Canadian any longer—and that's what I wanted you to be—pure Canadian through and through, doing something as far as in you lay for the literature of your own country, keeping your Canadian tang and flavour. But of course there's not many dollars in that sort of thing yet."

It is not, however, Mr. Carpenter's words that cause Emily to remain in Canada: rather it is her deep attachment to her own geography. As, reaching a decision, she wanders around the New Moon farm looking from the windows of her small room or gazing at the orchard from the garden, we realize that the outer landscape of these surroundings reflects exactly the inner landscape in which Emily's imagination finds its voice. To leave New Moon and Prince Edward Island would be roughly equivalent, for this Canadian girl, to committing literary suicide. As she tells the successful editor, "Some fountain of living water would dry up in my soul if I left the land I love."

Trite though that line, out of context, may seem, I wept when I read it at eleven and a half, I wept when I read it at twenty-five, and I weep when I read it now for the simple reason that I know it is the truth. Emily realizes that it is the spirit of the place that keeps her there; the same spirit that has enriched and will continue to enrich her writing.

This is what Montgomery has given us, then, in *Emily*, particularly *Emily Climbs*, a portrait of the young creative spirit of this country at adolescence—a time that is both immensely fertile and heartbreakingly fragile. Out of the raw materials of the best of her own life, she has created a world in which that young spirit can flourish and has peopled it with characters who either assist or resist the heroine and her calling, but who are, nevertheless, always drawn with great love. And she has given us a landscape, both inner and outer, that we are able to recognize as our own.

·6· Poetry

"The best words in the best order"
—Samuel Taylor Coleridge

Several writers have commented elsewhere in this book about their early memories of poetry, from nursery rhymes or nonsense verses to the lyrical whimsy of an A.A. Milne or Dr. Seuss. A child's first songs—for example, the traditional alphabet song—are almost always rhymed as an aid to memory. My children learned to count in French, in kindergarten, with "Un, deux, trois, quatre, cinq, six, sept, Violette sur bicyclette." It makes little sense, but was, for a four-year-old, a breeze to remember. Through the happy marriage and universal appeal of music and poetry, thousands of pre-school children unconsciously pick up the words and rhythm of entire CDs by talented performers such as Fred Penner, Raffi, Eric Nagler and Sharon, Lois and Bram. Older children and teens are similarly familiar with the music and lyrics of dozens, even hundreds of songs. They may not connect the relationship between language, rhythm and beat—as manifest in popular icons—and poetry, both traditional and modern, but the line between them is frequently very faint.

Before the nineteenth century, poetry for children, like most other literature intended for them, was almost entirely focused on their training and improvement. Virtually all was religious or didactic. Until, that is, around mid-century when the playful limericks, nonsense verses and hilarious illustrations of Edward Lear and the witty, funny poems of Lewis Carroll (Charles Dodgson) burst upon the scene and were eagerly embraced by delighted (English-speaking) kids and their parents.

Lear's original and highly influential verses, including *A Book of Nonsense* (1846), *More Nonsense* (1872), preposterous narrative poems such as "The Owl and the Pussycat" and "The Quangle Wangle's Hat" and a multitude of nutty limericks enjoy popularity today because of their sheer inventiveness, humour and imagination.

Carroll, as both a child and grownup, was enthralled by nursery rhymes and fairy tales. His two best-known poems, "Jabberwocky" (1855) and "The Hunting of the Snark" (1876), combined with his ground-breaking fantasy novel *Alice's Adventures in Wonderland* (1865), provided the first crucial (and welcome) strokes that would eventually sweep out a long, dull era of bleak, uninteresting children's literature.

The revolutionary writing, and especially outlandish poetry, of these two seminal authors heralded no less than the beginning of a new era: a change in philosophy and a golden age of writing and illustration for children. Lear's and Carroll's poems, with their unprecedented creativity and innovation, continue to captivate everyone who reads them. Modern children's poets like David McCord, Dr. Seuss (Theodor Seuss Geisel), Dennis Lee, Sheree Fitch, Shel Silverstein, Jack Prelutsky and others trace their own playful roots in the wordplay, delicious language and sense of fun of these two great originals.

It also seems entirely appropriate that works of poetry have inspired some of the most tender and romantic reminiscences in this collection. A few contributors chose material composed deliberately for children, such as the engaging rhymes and idealized illustrations in Robert Louis Stevenson's *A Child's Garden of Verses*. Others recalled compelling works by renowned poets such as Whitman, Frost, Longfellow and Lampman. The discovery of the flavour and rhythm of words invariably awakened sensibility and sometimes, remarkably, led to action. For some, poetry was a refreshing oasis; for others, it paved the way to creative pursuits such as painting or composing their own writing or music.

Many poets write for both adults and children. Whoever their intended audience, all poets, like young children, delight in playing with words and images. Poems for kids in particular seem to tempt the reader to try them out loud. It is a satisfying sensation to roll the words around in the mouth, hear the lines, taste the pleasing pop of alliteration. Some of the tongue-twisting, repetition and wordplay appeals particularly to the very young, but it's fun—and often challenging—for older kids and adults to read aloud single-poem picture books, narrative verses and collections of poetry, naturally with appropriate gusto and dramatic expression.

One of my daughters memorized Dennis Lee's "Lizzie's Lion" at the age of four or so. She was entranced by the rhythm, usually turned the pages at the "right" spot, and recited the book countless times over many months. Although she hasn't seen it in years, I doubt she will ever truly forget it. Similarly, without meaning to, I can still recall "The Giant" and sizeable chunks of "If," "The Cremation of Sam McGee" and "Casey at the Bat"—all primary-school assignments—with very little prompting. They are somehow part of me, stored away in some obscure cerebral recess, waiting to be called upon for whatever purpose. Although far more recently I memorized long passages of dialogue for roles in plays at high school and university, no paragraph of prose has remained locked in memory that securely.

Poetry has, it seems, a unique staying power. Of those who chose books of poetry for *Everybody's Favourites* many seem to be frequently, and happily, haunted by their selections.

Christina McCall (writer)

Before I was halfway through the letter asking me to contribute to this book, I remembered some nonsense rhymes that were read to a preliterate me and the recollection pierced me with something like the bliss they brought when I heard them first at the age of four.

For the rest of the day—when I was supposed to be thinking about the impact of Keynesianism on women in the industrialized democracies—I kept muttering to myself: *"So the sheep went to sleep/And the armadillo/Used him for a pillow/While the kangaroo/Tried to paint the roses blue/Till the camel swallowed the enamel/In Johnny Crow's Garden."*

Weeks later, when I was still plagued by lines like *"So the chimpanzee/Put the kettle on for tea,"* I repaired to the Osborne Collection of Children's Books at the Toronto Public Library to find out why this sweet doggerel had so captivated my imagination that I could remember it half a century on.

From among their stock of treasures, the Osborne librarians produced not one but three books of considerable charm and great good humour about an anthropomorphic crow named Johnny and the animals who cavorted in his glorious garden. Intended for children from three to five, they were written and illustrated by a famous Edwardian watercolourist named L. Leslie Brooke and published in London by Frederick Warne & Co.

As I leafed through them in the library's reading room, what flooded my mind was a startlingly vivid sense of what a British colonial outpost Toronto was when I was young and the Second World War had barely begun. When the best books were the English books. The best biscuits were Peek Freans. And the best and bravest race in the history of humankind were the English-speaking peoples standing alone against the Hun.

What Leslie Brooke and the dozens of other English authors who followed him in my childhood reading life (Edward Lear and Arthur Ransome, Emily Brontë and Jane Austen to name but four) induced in me was a case of anglophilia that I didn't get over for decades. What they left me with was a fascination with the suppleness and subtleties of the English language that pleasures me still.

Roy Bonisteel (broadcaster)

I have no difficulty selecting a favourite and important book in my young life.

As the youngest of ten in a farm family just barely scraping through the Depression, books were a luxury. My mother, however, had a great love of literature, especially poetry. My earliest memories are of her reciting long, narrative pieces as she did her housework and many farm chores.

So, when she gave me a beautifully bound copy of *A Child's Garden of Verses* (by Robert Louis Stevenson) when I was about five, I was in seventh heaven. I could sound out some of the words of the magical little poems (which I already knew by heart), but it was the illustrations in both pen and ink and warm lavish tones that entranced me so.

The words from every poem in *A Child's Garden of Verses* have stayed with me for over sixty years, like the lyrics of songs that haunt your memory. I don't believe I have ever climbed onto a swing in my life without the words "...Up in the air and over the wall/Till I can see so wide,/Rivers and trees and cattle and all/Over the countryside" on my lips.

The book was worn out from such loving use. But I found an identical copy many years later, which my children have adored and now my grandchildren are reading.

Stevenson excited my imagination by telling about the Great Wall of China, crocodiles on the Nile and jungles with tigers and cockatoos. "I should like to rise and go/Where the golden apples grow," and so did I. And I did. Years later when I found myself in Cairo, or Calcutta or Rome on some film assignment I'd wonder, "Where shall we adventure, today that we're afloat/Wary of the weather and steering by a star?/Shall it be to Africa, a-steering of the boat,/To Providence, or Babylon, or off to Malabar?"

Quite frankly I still would like to go around with Leerie and light the lamps at night...and I enjoy getting up early and leaving my shadow behind, "like an arrant sleepy-head."

Louis Applebaum (composer, conductor)

Mrs. Rae asked about "the book that stirred my soul or changed my life." The title came rather quickly: Walt Whitman's *Leaves of Grass*. It was Whitman who, in the early 1900s, was inspiring so many American composers to "Hear America Singing," who gave them soaring words to set to music, who demonstrated for them such an attractive, non-European, self-confident way of thinking and making art. But, in my case, the impact was quite different, having nothing to do with the emerging art forms across the border.

In the mid 1930s, at 201 Beatrice St. in Toronto lived a callow, romantic teenage pianist seeking anxiously to impress a lovely, blonde girl four blocks away on Euclid Ave., who read a lot and had a grand passion for books and music, who didn't scorn his romantic notions and who had a birthday coming up. There, on the shelf in the book store around the corner on College St. (owned by film-maker David Cronenberg's father), beckoned this impressive, elegant, green, boxed edition of Whitman poems, and, glory be, it was "on sale." It was obviously destined for her and my meagre allowance be damned. A deal was struck with Cronenberg and the book was mine, or rather, hers.

But what about the inscription? It mustn't be too mushy or presumptuous. It must, perforce, be in verse, unrhymed, naturally, and oh so subtle in hinting at an unstated but intense desire to savour Whitman's eloquence in a shared future of some kind. Hours and hours of creative agony for a wannabe poet!

Somehow, it worked in the end and the bond was miraculously made. In fact, she shortly thereafter was eagerly showing me a beautiful, old book of poems that she had found, a lavishly illustrated nineteenth-century edition, far more lovely and romantic than the Whitman, the poems were by Heinrich Heine ... in German. Somehow, our underdeveloped and hesitant Yiddish and primitive German enabled us to absorb the meaning of many of the poems, some even in precise detail. It was she who suggested that I set one of them to music, a poem that began:

Du hast Diamenten und Perlen,
Hast Alles, was Menschen begehr.

It was the first song I ever wrote. I submitted it to a CAPAC young composers' competition of which Sir Ernest MacMillan was the judge. It, together with a little piano piece, won a prize and that, more than anything, set me off on a composer's career.

The greatest and most life-stirring boon of all, though, was that Janet, the lovely, sensitive, talented, empathetic girl on Euclid Ave, became my wife fifty-six years ago. We no longer live in that College–Bathurst enclave, but her passions remain undiminished and we both are still moved by Whitman's overt romanticism. There is no question at all that the book that stirred my soul at that time and totally changed my life for the better thereafter was that boxed edition of Walt Whitman's *Leaves of Grass*.

Peter Cumming (writer)

Who can guess how what we read will weave its way through the rest of our lives? When, at age three, as a sort of parlour trick, I read aloud random sentences from the King James version of the Bible, how could I know that the structure of those sentences would haunt my writing for the rest of my life? At age ten, when I craved boys' action stories, wartime adventures of American fighter pilot Dave Dowson and British sidekick Freddy Farmer, how could I predict a lifelong passion for Canada and peace? At age twelve, when I shuddered as one of the Hardy Boys was in danger of being tattooed against his will, how could I know that one seemingly insignificant scene out of millions would remain absolutely vivid in my mind—in my very body—three decades later? As a young adult, when I first read Lin Yutang's *The Importance of Living*, or later when I discovered George MacDonald's *The Golden Key* (inseparable in my mind from Maurice Sendak's illustrations, and still on the shelf beside my desk), or later, when I first read the short stories of William Saroyan or the poems of e.e. cummings, or later still, when, one night in a library, I stumbled across Jonathan Schell's *The Fate of the Earth*, how could I know that in books I would meet companions, kindred spirits, fellow travellers as real and present and important to me as my parents, my brothers and sisters, my friends, my partner and my own children?

I am thirteen. I live in a small, flat Ontario village where sulphur water reeks on insufferable, humid, summer afternoons, where chickens are slaughtered on the edge of town, where false fronts thrust themselves up from the stores on Main Street. Except for the librarian, I am alone in the small, red-brick Carnegie Library. I kneel on the hardwood floor to get at a little-used shelf of oversized books. I pull out, touch, smell, open, skim, then sign out and pore over a book which will—though I don't know it then or fully understand it now—change my life.

The book is an old, tall, thick, heavy hardcover in a green box. Its cover is green linen, almost as coarse as burlap. The box and the spine of the book are faded, yellowed like dried grasses. The rest of the cover, protected by the box, is a bright, rich green, like the living grasses that blow in the salt wind along seashores. The book's cream-coloured pages smell musty, but from the delicate, green garland of grass of the book's frontispiece through the first unusual poem (its lines as long as life itself) through the first dramatic illustration of a larger-than-life human being rising out of an all-living world, this book brings a breath—a very wind—of fresh air into my life.

Leaves of Grass, a life-full of poems written and rewritten by Walt Whitman from 1855 to 1891. Published, in this edition, in New York by Doubleday, Doran & Co., Inc., in 1940. Heroic, full-page illustrations in colour and black-and-white (I liked then and I like now the charcoal, black-and-white ones best) of a solitary boy on the seashore, of crowds of people on a ferry, of strong, vibrant, naked, unashamed, intertwined bodies, of birth and death, of love and companionship and war.

Who can guess how reading changes lives? The first poem of this edition of *Leaves of Grass* is "Song of the Open Road"; later, after going away to university and finding and buying a copy of this same edition in a used-book store, I will travel my own open road, to Entry Island on Iles de la Madeleine to Framboise on Cape Breton Island to Iglulik in the eastern Arctic. Later still, I will buy a second copy of this edition to give to my younger brother on his thirteenth birthday (and he, mystified by what kind of birthday present this *Leaves of Grass* might be, will later become a professor of Victorian literature who published an article on Walt Whitman). In "Song of Myself" Whitman sings that "this (is) the common air that bathes the globe," and later, whether in political action to protect the environment, or writing children's books and plays, or exploring issues of gender and race in literary criticism, I will live (as best I can) with a tolerance and generosity of spirit worthy of the poet who wrote and spoke, across boundaries of time, national origin and sexual orientation to tell the small-town adolescent on the library floor, "Whoever you are, now I place my hand upon you, that you be my poem."

Who can guess how books affect each of us? My own children are now growing into their teenage years and though they are finding—as well they should—their own friends and their own books and their own way through the world, I realize now, as I write these words, that the time has come for me to seek out three more copies of the large, green, boxed, 1940 edition of Walt Whitman's *Leaves of Grass*—to give to those children who are who they are because of who they come from and because of who they meet in books and on the open road of life.

Raymond Souster (poet)

In 1881 a young, first-year student from Morpeth, Ontario, Archibald Lampman, was attending Trinity College of the University of Toronto. One night, much to his surprise, he found in the college library a book of poems by a young Canadian poet, which had appeared the year before. The book was *Orion and Other Poems*, the author a twenty-year-old at the University of New Brunswick, who was being hailed as the foremost Canadian poet of his day, both for his amazing technique and youthful maturity. That young man was Charles G.D. Roberts.

Archibald Lampman has left us in his own words the elation that swept over him at that moment: "I sat up all night reading and rereading *Orion* in a state of the wildest excitement, and when I went to bed I could not sleep. It seemed to me a wonderful thing that such work could be done by a Canadian, a young man, one of ourselves."

Perhaps it might be possible, he must have concluded, for one such as himself to become a distinctive Canadian poet. And almost certainly his full commitment to poetry, for the rest of his pitifully short life, can be dated from that eventful evening.

To complete the final link in this story we must leap ahead forty-two years to the Ontario of 1934. We are interested in a certain twelve-year-old boy in his second year at U.T.S., or University of Toronto Schools, whose venerable building still stands, very much in operation, at Bloor and Huron streets in downtown Toronto. His English teacher has given his class the choice of memorizing any one of the eight poems in the Canadian Section of W.J. Alexander's *Shorter Poems*, at that time the standard poetry text for secondary schools in Ontario. He reads each poem over carefully, and finds himself drawn to two by Archibald Lampman.

His favourite is "Morning on the Lievre," a vivid account of a sunrise during a canoe trip near Ottawa at the turn of the century. Although he has never been in a canoe, the poem seems to convey the spirit of the sport and the joy of good companionship; it almost comes alive right off the page.

The second choice, "A January Morning," conjures up a very identifiable picture of a bitterly cold Canadian day—what if those woodsmen's sleighs and struggling horse teams are back in 1899?—the frigid cold, red cheeks, frosty plumed breaths from both man and animal are really no different today, when you come to think of it.

He eventually decides, given past difficulty with memory work, that the fourteen-line winter poem seems a wiser bet than the forty-four lines of the canoe trip.

As it happens he never regrets his choice. Each time he rereads "A January Morning" the more he appreciates the subtle artistry behind it. And also, for some reason that he can't logically explain, that poem has awakened in him a kindred spark.

Much to his delight he found that there were four other Lampman poems in the same textbook. With such vibrant and communicative examples of the poet's art suddenly revealed to him like a new-found land, is it any wonder that this young lad is tempted to try his hand at making poems of his own? Helping to fan the flames is the fact that ten minutes from his door he can be transported into the rugged, yet unspoiled scenery of the lower Humber River valley (especially that stretch of the winding stream from the Dundas–Lambton bridge south to the last stand of bulrushes at Third Marsh's sudden ending). Or perhaps he will try to convey the breakneck pace, the combined joy and terror of a wild eight-car tram ride driven by a totally nonchalant employee of the Niagara Gorge Route Streetcar Company, causing sharp intakes of breath and the occasional scream among even the most blasé of passengers.

Over the next few months the boy gradually copies his best efforts and one day, gathering up his courage, leaves a small notebook on the crowded desk of his Canadian History teacher. Good old Mr. Daniher keeps him in suspense for only two days. His poems are returned with neatly pencilled notations, and a final: "So you have proved you have imagination and some talent—next you must learn about metre and rhyme."

Now that he has shared his secret with a stranger, there doesn't seem to be much point in keeping it from his family. His father is a great consumer of true-adventure tales and detective thrillers. He reads a dozen poems, selects one, copies it out in his very legible handwriting (a gift not shared by his son), and mails it in to the *Toronto Daily Star*'s "A Little of Everything" column, a filler of odds and ends on the editorial page. Five days later, to everyone's amazement (especially our budding author's), "A Field in Winter" appears at the top of the column, with his own name staring very nakedly out at him. He is fifteen and a published poet! That left only the world to conquer.

That same boy (his wife, Rosalia, of fifty years will tell you) has been writing poems ever since. And if he's very lucky he may still write a few good ones in the next year and the next.

An obsession? Obviously. But he wouldn't have it any other way.

Alexander Brott (composer)

Since my early youth, I have had the good fortune to benefit from excellent teachers, teachers who imbued respect for the arts and who could succeed in drawing every vestige of natural aptitude from their students. For example, when we were engaged in the study of poems by Wordsworth, Tennyson, etc., we were expected to know their form and metric subdivision, as well as their content. In my case, as a musician, it was quite common to be asked to set some of these poems to music—a function which I found challenging and very enjoyable. An early example of such creativity is to be found in my "Songs of Contemplation" which probed various facets of introspection and subjectivity and is based on texts by Milnes, Tennyson and Rossetti. The work was subsequently performed by sopranos Lois Marshall and Rose Bampton, and recorded by Maureen Forrester.

This incentive produced a number of other works in similar vein when I was inspired by Kahlil Gibran's *The Prophet* and was moved by his perception of life's cycles to the point of writing a cantata bearing the title "Love, Work and Beauty." This cantata was given its premiere by Pierette Alary and Leopold Simcreau. Biblical incentive produced Jeremiah's "Prophecy of the Dry Bones," as well as Solomon's "There Is a Time for All Things," which received its first performance in Bonn, Germany, under the direction of Elmer Eisler.

For all the foregoing, I owe a debt of gratitude to my teachers who first encouraged me to set poetry to music.

Joan Finnigan (writer)

From the beginning I was read to by a mother who brought with her as part of her "marriage dowry" classics she had collected as a teacher. I was the fortunate eldest of five so garnered more of her reading time. From the beginning I was a voracious reader. By the time I was nine or ten I had read almost "everything in the house," including the ones my mother censored by hiding in the linen closet:

Bulldog Drummond, murder mysteries, romantic and—I guess she thought then—"sexy" novels. McLeod Street United Church had a library from which, only on Sunday, we were allowed to borrow its strictly structured moral fables. Then I discovered the Carnegie Library, ten or twelve blocks away from my home in Centretown. I became a "bender" reader, all of G.A. Henty, all of James Fenimore Cooper, all of Ernest Thompson Seton. By that time my whole enormous clan recognized me as a "reader," understood that anything less than a book was entirely unacceptable for birthdays and Christmas. One of my American aunts sent me Hurlburt's *Story of the Bible*, and I hold it close to me yet. For an eleven-year-old it was an incredible and inspirational adventure story.

Since the age of seven I had been writing poetry and this, too, was clan nurtured. I still have on my bookshelves slim volumes of Robert Louis Stevenson, Edward Lear, James Whitcomb Riley and John Greenleaf Whittier, all gifts of supportive relatives.

When I began to attend Lisgar Collegiate I fell under the spell of a great teacher, Walter B. Mann, who was to remain my lifelong friend and mentor. With Shakespeare, Tennyson, Browning, Keats splendidly read, dramatized—and dissected—he enhanced my life immeasurably, and the lives of many around me. In 1993 at the Sesquicentennial Celebrations at Lisgar, Bill Pratt of Calgary and I sought out our beloved Wally Mann and quoted some of that old "memory work" to him, Bill doing Shakespeare and I, Tennyson, and "we damn near cried together."

It was Wally Mann who introduced me to one of the most influential books of my life, Louis Untermeyer's *Modern American Poetry*. I am sure it was not on the curriculum, but when he read from it to us I was infused with a feeling of New Age. I can recapture yet the excitement and exhilaration I experienced confronting the free expression, the liberated style, the unadorned realism, from the unrhymed rants of road-makers like Walt Whitman to the totally non-conforming "determined madness" of e.e. cummings. And I coveted that book. I wanted to have it in my own hands, to devour it in my own privacy. So I saved for it, and saved for it, because money was short back then in our family. I ordered it from Hope's Bookstore, and waited. Weeks later, one day when Ottawa was enjoying a torrential July rainstorm, Hope's phoned to say Untermeyer had arrived. I put on rainwear, climbed aboard the Bank Street streetcar, my hoarded money in my pocket. Emotionally and spiritually thereafter I lived with that book through my teens. True, one hundred and twenty miles away in an old Canadian city Modern Canadian Poetry was "being born." But, as a developing Canadian poet, it was American poetry which was to deliver the greatest influence on me.

Allan Blakeney (former premier of Saskatchewan)

When I was a young university student I did a lot of hitch-hiking. It was a safe and acceptable mode of transport in Nova Scotia at that time.

It is the nature of hitch-hiking that you spend quite a bit of time sitting by the edge of the road, and a book is a great companion. I used to carry a now-battered copy of *The Pocket Book of Verse*. I found it the other day and noted with nostalgia the directions "Buy War Savings Stamps and Certificates" and "Share This Book with Someone in Uniform." It was one of those books which has selected poems from Chaucer to the present day. I read and reread a few of the poems. As I look back they seemed often to be about sad themes. There was Thomas Hood's "I remember, I remember, the place where I was born," the theme of which is, I would say, lost innocence. A particular favourite was Gray's "Elegy Written in a Country Churchyard," which has given us a few of our most lasting epigrams, "The boast of heraldry, the pomp of power," "The short and simple annals of the poor," "Far from the madding crowd's ignoble strife." General James Wolfe is supposed to have said, before he led the attack on Quebec in 1759, that he would rather have written that poem than capture Quebec. In that context, one line of the poem, "The paths of glory lead but to the grave," is particularly poignant.

While still a student I got a small copy of *The Rubáiyát of Omar Khayyám*. I recently turned up this volume, with many verses underlined. It strikes a fatalistic theme with such stanzas as:

> The Moving finger writes; and, having writ,
> Moves on: nor all Piety and Wit
> Shall lure it back to cancel half a Line,
> Nor all your Tears wash out a Word of it.

I don't think I ever accepted either the pessimism or the fatalism, but perhaps they served to temper my persistent optimism.

Eventually my old copy of *The Pocket Book of Verse* collapsed into two parts and could not be carried. One Christmas, my older children gave me a replacement paperback book of poetry, all custom bound with my name embossed. It was beside the bed for years but somehow it wasn't quite the same. For one thing, it weighed quite a bit and I didn't throw it in my briefcase when I was out on the road, now not hitch-hiking but seeking votes.

One of the real virtues of poetry is its ability to capture a penetrating thought in a few words and then to give one the ability to recall it by remembering a verse or two of the poem. I spend most of my work day and my leisure reading prose, everything from legal judgements to financial reports to whodunits. But poetry has the unique quality of creating both a mood and a memory, and a few of these poems have been my constant companions for more years than I care to remember.

Mike Katrycz (broadcaster)

Books failed to stir me much until I was in high school. It was there that a very special teacher introduced me to a young new writer who had just won the Governor General's prize for a collection of poems entitled *The Collected Works of Billy the Kid*. The hot young writer was, of course, Michael Ondaatje, much hailed since then for his novels, including *The English Patient*.

With an amazing leanness of language he was able to inject fresh brilliance into characters, landscapes, events and an era that had been turned tawdry and tired by Hollywood. By becoming the "voice" of Billy the Kid, writing the poems in the first person, Ondaatje made this original rebel-without-a-cause into a human being, completely identifiable.

I read the book over and over and was so taken with it that when it was adapted for the stage I hitch-hiked to Stratford to see it. With barely enough money in my pocket for the show, finding food and lodging for the night became quite another adventure.

Years later, no longer thumbing but behind the wheel of my own car, I took a trip across the American Southwest and found Michael Ondaatje's book still echoing over the terrain. I never actually saw the Fort Sumner of William Bonney, Pat Garrett and Miss Angela D', but their images occasionally joined me like happy ghosts hitching rides of their own.

Liona Boyd (classical guitarist/composer)

As an eleven-year-old living in London, England, I was introduced in school to the epic poem "The Song of Hiawatha." Having spent three years in Canada I felt an immediate identification. Henry Wadsworth Longfellow's vivid images of natural scenery resonated within me, for I had experienced the translucent blue lakes of northern Ontario, paddled a canoe along her sunlit shores and crept through her pine-scented forests. That romantic poem had such an attraction for me that I stayed up several nights reading the entire epic and memorizing many of its verses. The poet's idealized fantasies of North American Indian life so fired my imagination that I was inspired to write a personal version which was published in the school magazine. My English classmates could only imagine the shores of "Gitche Gumee," whereas I had actually been there.

Years later, on a white-water canoe trip down the Missinnaibi River, Longfellow's rhythmic lines and repetitive phrases sang in my head: "Till he came unto a streamlet/In the middle of the forest,/To a streamlet still and tranquil/That had overflowed its margin,/To a dam made by the beavers,/To a pond of quiet water/Where knee-deep the trees were standing,/Where the waterlilies floated,/Where the rushes waved and whispered."

"Wah-wah-taysee little firefly, little flitting white-fire creature" danced around our campsite and "The Great Spirit, The Creator" guided us through the rapids and portages. Through this poem I learned to share Hiawatha's reverence for the mysterious forces of nature and our great northern landscapes. In my autobiography, I devote a chapter to this adventure—"The Ultimate Canadian Experience"—where Hiawatha had surely acted as my personal guide.

As a musician I once again called upon my muse to help compose a suite for solo guitar called "My Land of Hiawatha" ("Spirit of the Moving Waters," "Spirit of the Forest" and "Spirit of the West Wind") which I recorded and had arranged for orchestral performance. The reading of that poem has certainly left its imprint on my creative endeavours. I wonder when Hiawatha might resurface again in my life's journey.

Paul Kropp (writer)

In my second year of high school, I decided to use a makeshift printing press in our basement to produce some business cards for myself. After a little reflection, I hit upon the desired text: Paul Kropp, poet and philosopher.

At the time, my experience in both poetry and philosophy was fairly limited. Among poets, the only writer I had read with real relish was e.e. cummings, whose *Collected Poems* was the first expensive hardcover book I ever bought. Cummings's inventive punctuation and cleverly layered images inspired some truly terrible poetry of my own and led me to sign my name p.s. kropp for six months or so. Among philosophers, I had such a fondness for the last chapter of Henry David Thoreau's *Walden* that I tried, really tried, to enjoy the other twenty chapters on animals, ponds and solitary life in the woods—topics as remote to this city kid as descriptions of Aztec temples.

Nonetheless, I thought some combination of e.e. cummings and H.D. Thoreau would make a pretty extraordinary adult and announced these intentions proudly on my business card.

I might add, there's been a slight adjustment in goals since then.

·7· Popular Reading

"The point of literature is pleasure"
—Doris Lessing

Part One: Series Books

"A literary assembly line"—Edward Stratemeyer

If you read a book and develop a relationship with the central characters, if you dread coming to the final pages and yearn to know what happens after the book ends, it is thrilling to discover your new friends once again brought gloriously to life in another book. To the delight of their publishers, children adore sequels. Series of children's books have proven perennial best-sellers. Despite contrived plots and often predictable outcomes, mass-market series books are as popular today as ever (thanks to advertising, possibly more so). They continue to fly off book-store, supermarket and library shelves and are hotly traded in many a schoolyard.

The truth is some series are a good deal better literature than others.

The longest and most commercially successful serial dynasty began with American Frank Stratemeyer and the Stratemeyer Literary Syndicate. He composed his first book in 1890, and essentially never stopped. Soon he was churning out twelve or more a year under various pseudonyms. Then he hired a fleet of writers for whom he provided pen names and an assembly line of characters and detailed plot outlines.

Stratemeyer's daughter, Harriet Adams, is far better known by her pseudonym, Carolyn Keene. The still-popular (two hundred plus) Nancy Drew books began rolling off the presses in 1930. Since then "Carolyn Keene" and "Franklin W. Dixon" have become the general pen-names of numerous commissioned writers employed to pump out the wildly popular books. The family could not keep up with the enormous demand all by themselves.

The Hardy Boys began their adventures in 1927. Like the first three Nancy Drews, they were originally written by Stratemeyer, then Leslie McFarlane and later a stable of others. Essentially, all these idealized heroes and heroines fight crime and solve mysteries with spectacular ease and remarkable coincidence. Unfailingly courageous, courteous and bang on with their hunches, the predictable exploits of these upstanding but sadly static characters have filled bedroom shelves and the heads of young readers, perhaps benignly (but often too long) to the exclusion of other books.

It has been theorized that pre-teen youngsters—hovering as they are between the relative security of childhood and the anticipation of teenage and adult responsibilities—are especially drawn to junk reading including the trashiest of series books. They find them reassuring and undemanding at a time of great personal change and turmoil. Kids are also attracted to the independence of apparent "choice." They feel a new and heady sense of freedom in selecting their own books, sometimes in deliberate conflict with parents' and teachers' recommendations. Never mind that the rows of options are cut-out copies, all virtually identical in flavour.

Michele Landsberg has identified the ingredients of bulk reading as "speed, comfort, familiarity, a reassuring simplicity, devotion to surface actions and conventional behaviour, a complete absence of introspection." To that useful list I might add mindless dialogue, undemanding storylines and, perhaps worst of all, a possible dulling of literary taste and of the impulse for finding and reading better books.

To give some idea of the immensity of the operation, Stratemeyer's company produced more than seventy series, including Rover Boys (1899–1926) under the name of Arthur Winfield, Uncle Wiggly's Adventures and Tom Swift Books, both by "Victor Appleton" (really Howard Garis). Tom Swift was a young inventor and scientific genius whose forty crime/adventures sold more than six million copies in hardcover before 1935!

Horatio Alger's "rags-to-riches" sagas—dozens of them, all extolling hard work and good luck—date from the turn of the century. Laura Lee Hope's two sets of Bobbsey twins, Nan and Bert, and Freddie and Flossie, endured countless milder adventures programmed for younger children. Today the far-fetched escapades of these sticky-sweet twins have, predictably, lost their audience.

Slightly older children have found a sugary replacement in the glossy and silly teenage romances of Sweet Valley High and the (only slightly more palatable) patly predictable, disposable psychology of The Baby Sitters Club.

In defence of bulk reading: series books fill a need for volume by the voracious young reader. They are escapist "light" reading. "Social literacy" and peer pressure make children cry out for them—reading them may provide immediate kinship with up-to-date insiders (gloriously separate from judgemental grownups). Kids outgrow them. (I did, my kids too.) At least the kids are reading *something*, firming up new skills and improving their reading speed. In the best-case scenario they may whet the appetite for more and better literature (in the worst, they dull it...). They may be only a comfortable way station, cheap, harmless and temporary. We all ate simple food before we moved on to anything fancier. If reading leads to more reading, then, with a little luck and some direction, most kids will eventually seek out more satisfying, nourishing and better quality books.

On the other hand, the bar is lowered. Characters are uniformly shallow and stereotypic. The writing is rarely of a high quality. As in the past many are written according to a set recipe. Contemporary examples offer cheap thrills and easy resolutions. They manipulate and exploit the sensibilities of the reader. What passes for dialogue is utilitarian, lamentable and often stilted. There is virtually nothing to stimulate the imagination. In some series, the values espoused by the (alleged role model) heroes and heroines reveal dubious character quality—little depth and questionable morality. In the United States, in particular (and more and more here in Canada), through powerful marketing, series books have had a negative impact on the sales of smaller publishers and individual authors. The "low end" has virtually swamped the children's book trade, leaving "high-end" children's books scrambling for publishers, shelf space and readers. Series and sentimental Disney versions of their movies and videos crowd out books by virtually everyone else, including the best authors and illustrators.

Television situation comedies follow precisely the same formula as series books—familiar, often shallow characters who return week after week—like book after book—thrust into only slightly different scrapes and circumstances. Using similar methods and principles (with minor variations such as gags and the cult of "coolness") they too build up huge dependable audiences for their mindless entertainment, squeezing out quality programs. Viewer loyalty, like reader loyalty, ensures longevity.

Not all series are "bad" or lead to a life hopelessly mired in junk reading. As Robert Coles has noted in *Read for Your Life*, "fiction that is not 'classical' can still be important." It frequently gets kids in the habit of reading regularly, and may actually help with speed and proficiency. I confess to gobbling up Nancy Drew and Cherry Ames for a year or so as a pre-teenager. Once, just a few years ago, desperate for reading material at the cottage, and seduced by the price (twenty-five cents a volume), I actually bought a whole box of Nancy Drews at a summer garage sale in response to my youngest daughter's urgent demand. She was, I think, ten, and very satisfied for a month or two. We've all survived and moved on. Happily, what my kids and I both realized some time ago (okay, I pushed them a bit) was that there is so much more out there to choose from—a great cornucopia of wonderful books and stories to discover. Besides, there are better series available too.

That joyful sensation of encountering familiar characters in a new adventure may be satisfied through some remarkable, exciting and imaginative (admittedly often shorter) series of books.

Arthur Conan Doyle wrote about Sherlock Holmes and his partner, Dr. Watson, until they achieved a reality almost beyond fiction.

Arthur Ransome's *Swallows and Amazons* (see Chapter 2), the first book in a wonderful and stimulating series, appeared, interestingly enough, the same year (1930) as *The Hidden Staircase*, the first mystery featuring Nancy Drew.

Ransome's durable saga follows the creative escapades of two families of middle-class boys and girls through twelve fantastic adventures. This high-quality British series retains its popularity because the self-respecting characters, compelling plots and exceptional writing are satisfying from first to last.

Very young children continue to amuse themselves with the mischievous escapades of *Peter Rabbit*, *Squirrel Nutkin* and *Two Bad Mice*. Beatrix Potter wrote nineteen small-format books between 1902 and 1913, each one familiar but wholly unique. Older kids, especially earlier this century, loved L. Frank Baum's Oz series—often called the first American fairy tales and named for a filing cabinet (from O to Z). Today only the first of the fourteen, *The Wizard of Oz,* is well known, partly, of course, because of the movie.

Perhaps the best-known literary series for children is C.S. Lewis's Chronicles of Narnia. These seven fantasy classics, beginning with

The Lion, the Witch and the Wardrobe (1950), have earned Lewis a well-deserved reputation as one of the best-loved children's authors in the world. He claimed he was only trying to write the sort of books he would have liked to read as a youngster. Also hugely popular are Lewis's contemporary and friend J.R.R Tolkien's elaborate fantasy adventure *The Hobbit* (1937) and seventeen years later, its sequels, *The Lord of the Rings* trilogy. All are much loved by devoted fans.

Even the better quality series books tend to be inexpensive and widely available. Some publishers have grouped them conveniently into boxed sets. Many are available in libraries. Their escapist appeal and, most of all, the comfort and continuity of attractive and (usually) courageous central characters and action draw kids to them like bees to flowers.

Among well-known collections, still popular and praised for their enduring value system and literary quality, are series like Eleanor Estes's warm and insightful *The Moffats* (four books) and E. Nesbit's fantasy-based *Five Children and It* and its funny and creative sequels. Nesbit also wrote the three-volume spell-binder *The Story of the Treasure Seekers*, in which a family of motherless, independent, resourceful (and well-read!) children attempt to recoup the family fortune. Despite occasional stereotypical minor characters, these books endure because of their intriguing storylines, interesting and well-developed characters and Nesbit's adamant belief in the power of the imagination. Also far from run-of-the-mill are Laura Ingalls Wilder's earnest but engaging Little House books and Beverly Cleary's Ramona stories. Lynne Reid Banks's *The Indian in the Cupboard* combines fantasy, adventure and time travel in a lively and animated trilogy.

The first well-known series by a Canadian was Palmer Cox's hugely popular Brownie series (launched in the United States) beginning with *The Brownies: Their Book* in 1887 and continuing through twelve sequels. The Brownies even spawned commercial spinoffs—salt and pepper shakers, Brownie wallpaper, toys, games and endorsements for soap, medicine and a variety of beverages.

Lucy Maud Montgomery was somewhat reluctantly persuaded by her publisher to write seven sequels to *Anne of Green Gables*. Although arguably none may be as high in quality as the original, loyal fans remain undeterred. Readers continue to devour them eagerly, anxious to pursue Anne's career, misadventures and marital prospects.

What currently constitutes a quality series is often only a few books. One such charming and evocative Canadian series is Bernice Thurman Hunter's *That Scatterbrain Booky* and its two sequels. They form a lively episodic re-creation of the struggles and preoccupations of a sympathetic Toronto girl growing up during the Great Depression. Hunter's *A Place for Margaret* and its two sequels introduces, through its heroine, the love of horses—a persistent theme in children's literature.

Mordecai Richler's hilarious threesome, *Jacob Two-Two Meets the Hooded Fang*, *Jacob Two-Two and the Dinosaur* and *Jacob Two-Two's First Spy Case*, shimmer with irony, wit and the broad and gutsy literary strokes of a clever and accomplished writer.

Kit Pearson's *The Sky Is Falling* and its two sequels (*Looking at the Moon* and *The Lights Go On Again*) are an exceptional set of books about British "war guests," children who were sent to wait out the war in safety with Canadian families. Nora and Gavin are believable, realistic characters going through the complications and adjustments of growing up—but with the added stress and loneliness of being far away from home and family. In Pearson's skilled hands, their story, problems and choices come stunningly alive.

The mystery format continues to lend itself to series writing. A bunch of Eric Wilson's mysteries—each set in a different province or famous location (for example, Disneyland, the West Edmonton Mall, Casa Loma)—are somewhat more formulaic but curiously satisfying adventure stories for eager young self-readers.

Judy Blume's contemporary (American) problem novels, and Matt Christopher's sports knockoffs, despite serious shortcomings, remain constantly available. But no series of books have dominated the preteen market like the invasive American series *Goosebumps*. Canadian kids, as vulnerable to extensive promotion and peer pressure as their American counterparts, have swallowed heaps of these like so many kernels of salty popcorn. Reams of shallow "fear books," with garish covers and equally gross and awful storylines emanate hourly from the monster-like scary fiction factories of "pikenstine" (R.L. Stine and Christopher Pike). The ones for younger kids are into titillation and suspense, those for slightly older consumers evolve into senseless episodes of crime and murder. There are other even worse derivatives.

Compare these, at their peril, to one of the few Canadian collections that has crossed the U.S. border in the other direction—the Franklin the Turtle stories—a growing canon of gentle and endearing picture books for very young children by Canadian author Paulette Bourgeois, illustrated by Brenda Clark. Or, closer to the same playing surface, Roy MacGregor's Screech Owl series, a hockey-centred short list of fast-paced brief novels aimed at ten- to twelve-year-olds (both boys and girls) that briskly combine page-turning action, social issues, mystery and believable characters.

Young children continue to appreciate classic series including Ludwig Bemelman's saucy and delightful Madeline books, H.A. Rey's irrepressible and mischievous monkey, Curious George, and the consistently charming Babar stories by Jean de Brunhoff (series continued by his son Laurent).

Slightly older readers, especially horse lovers, will gravitate happily to Walter Farley's *The Black Stallion* and some of its twenty or so sequels. Each has a strong and independent plot, compelling action and high adventure.

There is a tremendous amount of poor series fiction available; the quantities are troublesome. My advice—I can't help but give a little about all this—is to always seek out and offer children the best books you can find. Capitulate for a time, if necessary, to the big American series (if the child insists)—but keep it to a mutually negotiated minimum. I don't like censoring books, and dislike telling kids not to read a few of the crummier books if they crave and demand them, but push the bar higher whenever you can.

I strongly recommend, for instance, keeping better books readily available and talking them up. Follow informed suggestions, especially raves, from librarians, reviewers and knowledgeable sales personnel. A parent might read aloud the first few paragraphs of an intriguing book—and then casually leave it on a table or counter, visible and tantalizing. (Perhaps you've hooked someone!) Resourceful adults can make deals too—barter alternate book selections with a series-addicted child. Grownups can continue to introduce good books whenever the choosing is up to them (for instance when reading to children, gift-giving, setting school assignments, and while making several selections in book stores or libraries). Some of these measures may seem devious, but consider the reward: the fostering and encouragement of a hungry, demanding and discriminating reader. Such a person will, eventually, only be able to satisfy their increasing need for stories with good ones, well told.

Alex Tilley (Pres., CEO Tilley Endurables)

Oh God, why do the Bobbsey Twins keep springing to mind!

Dennis Lee (poet)

When I was a boy, my favourite book of all time was the one I was reading that day. I would crawl into the secret hideout of words, and in spite of piddly distractions like eating and sleeping and school, I never really emerged till I'd finished the final page. A book was a bit like a splendid attack of the flu. It took you over, established a new reality of its own, and when it had passed you could scarcely imagine where you'd been. So you started another.

Which of all those books has the greatest resonance now? *The Wind in the Willows*. At the time, it was only one among hundreds of revelations. But it lasted. I savoured its incomparable drollery and heartache when I was ten, and I savour them even more at fifty-seven.

But when I think back to those years of passionate reading, to their hungry joy, the flash I get is not of a particular book. What I remember is a discovery I made when I was—how old? I no longer recall, but it was momentous.

The discovery was: *There were books that came in series.*

Peter Rabbit was grand—and the next night, you could have *Squirrel Nutkin*! Thornton Burgess went on and on. *Freddy the Pig*: how many glorious escapades did he and his friends lead me through? *Mary Poppins*. The Nesbit books. Swallows and Amazons. I can't recall how many series I burrowed into in the course of my childhood, but they were special kingdoms. Some came by author, like the Henty books; others were tagged to a hero, like Dave Dawson. Some looked as if they were endless, and you mentally checked off each title you read at the front of the book. Others gave out after three or four. Looking back, I can see that the series I loved ranged from formulaic junk to the real thing. But I was a vacuum cleaner! It was reading that had me hooked, not just reading great books. Though they were the ones that became friends for life.

What made a series so irresistible? It was partly the sense of security it gave. I couldn't have put it into words, but the promise was unmistakable. "This second life you're living—it won't let you down. You will never come to the end of the ride. You can live in the imagination, and books are the magic key."

And how do I feel about that now? I believe I only half understood what the promise meant. I had to give up the simplest version of the dream that enchanted me then: that settling into another new book, another new series, meant that nothing beyond it was real. That nothing would change.

But I still exult in the promise. The imagination speaks its luminous shapes of meaning. They're there to be entered, and books are a magic key. I still crawl in, with the same old hungry joy.

Sheila McCarthy (actor)

Don't laugh, when we were little, my two sisters and I read and reread and reread once again the entire series of Cherry Ames. Cherry was a nurse who managed to work at her profession in every walk of life. She nursed on remote islands in the Pacific, in private girls' schools and in every major city in North America, at every single hospital. What a gal!

Cherry was a good nurse, but she always managed to get into trouble and become entwined in mysterious espionage or danger of some sort. Her superiors were forever telling her to wipe that blush off her face, but Cherry just naturally had cherry red cheeks. She was fearless, single-minded, adventurous and kind.

I became Cherry Ames when I read her books. They may be dated now, but to me Cherry was a heroine of enormous proportions.

Sylvia McNicoll (writer)

As the daughter of German immigrants, I grew up with *Grimm's Fairy Tales* at home and *Fun with Dick and Jane* at school. I remember loving Hansel and Gretel best and being slightly perturbed by the differences between my family and Dick, Jane, Sally, Mother and Father. Even their dog, Spot, spoke a different language when he barked "Bow-wow."

Then one spring, we all accompanied my father to Connecticut on a business trip. We were to stay six weeks and my brother and I to attend school. A boy we met invited us to his attic to choose a book to read. "Here, you'll probably like this one," he said as he handed me a hardcovered blue book with black lettering. There wasn't even a picture on the cover. Still, I didn't want to disappoint him. He was older and the book looked grownup. I started reading it immediately and can't remember putting it down. My first real novel. Excitement, glamour, mystery! When I finished it, I returned it, and he gave me several more hardcovered blue books which I also devoured.

My father's trip was cut short to a week, but back in Canada I hunted for more of those books at the library.

Because literary élitism won't inspire reading and writing excitement in children, even though this is difficult and embarrassing as a Canadian writer, I'm going to admit that an American series launched my love of reading. That first hardcovered blue book which affected me most was *The Mystery of the Witch Tree Symbol*, the author: Harriette Adams, one of the many writing under the pseudonym of Carolyn Keene for the Nancy Drew series.

Pamela Wallin (television interviewer)

One of the questions I am most frequently asked is: "How did you get here from there?"

The "here" is Toronto, the self-declared centre of the business, cultural and media universe where I am president of my own production company and host of a successful television program.

The "there" is Wadena, Saskatchewan. Population 1,600. My home town.

The answer is some combination of chance, circumstance, curiosity and Nancy Drew. Allow me to explain. My parents taught me not only to think for myself but encouraged me to explore places and ideas through books. This was wise advice for many reasons, not the least of which was that the Wallin household didn't have a TV set until I was through grade 4. There are many long nights in a prairie winter.

I read everything I could find in our well-stocked house (Mom was an English teacher, Dad a voracious reader). But with the benefit of hindsight and foolhardy enough to risk public ridicule, let me confess that the books that whetted my appetite for far-flung places and risky business were the Nancy Drew mystery stories.

I'm sure I read them all. Dozens for sure. Author Carolyn Keene was the Charlotte Brontë of the fifties, implicity suggesting that girls had the same dreams and fantasies as boys about adventure and about making a difference. I'm not suggesting that Keene's works were feminist treatises. Instead, they worked their magic by example.

Nancy was independent, smart, respectful of her elders and always caring. Therefore, her father trusted her to pursue her own "good works" for those in need. Her efforts often saved lives and she always got the bad guys for crimes against humanity so infuriating to this young, self-styled Robin Hood. Above and beyond the appeal of her sense of adventure, as well as her compassion and fairness, was the compelling image of this girl, a mere teenager, who had her own convertible. In the fifties this was THE symbol of freedom.

Recent printings of the books have apparently been sanitized to meet current standards of political correctness. I hope they haven't banished the car. Every girl needs one, or the dream of one, especially if she's planning to take on the world (or dreams that she may). Nancy never gave in to her fears or yielded to self-doubt.

I loved Nancy Drew and I wanted to be Nancy Drew. I'm still striving to ensure that my journalism has heart. And now I'm passing on these treasured books to my young god-daughter so that she grows up motivated by those in need and believing that girls can have dreams too.

Brian Mulroney (lawyer, former prime minister)

My earliest memories of reading books actually involve my older sisters, Olive and Peggy, in Baie Comeau. They were both great fans of the junior detective series and read to me, their younger brother by two or three years, regularly after school. In my mind's eye I can still see the brutal February winds swirling off the St. Lawrence River and sweeping snow banks even higher against our snug mill house as my sisters alternately performed—the word "read" does not adequately describe their sense of theatre—chapters from the latest brilliant exploits of Helen, Nancy or Mary—girl detective! I suppose I was about four years old.

After I eventually improved my own reading skills at school, I developed a taste for the Hardy Boys and reciprocated the earlier courtesy from my sisters by reading aloud from my latest book (sent down by boat from Montreal by my Aunt Ena). Olive feigned interest but Peg usually fell asleep—a hazard I was later to encounter at various stages of my political career.

But the words from those books made pictures in the sky that enthralled me then and remain vivid even today. I became a regular at the little library in the Baie Comeau Community Association with the gentle and encouraging Alice Lane (wife of our mill manager, Jim Lane) as volunteer librarian.

My respect for books and my love of reading, born in those cold northern Quebec winters, have stayed with me for a lifetime.

Don Cherry (hockey expert)

I believe in the power of books. Books helped form my personality and definitely affected the way I am today. When we were little, my father would read to my brother and me every night. We would sit on the floor beside him. He was in a chair and I can still see him sitting there, peering at us over his glasses, a bowl of delicious "bridge mixture" balanced on his chest.

He read several "rags to riches" books by Horatio Alger, Jr., and I loved them all. Books with titles like *Ragged Dick*, *Sink or Swim*, *Strong and Steady*, *Strive and Succeed* and *Risen from the Ranks*. Alger wrote about a hundred books. Though the stories were all different, they each, in a sense, promoted the same idea: hard work, courage and determination will continually pay off. The boy heroes start low but always move up in the world. They make their way by sticking things out through tough times. Their hard work, honesty and perseverance rise up over whatever gets in the way. They never give up.

Our dad read about half a chapter a night. Sometimes he'd treat my brother and me to one of the chocolate candies. I always hoped I'd get one of the pink ones with a sweet centre. Sometimes Dad would check if the message of the book had sunk in, asking if we understood the stuff about courage and honesty.

Sometimes the boys in Alger's stories ran into trouble with higher-ups, bosses and the like. That part of the story must have affected me too, because I'm always having run-ins with authorities. But more important, the "never complain and work very hard" philosophy was ingrained in both my brother—a high-school principal for thirty-eight years—and me very deeply because of the lessons learned from my father and the characters in the books he read to us.

Part Two: Sports Books

"The real contest is with yourself"—Jay McInerney

Thank goodness for sports books. The fact is, kids like to read them, especially pre-teen boys. For some kids, it's the only thing they will read for a while. If a child is living, eating, breathing hockey, for example, or if he or she spends every spare moment at the rink (or the ball park, the basketball court, the field or the gym ...), it is logical that the only books that child will tolerate for some months, possibly years—and then only in a blizzard or a downpour, or late at night—are sports books, especially those about their current obsession.

Because sports are as familiar to young people as school and music, these stories tend to connect well to their experience and other interests. Sports stories are often about developing values. As with real-life competition, there is the opportunity for dramatic tension between sport for the sheer pleasure of it and the will to win. This is a logical genre for stories about commitment, determination, accepting defeat and striving to be the best one can be.

There is a considerable body of sports fiction and non-fiction available for youngsters and adults alike. The 1940s American author John Tunis (*The Kid from Tompkinsville*) has been called the "father of modern sports fiction." His star character, Roy Tucker, is a centre-fielder and hero of a number of baseball-centred novels.

Sports attracts extremely capable writers. There are numerous sports writers who, in newspapers and magazines, as well as in books, make the details of a game, the conflict of participants (both teams and individuals), as well as the surrounding ambience and mitigating circumstances, a beautiful thing. In any library or book store, readers will find captivating sports anthologies brimming with stories and essays. The expertise, variety of authors and readable style are hard to beat.

Beware the cliché children's book—these often come in series such as the Matt Christopher novels—that leads inevitably to the "big game" and a hero who miraculously and against tremendous odds surpasses all obstacles to save the day. Except in rare circumstances (an early example is Edith Bagnold's *National Velvet*, 1935) this plotline is not only predictable but slightly ridiculous. Sports books may well be action packed and exciting, but sometimes the wish-fulfilment fantasy gets a little out of hand. For pure fun something like Gordon Korman's *The Toilet Paper Tigers* or Jerry Spinelli's *There's a Girl in My Hammerlock* can (unpretentiously) fit the bill.

Baseball fans will rapidly gravitate from American Ernest Thayer's famous poem "Casey at the Bat" to Alison Gordon's *Dead Pull Hitter*, W.P. Kinsella's *Shoeless Joe*, Bernard Malamud's *The Natural* and a host of other novels. They will, in their quest for more sports stories, discover masterful writers like Roger Angell, Thomas Boswell, Peter Gammonds and others.

Chris Crutcher (*Athletic Shorts*, *Running Loose*, *Stotan!*) is an American writer for young adults whose realistic style and convincing psychology have won him many fans. His books deal with swimming, basketball, football and other activities, but use sports as a springboard to deal with issues as diverse as racism, physical handicaps, ethics and self-esteem.

Young Canadian readers who appreciate hockey stories will be familiar with Roch Carrier's classic story "The Hockey Sweater." They will also likely soon discover Scott Young's memorable novels such as *Scrubs on Skates* or *A Boy at the Leafs' Camp*. Roy MacGregor's vivid new Screech Owl series for pre-teen enthusiasts are clear winners by any assessment.

Steve Paikin (television interviewer)

Not only can I remember a book that was tremendously important to me as a child, but I also believe it was the first book I ever read.

I can remember attending my first National Hockey League game at Maple Leaf Gardens in 1966. I was six years old. The Leafs beat the Boston Bruins 3–0. Johnny Bower got the shutout. My brother, who was four, slept for most of the third period on my father's lap. We have pictures to prove this!

In any event, I developed such a love of hockey that my parents bought me Scott Young's novel *A Boy at the Leafs' Camp*. That book started me thinking about the career in pro hockey that I'm sure still awaits me. (Thirty-six-year-old rookies aren't *that* rare, are they?)

Even at my advanced age, I still play hockey once or twice a week, despite having no skill, ability, speed or any of the other things one would wish to have on the ice. Although I am the same age, height and weight as Wayne Gretzky, I'm told by knowledgeable hockey observers that the similarities end there.

I'm convinced that much of my love for the game and its history stems from my recollections of Scott Young's classic. In fact, one of the best moments of my journalistic career came last year when I met Scott Young for the first time. The interview was supposed to be about his new autobiography. But all I wanted to talk about was *A Boy at the Leafs' Camp*. He seemed genuinely moved that, nearly thirty years later, I was recalling one of his books with such affection. He told me one of the smartest things he ever did was write that book. Each generation has loved it, then purchased it for the next.

I've now taken my oldest son to see the Leafs at the Gardens. The blue-and-white brainwashing continues. Perhaps it's time to get him his own copy.

Trent Frayne (writer)

I became a lifelong sports fan at the age of six when my Uncle Fred Trent gave me a book for Christmas called *Baseball Joe of the Giants*. Joe was Joe Matson. He wasn't nearly as accomplished as his literary contemporary Frank Merriwell (who could do anything, including throw right- *and* left-handed) but he gave his BEST at everything he undertook. He pitched for the New York Giants and he was a quiet hero, the best kind. He didn't always strike out the opposing slugger but he always came back from the jaws of defeat to the joys of victory. In later years it often seemed to me that the famous Yankee pitcher Lefty Gomez had been aware of Joe Matson, because one day, when asked the secret of his success, Lefty said, "Clean living and a fleet-footed outfield." Modest to a fault, Joe would have said something like that.

Christopher Moore (writer)

We were immigrants. When I was a kid in the Kootenays in the 1950s, relatives in Scotland and England kept their colonial kin supplied with reading material from home. I had the Noddy books (still available, though my daughters didn't like them—what are those creepy Golliwogs) and the magazine *Robin*, as well as *Rupert Bear*—who recently turned up animated on YTV! My older brothers got Enid Blyton adventure books about the Famous Five and the Secret Seven. I remember reading one that was set at a castle when I was too young to know what a castle was. We had a big fieldstone fireplace in our home then. I associated that somehow with what a "castle" might signify, and it seemed to work just fine (I've often thought of telling this story to Roland Barthes).

At Christmas, we received a thick hardcover anthology called *The Commonwealth and Empire Annual.* The annual must have been a last gasp of Britain's literary empire (if you don't count the Booker Prize) and its politics were probably quite incorrect, but I remember it fondly. Having crossed the ocean when I was three, I always knew the world was a big place, and the *Annual* was full of bits and pieces from all sorts of places I'd never otherwise have known.

We are supposed to believe Canadian books did not exist before the Canada Council gave them permission about 1967. Yet for all my British influences, I never understood writing must come from away. There was a big house down the lakeshore from us, and somehow I always knew it had belonged to a writer, though I see from the *Canadian Encyclopedia* that Frederick Niven had been dead ten years before we came to Nelson. There were Canadian books in small towns in the 1950s. I particularly remember the Dale of the Mounted series: *With the Musical Ride*, *In Newfoundland*, *On the West Coast* and so on. I devoured those books, right along with the Hardy Boys and whatever came from the TAB Book Club at school. The summer we went back to Britain, a Mountie rented our house from us. Dale seemed pretty real to me.

In my mother's attic, I recently found a copy of *Dale of the Mounted*, by Joe Holliday. It was published by Thomas Allen in

Toronto in 1951, the first of a substantial series that sold in hardcover for $1.50 each. Joe Holliday, who seems to have been a journalist and magazine writer, and his character Dale, and the publishing and marketing conditions that brought them into print and into my small-town home, all seem to have vanished entirely from our literary history. I have to say that today Joe Holliday's prose sets my teeth on edge, and I can hardly bear to reread Dale's adventures. But I didn't think that then, and I'm glad Joe and Dale were there for us.

The book I really wanted to recall was *Scrubs on Skates*. God bless Scott Young, who knew about the hockey we played, and the schools we went to, and who even knew there were immigrants before there was multiculturalism. Out of those elements, he made some kind of a story. Seeing how he made Bill Spunska, at first just one of the kids in the crowd, not even on a forward line, gradually skate out of the pack to become the hero of the series may have been my first discovery of literary technique.

The other day I spotted *Scrubs on Skates* and *Boy on Defense* with snappy new covers on the paperback rack on the kids' side of the local public library. I knew a piece of my childhood was immortal.

Part Three: Humour, Comics, Light Reading

"A relief from chaos"—Joseph Gold

Why are there so few funny books for teenagers? Kids love humour, but so many books—especially for older children—are unrelentingly serious and singleminded in their treatment of issues and social problems. There are stacks of books about teenage suffering, kids in crisis, family breakup. Fine. But satire, irony, juxtaposition and other humorous techniques will make a point or advance a story far more effectively than the most well-intentioned prose. Don't teens get enough problematic, earnest and world-weary material in their daily lives and the nightly news?

Brian Doyle is a gifted Canadian writer who seamlessly blends humour and issues in his carefully crafted and captivating novels for young adults. His comic/serious books (*Uncle Ronald*, *Spud Sweetgrass*, *You Can Pick Me Up at Peggy's Cove*) pull no punches, but never stint on the lighter side either. Working in the same attractive genre are accomplished humorist Jerry Spinelli (*Maniac Magee*), Richard Peck (*Secrets of the Shopping Mall*) and Canadian Sylvia McNicoll (*Bringing Up Beauty*), they write novels that are both funny and relevant. Gordon Korman began writing his own hilarious and very popular novels—some in a series—because of a personal desperate search for books that were funny. His novels *The Zucchini Warriors*, *The Twinkie Squad* and many others draw laughs above all. If not deep literature, they are at least widely accessible and very readable.

Included in this grab-bag section are the (ever-popular) comic books whose attraction, I confess, has always eluded me. They have been around for just over a hundred years, and since their inception have doubtless formed a significant part of children's culture. One theory is that comics extend the picture-book format to children who have suddenly (and unhappily) graduated (only by virtue of their age) to books without illustrations. Another appeal is, apparently, their exaggerated language, "bop whap bang" kind of violence and cast of one-dimensional or cartoon characters. There is also, of course, a galaxy of superhero stars, swift justice and outrageous plot twists and developments. Some devoted followers find them a refreshing break from stories with "meaning." Thin in substance, exaggerated in heroism, overly simplistic in plot and dialogue, they continue to have followers and fans of all ages.

From Detective Comics to the great superheroes—Marvel Comics—to Classics summaries, comics are easy to read, foldable, hideable, apparently highly entertaining and generally inexpensive booklets. They are the definition of light or escapist irrelevant reading. Some ardent devotees read virtually nothing else. Some of the older ones—first editions—are collected and traded among aficionados (at dedicated conventions and specialty shops) in the same manner as rare books.

They have certainly affected television and film—cartoon comedy, superhero dramatic series, and science fiction and special-effects movies from *Batman* to *Star Wars* all have evolved and owe part of their identity to the lowly little comic book. Critics Tim Retzloff and Patrick Jones have suggested that comics are fairy tales for adolescents that "may help them cope with the changing world around them." Perhaps, but surely there are more satisfying sources of insight available in addition or as an alternative.

Included in this section are books of lists, humour and other light reading in which everyone indulges more or less often. Sometimes just the right book happened to find the right person at an appropriate (or vulnerable) time. This seems, in a significant way, to have set off an interesting variety of creative sparks.

Don Harron (writer, performer)

My father started me reading at an early age. It was the height of the Depression so I got all my books from our public library. I remember boys' adventure books by R.M. Ballantyne (*The Mysterious Island*, or was that by Big Julie Verne?) and G.A. Henty (*A Hornet of Course* or was it *A Cornet of Horse*?). I sold *Liberty* magazines to get a meagre allowance, and my money went mostly into English boys' weekly adventure magazines like *Triumph* and *Champion*. American comic books had not yet made their appearance in my life, although the Big Little Books, based on American comic strips like "Little Orphan Annie" and "Moon Mullins" were very popular gifts at Christmas.

But the book that brought me the change of life at age twelve was called *Low Company*. It wasn't pornography but a collection of political cartoons by David Low, a New Zealander who worked in England for Lord Beaverbrook's *Daily Express*. My father was an amateur cartoonist who had been published regularly in the *Varsity* in his college days, and he collected cartoon books. In fact, I began my professional career at the age of ten by doing chalk talks with coloured chalks on huge sheets of white paper at banquets. But I learned everything by rote from my father.

It was the David Low cartoons that set me ablaze with an ambition to do my own someday. I did become a temporary cartoonist a couple of years later for the *High News* but I was never able to develop my own style. To this day the people who manage to do this are the Canadians I most admire: Duncan Macpherson, Aislin, Brian Gable, Anthony Jenkins, Andy Donato, Roy Peterson, Lynn Johnston and a brilliant newcomer from Halifax, Bruce McKinnon. Alas for me, I am reduced to doing caricatures with my voice. However, it has given me a sixty-year career, and for that I will always be grateful to the inspiration provided by David Low.

Ted Staunton (writer)

Classics, of course, were generally nothing of the kind, either as literature or comics. Mostly they were chestnuts like *The Prisoner of Zenda* or *The Three Musketeers*, with an occasional *Silas Marner* and *The Song of Hiawatha* for tone. The quintessential *Classics* author was Jules Verne: *The Mysterious Island*, *Off on a Comet*, *20,000 Leagues under the Sea*. Oh, yeahhh.

Now I know that for many of us, *Classics* were the comics equivalent of broccoli. From the cheesy yellow and black logo to the kiss-of-death tag "DON'T MISS THE ADDED ENJOYMENT OF READING THE ORIGINAL. OBTAINABLE AT YOUR SCHOOL OR PUBLIC LIBRARY" they were tainted with the implication that responsible grownups would probably approve. Any kid or ex-kid knows that adult disapproval is the whole point of comics.

So why did I like them so much? Partly, it was their very unpopularity. *Classics* were my secret; if nobody else liked them, that just meant they were mine. The marketing savvy that made *Classics* the soggy green vegetable of comicdom guaranteed their invisibility at the corner variety store. The only place I was sure to find them was on a revolving stand in the A&P near our summer cottage. The rest of the year I'd reread them, one every lunch hour.

But the real key, of course, was that they launched me into the rich fantasy world we all need. If a *Kidnapped* or a *Covered Wagon* popped up Friday night at the grocery store, I was set. The comic would be read in no time, but then the real fun began.

It seems to me that the way kids really tell their own stories is by playing wonderfully repetitive variations of the stories that set their imaginations on fire. I rode the Time Machine, fought Under Two Flags, joined the White Company, Journeyed to the Centre of the Earth, found King Solomon's Mines, all on a beach near Port Hope, Ontario.

At eight years old I was ready for adventure, but not unabridged translations of Victor Hugo. For all their failings, *Classics* got the high points across with admirable economy, and as little kissing as possible. And, refreshingly, they never tampered with a tragic ending. What more could you ask? They set me free.

Currently, my son, an excellent reader at seven, has taken possession of the boxful of *Classics* I tracked down in the basement. Last week I found #42, *Swiss Family Robinson*, in the family room. He and a buddy were playing shipwrecked on the moon. Oh yeahhh.

Phoebe Gilman (writer, illustrator)

After much digging and delving into the dusty, dim past, I was ready to give up in despair and confess the bitter truth: there wasn't one book that gleamed as a beacon, one light that remained undimmed from childhood to the present, because, oh, the shame of it all, I was a comic-book addict in my pre-teen years.

I have only myself to blame for this. My mother loved reading and set us a proper example. When I close my eyes and bring her beloved image before me, she is not stirring chicken soup, she is reading. Each week we made our pilgrimage to the public library. I, too, took out books, usually fairy tales. I went through all the Andrew Lang coloured fairy-tale books...dipped into Andersen and Grimm too, but the pictures in comic books always lured me away from the more substantial fare to be found in the stacks of the public library. I spent some of my happiest hours meticulously copying comic-book pictures.

I remember getting quite upset by the illustrations in the fairy-tale books I read. They never matched the incredible imagery that the words conjured up. In fact, I distinctly remember covering them up with my hand while reading. Comic-book pictures did not suffer from this schism. The words were strictly unmemorable, with the exception perhaps of the "egads and gadzooks" sort of stuff. In fact, for years I read the "Jr." abbreviation in Captain Marvel Jr. as Captain Marvel Jerk, never noticing the incongruity of his name as I interpreted it.

All these thoughts have been burbling about in my brain for the last few weeks. Should I lie? Should I invent a favourite? That would be easy enough to do. I have many favourites today...*Charlotte's Web*, *The Lion, the Witch and the Wardrobe*, *The Secret Garden*...no, no, no, that wouldn't be honest. The other day, I was in the book store, browsing around for a baby-shower gift, still secretly puzzling over what to do, when, lo and behold, my eyes lit upon *Mother Goose*!

Eureka! That's it! How come I didn't think of it before? Of all the books I've ever read, none has had as profound an impact on me as *Mother Goose*. The rhythm and cadence of the language, the sheer delicious, delightful silliness of the message...the book I loved in childhood and have never stopped loving is *Mother Goose*.

John Robert Colombo (writer, Canadiana expert)

"If all the Chinese in the world were to march—four abreast—past a given point, they would never finish passing though they marched for ever and ever (based on U.S. Army marching regulations)."

If you can place that passage, you can identify my favourite book.

Before naming it and identifying its well-known author, let me share with you how I discovered that prized possession—or how that book discovered me.

I must have been about eleven years old at the time. It was a Sunday afternoon in the winter of 1947. My parents had taken me on a drive to visit my Aunt Marie and Uncle Stan who lived in a small house on the outskirts of my home town, Kitchener, Ontario.

All afternoon the adults gossiped about adult matters. I was bored and cast about for something to do or something to read. A copy of *Life* magazine lay on the coffee table, but my parents subscribed to it so I had already leafed through that issue. But beside it lay a Pocket Book, an early paperback, complete with the insignia of the kangaroo on the cover. The cover price was given: 25 cents.

I picked it up, and in a sense I never put it down again.

The illustration on its bright yellow cover, trimmed in orange, captivated me. It depicted "The Marching Chinese." I stared at the spectacle in wonder...a never-ending column of human figures trudging, four abreast, past a given point. The human column, appearing from beyond the distant curvature of the Earth, advanced into the foreground. It seemed the column would never end—ever.

"The Marching Chinese" is the most imaginative of the ingenious cartoon features written and drawn by Robert L. Ripley, the New York newspaperman, broadcaster, and world traveller. The book was titled *Ripley's Believe It or Not!* Ripley's first collection of columns, it was originally published in 1929. The Pocket Book edition that I held in my hand was the first paperback reprint, released in 1946. It took a year to reach me.

My aunt realized that I would be unhappy to be parted from the precious volume. "Keep it," she said. "I've read it." I took it home protectively, and over the next few days I read it from cover to cover. Over the next weeks and months I reread all of it. I have dipped into it repeatedly ever since.

Today's newspaper reader may be familiar with the Ripley cartoon feature and with the Ripley "odditoriums" at Niagara Falls and elsewhere. But today's reader will never sufficiently appreciate the imaginative shock administered by Ripley's early BIONS—his "Believe It or Nots!" They created newspaper headlines around the world.

It was Ripley's mix of showmanship and scholarship that astonished me when I was young. In later years I came to appreciate that the man and the artist was more showman than scholar. A case in point is the business about "The Marching Chinese."

It was Ripley's genius to realize that vital statistics could be put to dramatic use. As he explained, one evening he subtracted China's mortality rate from its birth rate, divided the result by four (everyone is marching in platoon-squad formation four abreast, remember), estimated how many people there are in a mile, divided by fifteen—the number of miles walked in a day—and, surprise!—it takes over twenty-two years for a living Chinese to pass a given point. That period of time is considered a generation in China. Therefore the column of Marching Chinese will never end...

I have no idea whether or not the notion is mathematically or demographically sound, but I do know it packs imaginative appeal. Once heard, it is not readily forgotten.

I found all this great entertainment when I was ten years old. That impressionable youngster lives inside me to this day, for I continue to find Ripleyisms exciting and stimulating—and so do millions of other people around the world.

Indeed, I have long cherished the desire to compile a collection of *Ripley's Canadian Believe It or Nots!*

Should I ever be permitted to do so, it would realize my childhood fantasy of being Robert L. Ripley. Hum, now let's see: "If all the Eskimos in the world were to march—four abreast—past the North Pole..."

Greg Hollingshead (writer)

I can't recall the title of the book I remember most vividly from my early teens. It was something like *Great Science Fiction by Scientists*. It was just one, I think, of several such collections edited by a man named Groff Conklin. I will never forget the name Groff Conklin, and I will never forget where *Great Science Fiction by Scientists* (or whatever it was called) stood on the shelves of the school library: directly to the left of the door as you walked in. I will also never forget the smell of that book: musty pasteboard and old glue and human-skin dust and mouldering paper, the smell of used-book stores. It was a great fat anthology-sized volume with one of those anonymous solid-colour (green, I think) rebound covers with reinforced tape (brown, I think) down the spine. The original cover must have fallen off from years of use. It was a massive book to hold in the hand but unwholesomely light for its size, printed as it was on spongy paper not a lot better than newsprint.

I imagine *Great Science Fiction by Scientists* was a gathering of recent magazine science fiction, intended for a general audience. The stories were fantastic and clearly written. Most of them were moral fables. Probably they were by science fiction writers famous at the time, though I recognized none of the names then and have remembered none since. To me the stories seemed simply vivid and fascinating, and that made them as good as great. They were stories that taught me a writer can do anything.

A few have stayed with me when everything else except Groff Conklin, the smell and heft of the book he edited, its possible colour and its location on the shelf have disappeared. Here is my favourite...

What seems to be a meteorite lands in a man's backyard, burying itself deep in the ground. He digs down and discovers a turtle of enormous density. Next he's in the kitchen, feeling a little smitten, fetching something for the creature to eat. When he takes a can from the shelf he accidentally crushes it in his hand. Then he falls through the floor.

Does fiction get any better than this? Not when you're thirteen. When you're thirteen it's your first brush with The Force. Thank you, Groff.

Robert Priest (writer, songwriter)

I had been a good boy for fourteen years straight. When people met me they would comment on my manners, my punctuality, my intelligence. I was top of the class always. Teacher's pet. And small, very small. The Beatles, and most particularly John Lennon who gave their cheek its necessary "fang," came along just in time. I received *The Penguin John Lennon* (which collects both of Lennon's early books—*In His Own Write* and *A Spaniard in the Works*) for Christmas when I was fifteen.

These grotesque and cruel parables with their equally bizarre drawings create an atmosphere of the world as bedlam—full of the deformed, the misunderstood, the diseased and disconnected. This was the first book in my life to challenge a way of reading—it had to be read slowly to be figured out. You wanted to catch every rude double meaning and all the hidden jokes. Lennon was constantly smuggling deranged other syllables inside well-known words. There are hanging adjectives, nouns that are verbs, and what a book of misspellings! It is never "people" but "peotle peebles peofle..." Bringing out the edge in language, bringing out the etymology. "Make an honest womb of her."

My friend Michael Manuel and I, who were both deep fans, had a whole patois based on it. We were always saying "You might well arsk" and "Elephants Gerald my dear whopper!" Let us put up some "dessicrations" and I still say "Merry Kruschove" on appropriate occasions. In fact my own writing was never the same after Lennon. That whole good-boy, polite and acquiescent part of myself was out the window, good only to be heaped with abuse and sent on its way. Yes Johnnie helped me be "bad."

If he hadn't written *I Am the Walrus*, and about twenty-five other immortal songs, I don't know if these books would still mean as much to me, but coming back to them now I'm still laughing out loud. I'm still getting that sense of discovering bits for the first time. And again I'm stunned by the constant inventiveness, charmed by the excoriating wit. Unable to put the book down, I run to show my Lennonesque six-year- old the funny pictures and we laugh and marvel together.

Rick Salutin (writer)

When I was twelve or thirteen, I stayed home from school sick and noticed a book called *Twice Over Lightly*, which I guess someone had given my dad when he was in hospital with appendicitis. It was a collection of newspaper columns by Vancouver humorist Eric Nicol. I didn't really get the title, since I'd never heard the phrase, once over lightly. But I opened it, read the dedication—"This book was written for the money"—and cracked up. I guess it was the first time I realized you could be funny on a page.

I still recall some of the pieces, like one on Columbus discovering (sic) America. As Nicol had it, the lookout yelled "Indians," so Columbus ordered his ships to form a circle with the women and children in the middle, while the women and children were splashing around and drowning...Before long I was writing wittily scathing (I thought) school assignments on *Jane Eyre* (the novel) and *The Ten Commandments* (the movie).

Many years later, when I began writing for the money myself, one of my first regular jobs was doing satirical sketches for a CBC radio program called "*Inside from the Outside.*" One of my co-writers was Eric Nicol.

·8· Transition to Adult Literature

"Thou hast nor youth nor age"
—William Shakespeare

There is no clear moment of transition from children's books to adult literature. However, the relatively new genre called "young adult" books has done a great deal to fill the gap. These novels and non-fiction books are written especially to reflect the interests (and attributes) of the teenage reader. They have succeeded beyond all expectation. They are available in virtually all genres—fantasy, history, adventure, sports, biography, mystery—but most pervasive perhaps is the problem or issue novel. A great many books for this age group reflect school life and the language, situations and preoccupations familiar to high-school students.

But there seems to come a time when, if a book looks or feels like a children's book, even of the "young adult" designation, the oh-so-cool fifteen- or sixteen-year-old will not even consider it. Despite themes deliberately chosen for them and, usually, protagonists their own age or a little older, significant numbers feel they have matured beyond a literature intended especially for them. They demand to read grownup books. But which ones?

When, how and with which books a young person takes the leap into the huge body of adult literature is largely affected by one major influence, their peers. Will their first forays inevitably be borrowed potboilers, popular best-sellers, schlock about movie stars, sports celebrities and music-industry icons? Or will they manage also to find extraordinary and exciting literary adventure—moving, timeless and important books? Does that potential for the knockout impact of a special book have to end with childhood?

Sometimes a book hits like a bombshell—the lights flash and a bond is sealed. Sometimes the book is a gift, other times it's been lurking on a shelf somewhere. But most people—including growing teens—frequently choose their reading material because of recommendations.

Young people share popular novels and all manner of other reading material with their friends at school. To a somewhat lesser extent, they are also drawn to suggestions from parents and teachers (especially teacher-librarians). Indeed word of mouth is the single most powerful incentive to read a given book. Kids see books (I hope) lying around the house. They occasionally read or hear reviews. Frequently they are drawn to a book because it has been transformed into a movie or television adaptation. The recent popularity, for example, of film and made-for-TV versions of *Persuasion*, *Pride and Prejudice* and her other four novels has rekindled enormous interest in the original books by Jane Austen. Theatrical productions, for example of *Les Misérables*, *Phantom of the Opera* and *Jane Eyre*, have done the same for original works by Victor Hugo, Gaston Leroux and Charlotte Brontë respectively. Sales of Michael Ondaatje's *The English Patient* soared after the success of the film. Adaptations are in the works for Thomas Hardy's novels, Montgomery's Emily trilogy (a TV series), Sir Walter Scott's *Ivanhoe* and other classics. They too are expected to attract a huge new audience to the original works.

No one would seriously suggest substituting the film *Clueless* on a school curriculum for Austen's *Emma* (although the movie is clearly based on the novel), but there is nothing wrong with viewing the former and using it to spark discussion or enhance a study of the latter. By drawing analogies, some kids may better appreciate a novel they might otherwise not have read (or fully grasped) at all.

One of my daughter's English teachers cleverly incorporated the musical *West Side Story* and a recent popular film adaptation of Shakespeare's play to explore the themes of *Romeo and Juliet*. Within limits, these are good ideas. Unfortunately, too many books get sentimentalized, watered down or hopelessly altered for TV or cinema. They are not a substitute; each is a unique and very different medium.

Many books, both now and in the past, were not specifically written for adults or children but for anyone from a wide, general audience who was interested in their plot, subject, characters or style. Some authors (Stevenson, Twain, Verne) intended much of their work for adults. Nevertheless, a younger—and eager—audience claimed it for their own. If a book continues to appeal to all ages, whole families and, in translation, to other nationalities, it has the makings of a classic. There are also many fascinating and significant books—frequently "best-sellers"—that are understandable hits for some time, and then fade in popularity.

Growing teens sometimes like to read material that concerned adults consider inappropriate (too difficult, too harsh, too graphic). There are also both groups and individuals who would curb the reading material of young people for their own ends. There is nothing like the whiff of controversy to create interest, garner publicity and enhance sales. There is no question that some books reflect negative stereotypes or attitudes understandably questioned or discounted today. It is my feeling that it is better to encounter the tough issues vicariously, through literature, than to experience real danger, violence or pain. I think it best to censor as little as possible, but to use books as springboards to discuss the problematic issues that may arise within and about them. I am reminded of the comment by popular thriller writer Stephen King: "If you encourage young people to read my books, some of them will, but if you tell them *not* to read them, they will flock to them in droves."

It may, sometimes, be possible to direct adolescents to other books with similar themes. Two books may be about the same "thing" but treat a subject with vast discrepancies of depth or sensitivity. Not long ago, one of my daughters, age fourteen, read a flimsy book describing the life (including drugs, depression and the ultimate tragic suicide) of pop star Kurt Cobain. After she finished it, I recommended Charles Dickens's *A Tale of Two Cities*, because it is a book about, among other things, a suicide/sacrifice of an entirely different kind.

Many adults (I know I'm one) take great comfort in rereading the books we loved best when we were younger. By recommending our personal favourites to children and students, we are telling them important details about ourselves and our upbringing. We are offering glimpses of the experience, world views and ethical framework that formed us and the world in which we grew up. Older people worry, understandably, about imparting standards and teaching virtues such as kindness and integrity to each younger generation. One avenue, through memorable books, goes some distance towards establishing a sense of history and place as well as expressing traditional, even noble ethics and ideals.

Part of the attraction of modern young adult fiction for me is that the stories are rarely resolved without hope. However well hidden, there is usually (even in the most disturbing "issue" books for young people) a sense of optimism. There is often a sign or signal pointing the way out of trouble. In the better books, there is encouraging growth, occasionally clear and insightful moments of recognition that will help the protagonist(s)—and by extension the reader—cope with the world.

The best stories for readers of all ages are not those that blatantly deal with faddish problems or transitory causes, but those that stir the heart and awaken deeper sensibilities. To the extent that this is their goal and their achievement, the best young adult or "transitional" books are wonderful by any measure, essentially no different from the best and most memorable "adult" literature. It is not really so big a step from one to the other. I for one will continue to seek out good books at all levels.

Rollo May has written in his *Cry for Myth* that myth is the child's endeavour to make sense of experience. Isn't all great literature attempting to do precisely that?

Peter Gzowski (broadcaster)

If you really want to hear about it, I was seventeen when *The Catcher in the Rye* was published, a year or so older than Holden Caulfield, and I'd just finished up at a school in Ontario that was uncannily reminiscent of Pencey, in Agerstown, Pennsylvania, which was where Holden was going, except he ran away, as we know, and I never did, although, to tell you the truth, I thought about it a few times.

Right from the first words, which are, of course, "If you really want to hear about it" ("the first thing you'll probably want to know is where I was born, and what my lousy childhood was like..."), the book hit me like a cricket bat. It changed the way I thought about school, about honesty, about families—it made me ache to have someone in my life like Holden's sister Phoebe—and about books and the people who wrote them.

I was scarcely new to reading. I grew up with books. My mother, who'd died just a couple of years before I discovered *The Catcher in the Rye*—it occurs to me now that *she* was my Phoebe—had been a children's librarian, and I knew *Doctor Dolittle* and *Winnie-the-Pooh* before I could throw a ball and how to read for myself before I went to kindergarten. Except when the lousy parts of my own childhood got in the way, I did reasonably well at school, too, certainly in English—I had one teacher in grade 11 who was quite a lot like Holden's Mr. Antolini, who'd taught him at Elkton Hills before he went to

Pencey—and books of all sorts, from the classics they pounded into our heads in the classroom to the Dorothy Parker and F. Scott Fitzgerald my mother loved, to the *Amboy Dukes* and Frank Yerby novels I hid even from her, were important to me. But *The Catcher in the Rye* was more than important. It was *me*. There was someone on the printed page who thought exactly as I did, who thought the same things were funny and the same things crazy, and wasn't afraid to say aloud what I could only imagine. It touched me in a way nothing else I'd read ever had.

Since then—it was 1951, to save you the trouble of looking it up—there have been a thousand other books that have hit me hard, from Jane Austen (no, I never read her when I was young) to Mordecai Richler, from *Gulliver's Travels* to *Who Has Seen the Wind*. But nothing, not even J.D. Salinger's thin list of later stories and novellas, has ever quite matched the experience of first reading *The Catcher in the Rye*. I still return to it every few years. I'm still Holden Caulfield, nearly half a century later, and I still wonder what the original Holden would be like if, like me, he'd ever read the lovely, funny, poignant, painful, sad and unforgettable chapters of his early life.

Tim Wynne-Jones (writer)

Graham Greene once said that only in childhood is one truly affected by books. Something like that. Ironically, it was Greene's own novels which most deeply moved me and infected me with the desire to write. I read them all, but not until I was in my twenties. Mind you, Greene never did specify when, exactly, childhood ends.

As a much younger child I read a lot but mostly junk. I poured over the Rupert Bear books sent from back home by my grandparents until long after I had outgrown picture books, let alone plaid pants! I laughed out loud at the episodic antics of Walter R. Brooks's *Freddy the Pig*. I climbed mountains and plumbed caves with Enid Blyton's various quartets and quintets of adventurous "blyters." I like the food in the Blyton books: picnics with canned hams and ginger beer. To this day I am suspicious of any book in which there is no mention of victuals. I did read some better things, too. Jules Verne, I remember, fondly; and, in a similar vein, Arthur Conan Doyle's *The Lost World*. There must have been others, but they were just books, I guess, not events.

Pooh was an event. We were just recovering from a time of being very poor. My father had been injured on the job and received no compensation. We had been living in a basement, all eight of us, with sheets for wall dividers. Then Dad was on his feet again, and we moved into a tiny bungalow. And one day the Milne books arrived. It wasn't Christmas or anyone's birthday. It was just a celebration.

Winnie-the-Pooh, *The House at Pooh Corner*, *When We Were Very Young* and *Now We Are Six*. The text is still wonderful, still fresh. And Shepard's drawings are a more poignant marker of childhood than most of the photos my family has of those less than halcyon days. Eeyore's house is my favourite. I suppose that after living in a house of sheets, myself, it seemed very homey indeed, and more substantial.

But if I were forced to point to a book that woke me up, that changed me, it would have to be Franklin W. Dixon's *The Missing Chum*. It was, without a doubt, the single most important literary moment in my young life.

We used to spend two weeks of every summer at a beach resort in Ocean Park, Maine. There was a lending library in Ocean Park and I remember running there as soon as we had unpacked, with the intention of finding a Hardy Boys book for the beach. I was sixteen that last summer in Ocean Park. There weren't many books left in the series that I had not already devoured. Thankfully, the little library was well stocked. There were enough to last me the whole holiday.

I grabbed *The Missing Chum*, plunked down my nickel, and beetled down to the beach, little realizing and totally unprepared for the fact that it was to be the last Hardy Boys book I would ever open. I threw myself on my towel, tingling under the sun with that anticipation a new book in a series is apt to bring upon the avid reader, young or old. I flung open the cover, leapt in, ready to be whisked away to mystery in one of the veritable squadron of vehicles the boy adventurers owned.

I read the first paragraph. I read it again. Something was wrong. Maybe it was the sun. I pushed on, turned the page. Went back. It was no good. I began to realize, with a sadness bordering on melancholy, that I had been deserted. Stranded on the sunny beach. The boys had left me behind. There they were off on another stunning romp and there was I in the first full blush of unqualified detachment. It was happening to me. I'd heard people talk about it, but I'd never believed it could be true. I knew that I was not going to read *The Missing Chum*. I knew, what's more, that I was not ever going to read another Hardy Boys book. I would never learn what happened to Chet. And, it seemed, I didn't really care. Suddenly I wouldn't have cared if Frank shot his famous father, or Joe came out of the closet. I closed the book. It was over between me and the Hardys.

I dragged myself back to the library. My nickel was still good. I perused the shelves aimlessly, landing, somehow, at *Travels with Charley,* a story about which I knew nothing. There was a dog in it; that seemed hopeful.

Well, as it turned out, I spent that whole summer reading John Steinbeck. Who can say how these things happen. But if it hadn't been for the utter banality of *The Missing Chum*, the hopelessly plodding text, the "Hey! What's going on here" excuse for dialogue I might to this day have been a reader for whom euphony was only a curious misspelling of a derogatory remark. Chet—wherever you are—thanks for getting lost.

Jack Rabinovitch (businessman, founder of The Giller Prize)

In our house my brother and I, when we were kids, anxiously anticipated Friday night—Sabbath eve; but not for any religious purpose, mind you. Friday night was comic-book night.

My father was a "newsy." He operated a kiosk, a small enclosed green-and-white hut measuring three feet by six feet on the lower part of "The Main" in Montreal, at the corner of Ontario. He sold newspapers, magazines, pocket books and most important of all, comic books.

Most new comics arrived on Friday, so on Friday night we read every comic book available—action comics highlighting Superman, Batman and Robin, Captain Marvel (Shazam), Sheena the Jungle Woman, Namur the Submarine Man and many others. Saturday morning they went back to the kiosk to be sold.

We quickly learned to treat every book respectfully. Each book we read had to be sold as new. Any youthful exuberance that resulted in mutilation would lead to a discontinuation of the comic-book flow.

At about eight years of age, like my brother before me, I started to work with my dad in the kiosk. Slowly I graduated from comic books to Westerns—Zane Grey, Max Brand, Jack Slade, Louis L'Amour were devoured. Then came mysteries; Erle Stanley Gardner and Rex Stout were the hot items.

When I was about twelve or thirteen my brother Sam, three years older, won a membership to the Book of the Month Club. He stumped the panel of a radio program. "Information Please." I still remember the question: "What language is on the Swiss stamp?" The answer the panel could not get was Latin.

Because of this windfall we started to receive hardcover books. One of the first to arrive was *A Tree Grows in Brooklyn* by Betty Smith.

My brother and I shared a room and one day I found the book on my bed. "What could a woman author write about that would appeal to me?" I thought disdainfully, a soon-to-be teenager brought up on the best escapist literature available. My brother noticed my disdain.

"Try it, shmucko," he said chuckling and waited as I picked up the book. "Up yours," I replied, waggling my two fingers in the traditional sign. I turned my back, opened the book and prepared myself for a short and boring ordeal.

An hour later I was completely engrossed.

Previously everything I had read served an instinctive purpose: take me away from where I live, concentrate on action, not feelings. Western heroes are strong, silent and quick on the draw. Perry Mason and Ellery Queen work in posh surroundings with elegant assistants.

Contrariwise, *A Tree Grows in Brooklyn* tells the story of an Irish family, the Nolans, growing up in a poor section of Brooklyn. Today it would probably be called "culturally enriched." Then it was "slum international." The book relates the story of a needy family and the inner feelings of one child. That anyone would and could write honestly, insightfully and with wry humour about my kind of neighbourhood and about feelings that I thought were unique and private was both a disturbing and exciting experience. How could truth disguised as fiction be so insightful and captivating? How could personal feelings be so universal?

A Tree Grows in Brooklyn highlighted my graduation. Maybe in another time or place another book would have done the same. But as I write this essay fifty years later I still remember that book and how it changed me.

Bernice Thurman Hunter (writer)

When I was a kid, back in the hungry thirties, you needed to be twelve years old to have a library card in your own name. And my dad was out of work so there was no money for books. So what was a ten-year-old who loved to read to do?

Well, the first day of school had one redeeming feature…you got your brand-new Reader! I'd sneak it home (you weren't allowed to) and read it cover to cover, over and over again.

It was my big sister who first noticed how much I loved to read.

I was surprised that she noticed, because she usually paid no attention to me at all. Except for giving me heck for being messy.

One day she came home from the library...she was fifteen and had her own card...and handed me a black, hardcover book. There were no colourful paperbacks in those days.

"Read this," she said, her voice dead serious. "But don't you dare eat an orange [where would I get an orange when it wasn't even Christmas?] or turn down the corner of a page. If a library book gets damaged the owner of the card [she poked herself in the chest] has to pay for it. So if I see one single smudge or one dog-eared corner you'll be sorry!"

"I'll be careful," I promised breathlessly.

The book was *A Girl of the Limberlost* by Gene Stratton Porter. I liked it a lot and I took such good care of it that my sister promptly got me another book. And another and another. And she didn't discriminate between boys' and girls' books either. She said variety was the spice of life. So by the time I reached the magic age of twelve, and was awarded my very own library card, I had already galloped with cowboys over the purple sage and flown through the trees with Tarzan, thanks to Zane Grey and Edgar Rice Burroughs.

It was our librarian, Mrs. Orr, who introduced me to L.M. Montgomery. I devoured her books as fast as she wrote them and *Anne of Green Gables* soon became my all-time favourite...until I discovered *A Tree Grows in Brooklyn* by Betty Smith.

The very name captivated me. I had no idea where Brooklyn was. I didn't find out until fifty years later, but as I gobbled up the chapters I was there! And I soon realized that, for me, Anne Shirley couldn't hold a candle to Francie Nolan. We were more than kindred spirits, Francie and me, we were soul mates.

Francie was a poor city kid, just like me. And she wanted to be a writer when she grew up, just like me. Francie lived in a cold-water flat three floors up in a New York City tenement. I lived in a cold-water house, fitfully heated by two coal-stoves, in the city of Toronto. There were no leafy "Lovers' Lanes" or fragrant apple orchards in our neighbourhoods. This was no fairy tale. This was life!

Francie's father was a singing waiter. (Oh, how romantic! I thought.) Her mother was a scrubwoman who was often tired and cranky, but her "Papa," handsome Johnny Nolan, the singing waiter, would come whistling tipsily up the stairs with leftover treats from someone else's party. And Francie's heart would sing as she ran to meet him.

On sweltering hot New York summer days we would sit cross-legged on the fire-escape, Francie and me, scribbling in our copybooks in the shade of the ailanthus tree. Brooklyn people called it the "Tree of Heaven" because it burst right out of the sidewalk and headed straight for the sky.

I have just reread *A Tree Grows in Brooklyn* and Francie and I had a wonderful reunion.

Recently an eleven-year-old girl, who had just finished reading my Booky trilogy which is based on my childhood during the Great Depression, wrote me a letter. It ended with this p.s.: "I wish I was a kid when you were a kid so we could have been best friends."

That's exactly how I felt about Francie Nolan.

p.s. Belated thanks to my big sister for the gift of a lifetime, the wonderful world of books.

Sam Sniderman (businessman, owner of Sam The Record Man)

In my early years I did not do much reading. I did not have the time. I was much too busy with working. But I could not get enough of the writings of Sholom Aleichem. And it was your request that made me think—why?

I was born in Toronto—and my first week was in my bubbe's house on Augusta Avenue. Then I lived with my older brother and parents in the back of my father's tailor store on College Street. That was in 1920. Eighteen years later saw this location as the birthplace of the record department that grew into Sam The Record Man.

My mother was born in Toronto in a religious family. Her father was a baker and in my mind I picture a closed wagon pulled by a single horse.

My father was from the group of immigrants whose parents escaped the pogroms of the Ukraine and eventually settled in Canada. I do not remember those grandparents that well; they would have been typical shtetl folk.

So my roots were Jewish and I was born, went to school and lived in an ethnic neighbourhood—half Jewish—half Italian. But, for some reason, though you would have thought it would be, my home life was not Jewish. When the holidays were celebrated, they were at the uncles' houses—Passover, Chanukah, Rosh Hashanah, etc. I did not study the language, although I remember my grandfather tried to teach me. I did not go to Kheyder and I did not have a bar mitzvah. My friends were Jewish, but I felt left out. And as I looked in their windows, I was envious.

I realize now that Sholom Aleichem's vivid writings of Jews and Jewish life were the link with the life I was missing. In the reading I could become part of the happening. I am the Fiddler on the Roof.

Bruce Kirby (designer of Laser sailboats)

The Ottawa high school was wise in choosing the autobiographical novel *Youth* as an introduction to Joseph Conrad. Not only was the story short, but on the surface it was a simple adventure—man against the sea and man against fire. It was the romance of adventure, a story any high-school boy could delight in; but like most of Conrad's work it was also a story with insight and depth—a tale of sunlight and shadow.

As one who had adored the recreational and competitive aspects of sailing and had devoured sea stories from an early age, *Youth* was a powerful incentive to pursue a life on the waters of the world and to write about it as well as I could. Like everyone else in the twentieth century who raised a pen or sat down to a typewriter I knew that I could never aspire to Conrad's heights, but even as a teenager I had become aware that if you set your mind on very high goals you would achieve far more than if you were satisfied with what you knew was possible. This course can lead to frustration, but can also unlock doors and reveal vistas that would otherwise remain hidden forever.

Conrad himself aimed high and surely achieved far more than he had dared to dream. Born of Polish parents in the Ukraine as Teodor Josef Konrad Korzeniowski, he did not go to sea or speak English until he was twenty-one. He went on to become a distinguished officer aboard British sailing ships, and along the way he developed a mastery of English that made him one of the giants of literature. He was not only a hero of my youth, but a lifelong inspiration who remains today, as I approach my seventies, the mysterious, unattainable but fascinating apogee.

It was in that ground-floor classroom at Lisgar Collegiate—the high school attended by Lorne Greene, Rich Little and Peter Jennings—that English teacher Walter Mann introduced me to the sailor/novelist who opened the door to his world of beautiful ships and exquisite words and allowed me to step inside.

For *Youth* is a story that can be taken as a fascinating narrative of the sea, or as a microcosm of life with its hopes and optimism, its fears and apprehensions. Has any writer in any language ever expressed life's total message as well as Conrad did in the final sentence of *Youth*? "... our faces marked by toil, by deceptions, by success, by love; our weary eyes looking still, looking always, looking anxiously for something out of life, that while it is expected is already gone—has passed unseen, in a sigh, in a flash—together with the youth, with the strength, with the romance of illusions."

Marian Fowler (writer)

I was six years old when I first experienced the intense joys of reading, and I've had my nose in a book ever since. By the time I was ten, I was devouring a steady diet of adult fiction, two or three books a week borrowed from the Richmond Hill Library which, in the 1940s, was modest indeed. The entire collection was housed on the second floor of an old brick building, in one long, narrow room which smelled of dust and dry paper and floor wax.

Round about the age of twelve, in the course of browsing along the library shelves in search of something I hadn't already read, I picked off the shelf a book entitled *Pride and Prejudice* by Jane Austen. I opened it and read this opening sentence, which I still think is the most perfect beginning of any novel: "It is a truth universally acknowledged, that a single man in possession of a good fortune must be in want of a wife." I read the book at one sitting, in a state of ecstasy. It wasn't just the characters and plot of *Pride and Prejudice* which made me smile and chortle, it was Jane's style: the delicious irony, the incredible elegance and economy of every sentence. How could any writer achieve such perfect felicity of phrase? I was in awe, and read her other five novels which, along with *Pride and Prejudice*, I have been rereading on a regular basis ever since. I consider Jane Austen the greatest English novelist of all time, and I divide the world into those who adore her and those who don't. "Do you like Jane Austen?" I ask every potential friend, and hold my breath for the answer. If they screw up their faces as if biting into a lemon, and spit out the word "NO!", I sigh deeply, knowing we can never become true soul mates.

Little snippets of Austen prose are permanently lodged in my head, like bright bits of ribbon peeping from a lady's sewing basket. They never fail to cheer me on dark days. After I'd married and had two children, I went back to the University of Toronto and earned a doctorate in English Literature with a thesis on—who else?—Jane Austen. And when I began to write myself, at the age of forty-nine, books of biography, not fiction, it was Jane Austen's marvellous prose rhythms which danced in my head. To date, no critic of my work has ever detected this major influence, but I keep hoping...

Marianne Brandis (writer)

I have read Jane Austen's *Pride and Prejudice* perhaps two dozen times. The first time was when I was about twelve. It is not usually considered a book for young people, but in Terrace, in northern British Columbia, in 1950, nobody paid much attention to things like that. Books were few, and bookish people of all ages read what there was.

In Terrace, which was then just twenty-five years old, life was basic and barely civilized. *Pride and Prejudice* depicted a world that was different in some ways—subtler, with more human variety—and similar in others—characterized by small-town life, family, neighbours and mud. At the time I paid no attention to the gap of nearly 150 years that separated me from Elizabeth Bennet: the world inside a book was expected to be different from (and similar to) the real world. To any young reader, book time is now and always, book places are here and elsewhere and nowhere.

Since then I have read *Pride and Prejudice* again and again, sometimes as frequently as once a year. It is like an often-heard piece of music, growing more loved with familiarity. I read it for comfort, for forgetfulness, for remembering, for renewing an old friendship and reconnecting with my past self. I read it for re-examining and deepening a valuable experience.

Each time, as well as being familiar, it is different and new in minute or major ways, because I am bringing new things to it. In the beginning I was younger than Elizabeth Bennet; later I was older. I read it sometimes in happiness, sometimes in bitterness and despair. I read it at times when confusion in my own life made me long for the orderliness of Jane Austen's world, and at times when I was interestingly and constructively irritated by that world's limitations. I read it when I was Elizabeth Bennet and when I stood outside her.

I read it when I was a teacher of literature; I read it now that I am a historian and writer, now that I am myself a constructor of worlds that are fictional and true. As much as family or an old friendship, as much as a shining or scarring memory, *Pride and Prejudice* is a vein running through my life.

Ralph Klein (Premier of Alberta)

Actually, one of the books that has most affected my outlook is one I read as an adult—*Trinity*, by Leon Uris. In fact, Mr. Uris is one of my favourite authors.

The reason Uris's novels are so special to me is that they deal with humanity's struggle for political and religious freedom. Reading them made me realize how fortunate Albertans and Canadians are to live in a country where we have the freedom to worship as we see fit and to voice our political opinions without fear of persecution. Uris's compelling tale of the Irish people's fight for independence renewed my own desire to be in politics, to do what I could to ensure our political system remains essentially honest, open and decent. Living in such a wonderful country, we can forget that our cherished Western freedoms were won by our ancestors at a steep and personal price. Mr. Uris reminds us of that in a powerful, unforgettable manner.

Yasmeen Ghauri (supermodel)

It's been a while since I read this book, but one of my favourite books of all time is *The Fountainhead* by Ayn Rand. I seem to remember the lead character, Howard Roark, as being this extraordinary individual dedicated to his own higher ideal. He dared to dream and to pursue this ideal even when it went against the tide of conformity. We are often misunderstood in the pursuit of our goals, and here we see a man who stays true to himself and to his ideal at the risk of being seen as selfish, egotistical and everything else in between. This book just served to reinforce for me who and what I am and can be, without the perception of others. Which is one of life's toughest obstacles.

Dinah Christie (singer, performer)

When I was eleven or so and had been reading all the Nancy Drew—like appropriate perfect-pretty-girl stuff all the way along my childhood—my grade-school librarian gave me *Precious Bane* to read.

Mary Webb's sad but romantic love story was about a young woman who, because she had been born with a cleft palate, was considered a freak. Oh! Shock and Surprise! A story about someone with an "imperfection." They'll try to burn her for sure. How will it end and do I have the courage to continue reading.

An exquisite book with a most perfect ending. It changed my reality on what subjects *could* be written about and opened another big door for me as a reader.

I'm looking for it all the time. I must read it again and compare my reactions.

Julie Johnston (writer)

At some point in my early teens, home from school with a mild case of the flu, I found that I had nothing to read. I'd read all the fiction in the magazines we took, read all the L.M. Montgomery books we had and all the Louisa May Alcotts. I'd read everything else we had around the house—*The Yearling*, the *Reader's Digest's* annoyingly condensed books, *Chicken Every Sunday*, *Bells on Their Toes*, *Cheaper by the Dozen* and *Daddy Longlegs*. I was really quite bookless. What I wanted was something gripping to see me through a few days of aches and chills.

After everyone had left the house that day I went downstairs and prowled around my father's study looking for something meaty to read. His book shelves, for the most part, were packed with fat brown law books, and books relating to history, war, heraldry and other such alluring topics. On one shelf, however, stood a set of identically bound books covered in black cloth over a flexible cover called *The Harvard Classics*. I knew they were there. My father had tried to promote them from time to time, but I had avoided them like a tonic, afraid they might be good for me. But I was out of books, after all.

None of the books in the set had illustrations, no dust-jacket picture to lure one in, nothing but page after page of relentlessly dense print. The first one I opened began, "It was the best of times, it was the worst of times... " I closed that one up and tried another, but it was full of hard-to-pronounce Russian names like Karenina. The next one was called *The Mill on the Floss* by some guy named George Eliot. I skipped the biographical notes and ploughed through a page or two of heavy-duty description until I came to a conversation between Mr. and Mrs. Tulliver about their son, Tom. It struck me that I wasn't just reading it, I was hearing it. Their speech rang so true that I could almost see the characters. When Maggie, the family misfit, entered the scene, I was well and truly hooked. I took the book back to bed and didn't get out for three days.

George Eliot, I discovered when I finally got to the notes, was actually a woman—surprise number one. Formidable as the book appeared closed, inside it was vital and passionate. Beyond the verbiage existed characters so real that they seemed to hang around with me, even after the book was finished—surprise number two. And, surprise number three—the other books in the set turned out to be equally absorbing, in their own way, as *The Mill on the Floss*, especially *A Tale of Two Cities* and *Anna Karenina*.

That was a number of years ago. Like many, I guess, I'm suffering from grey-matter overload (some call it aging, but I don't) and, as a result, have forgotten much of what I've read in my youth. This doesn't alarm me. It simply means I can now start all over again, and have. I'm up to page 157 in *The Mill on the Floss.*

Kristine Bogyo (cellist)

I grew up in a house full of good books, but up to the age of fifteen I mostly read fairy tales, nurse stories and comics. On my fifteenth birthday my favourite aunt presented me with a copy of *Anna Karenina*, saying, "I envy you that you will be reading this for the first time!" It was with great misgivings that I attempted to make sense of endless and complicated Russian names, but suddenly one day, as if by enchantment, I was caught under its spell.

Tolstoy's people live and breathe, they are simple and true and quickly became my internal friends. In fact I felt that this book and all its characters are really about me. I recognized familiar life situations, thinking, "yes, that's how it really feels, I had that same experience."

Levin, my favourite character, was always searching for something higher, more noble, more spiritual—he was searching for God. I was searching for God. Anna was searching for love and she found it, even though she was far from perfect. In fact she was committing adultery and even abandoned her child. It struck me that you don't have to be totally good to be loved. If you expose your faults, show your weaknesses and your true self without veneer, you will ultimately know a deeper love.

Anna Karenina was the door that opened my soul to great reading, and I've never turned back. Tolstoy has made me a better human being.

Anton Kuerti (pianist)

One of my first truly independent intellectual/political acts was subscribing to a radical American magazine, *Liberation,* when I was about sixteen years old. In one of the first issues I received, there was a review of *Summerhill School* by A.S. Neill, which whetted my interest enough for me to procure myself a copy. This book certainly changed my life.

Summerhill School made clear to me, very suddenly, how essential it is that the motivation to learn and explore be internal, not external, and that excessive pressures from outside—i.e., examinations, grades, parental threats and demands, etc.—can distort and suffocate one's natural curiosity and eagerness to educate oneself.

Summerhill School helped me develop a different set of values which were truly my own, and to free both my spirit and my body to try to live by those values. And it taught me, in dealing with others, that there is no point in trying to compel them to achieve. To help a child develop a positive attitude toward learning and culture, stimulating and awakening their fascination, and setting a good example, are all more effective and more pleasant than intimidation.

Of course this theoretical attitude needed much modification in the practice of child-raising and educating. This was a further lesson: What worked for A.S. Neill at his school could utterly fail when applied in a doctrinaire way by others, especially if they lacked his insight and empathy. Freedom without any structure, and avoidance of any strenuous effort or pain in learning, can be just as destructive as the rigid, brutal indoctrination which passed (and still passes) for education in some places.

Theory is fine, but it should not be allowed to completely overwhelm instinct—which also applies beautifully to my own work!

Tomson Highway (playwright)

Well, you see, up where I was born and grew up—the wilds of northern Manitoba and the Territories, everybody born in tents, dogsleds, caribou herds, etc., Cree country to the hilt—there weren't any books. So I never grew up with those little kiddie books that all other kids did. Plus, English wasn't our language. Our version of books was "oral" storytelling sessions with elders, in the Cree language, fabulous, mystical, hilarious tales about the Trickster, mostly, and about other mythological beasts, creatures and heroes. That was our world of magic.

By the time I got comfortably conversant with the English language, I was about fifteen years old. I just could never learn the goddamn thing before then.

So I remember reading the summer I was fifteen, late into at least three nights, back on "the Rez," a ratty old copy of Victor Hugo's *The Hunchback of Notre-Dame*. Really the first novel I ever read. And I couldn't stop. I remember that, back in those days, there was no electricity on the Rez so I read by the light of one candle until five in the morning, as I say, three nights in a row. I started wearing glasses the next year—and have ever since. So that's one way that book changed my life. Darn!

But I couldn't stop, because I was so enthralled by the tale. Just a plain, rollicking good yarn. I was amazed, more than anything else, at the skill, the magic, the spell that a really good storyteller wields. Ever since then, I've always wanted to be like Esmeralda when I grow up. Just kidding...

Knowlton Nash (broadcaster)

I was ten years old and shivering with exhilaration as I raced through the pages of the globe-trotting adventures of a foreign correspondent by the name of Webb Miller. Through his autobiography, he became my hero, my idol, my ideal, and his book *I Found No Peace* catapulted me into a lifelong love affair with the news. As I read of his journalistic exploits in distant, exotic parts of the world, there was no soul-stirring philosophical revelation or commitment, but a lightning flash of what I wanted to do with my life: be a foreign correspondent.

In a "gee whiz!" style of writing and an almost naive wonder at how much he enjoyed his job, Miller, who was a correspondent for the American news agency United Press, captivated my young heart with his stories of reporting from the trenches of World War One, chasing Pancho Villa in Mexico or the Riffs in North Africa, covering the Italian invasion of Ethiopia, crossing the Atlantic in the zeppelin *Hindenburg* and talking to everyone from Lloyd George to Mussolini, Gandhi and the Grand Mufti. The Valley of Jehoshaphat, Khartoum, Verdun, Jerusalem, Cairo, Rome, London, Berlin, Paris all danced before my entranced eyes as I read on.

For me, Miller vividly portrayed a magic world far beyond the Depression-ridden Canada of the 1930s in which I grew up. Like today's kids who idolize the stars of rock and *Star Trek*, I fantasized about being a foreign correspondent like Webb Miller. His life seemed so richly exciting and fulfilling. Maybe it was the glamour; maybe it was seeing at first hand world-shattering events; maybe it was being the first to know what was happening; maybe it was being able to see and talk personally to world leaders; or maybe it was the camaraderie of that band of foreign-correspondent brothers chasing the news. Whatever the reason, reading Webb Miller's books set me on a determined campaign to be, if not just like him, as close as I could possibly come as a trench-coated searcher of news around the globe.

Don Tapscott (cyberspace expert, writer)

Choosing a book that influenced me in my youth was easy: *Manchild in the Promised Land* by Claude Brown. The book changed my life.

The hard part of this assignment was that I read it in 1965, lost my copy, and many details were foggy. I had forgotten the name of the author, for example. Had anyone else read this book? I wondered. Would I be able to find a copy? Surely it was out of print.

I turned to my computer and typed the name of the book into a World Wide Web search engine and to my delight dozens of sites and references came popping back. The first citation was someone who had created a Web site for the book: "*Manchild in the Promised Land* by Claude Brown—the most influential book I have ever read." It turns out that I was not alone in having been moved by this work. I learned that it is judged to be one of the most extraordinary biographies of our time and one of the most important works of black literature ever.

This is the powerful story of a Harlem youth who faces violence, drugs, street gangs and murder in his neighbourhood. He struggles with this world and eventually finds a way out—becoming a law student.

I was an eighteen-year-old Orillia high-school student, trying to get through grade 13 so I could set out into the world for myself. Life was pretty sheltered and good. The worst violence I had seen was as captain of the school football team. Drugs were what you took when sick, and murder was Perry Mason.

The brutality of life in the ghetto blew me away and I was deeply moved by the plight faced by many urban blacks, called "Negroes" in the book's foreword (it was the early sixties). The book deeply reaffirmed my support for the civil rights movement and I remember I wrote a song about the ghetto—most of the melody and lyrics come back to me today.

To this day I remember the passages in the book about his personal experiences with cocaine and heroin. I swore to myself at the time I would never take hard drugs—a promise which I kept.

I was also inspired by how facing such obstacles he had triumphed. I had no obstacles. I could do anything I wanted to do. This revelation sent me down the slippery slope of logic to an extreme conclusion. I wasn't going to waste my life—I was going to change the world. My parents patiently waited out the next decade during which I became a social activist, not having a "real" job for years after graduation from university. In retrospect I don't regret a minute of those years of struggle. In fact I attribute much of whatever success and impact I have had during my professional life to those years of working to end the kind of inhumanity which Brown thrust at me with this magnificent book.

Douglas Fetherling (writer)

When I was about fifteen I stumbled upon *Emile Zola, Novelist and Reformer; An Account of His Life and Work*, published in 1904, a couple of years after the great French novelist's tragic end. (Zola died while writing, after accidentally kicking open an unlighted gas jet—as depicted by Paul Muni in the last scene of *The Life of Emile Zola*, a once-famous Hollywood film.)

The book I pulled from the public library shelf turned out to be straightforward in the extreme, though it had the advantage of being written by someone who had known the subject personally: Zola's English publisher, Ernest Vizetelly. Indeed, it was into Vizetelly's arms that Zola had fled France for a year in the late 1890s to escape arrest for publishing *J'accuse*. The charge against him was criminal libel. *J'accuse*, of course, was Zola's famous pamphlet in defence of Capt. Alfred Dreyfus who, as Zola helped to prove, had been drummed out of the army and imprisoned on Devil's Island on a phoney espionage charge in what was actually an anti-Semitic frame-up. I later learned that Vizetelly had also published an account of these troubles, *With Zola in England*. In any case, I found Zola an immensely and immediately admirable figure.

I tried reading any number of his novels any number of times (the translations were poor and I was young and easily distracted); all I recall vividly are parts of *La Débâcle*, which tried to do with the Franco-Prussian War of the 1870s what Tolstoy had done with the Napoleonic Wars. At his best, Zola was a tough-minded and honest critic of his fellow citizens, yet also a person of great humanity and compassion.

In the end, alas, he grew sentimental, which was ironic. So was the fact that ultimately, after a long career as the public receptacle of abuse and disrespect, he was honoured with a state funeral. But even though it was a period in my life when I was searching hard for proof of meritocracy, Zola's rise through the society he chronicled so unflinchingly interested me less than the fact that he was so perfectly *engagé*, working.

I doubt that I could read any Zola today (he is one of those writers who comes with a lifetime quota). But I recall him, and Vizetelly's book about him, with affection.

John C. Polanyi (winner of the Nobel Prize in chemistry)

When I was eight, and helpless, I was shipped to a boarding school in the Lake District. This is the remote region of northern England in which Wordsworth rhapsodized about daffodils. I saw no daffodils, and don't suppose that he did; it is much too cold up there. It is, however, a popular spot for schools. This is because the terrain, like that of Dartmoor in the south, provides a natural barrier to those contemplating escape.

There were many such. A few were brave enough to attempt it. They fled at night on foot. Of course the police pursued them and brought them back. This, it was explained, was for their safety. Everybody was very worried about them. They wanted them returned so that they could thrash them prior to expelling them.

I was too much of a coward to make a run for it. Instead I escaped into the school library. This too was fraught with peril since, understandably, profligate reading was discouraged. It could make one unaware of the ringing of bells. It not only could, but in my case, repeatedly did. Each time, I was punished. Reading has remained, to this day, a guilty pleasure; no less pleasurable for that.

A moment of intense delight at the age of ten (I left that school when I was eleven) was occasioned by my chance encounter on the library shelves with Winston Churchill's first attempt at autobiography, *My Early Life*. The book, written in 1930 when he was fifty-six years old, had been out for only nine years when I happened on it. It was one of the most recent books in that library. I was not surprised, therefore, to find it full of immediacy. Recalling it today, I am conscious that it was about an individual born in the heyday of Queen Victoria, but it still has the same hold over me.

I was drawn irresistibly, but unresisting, into Churchill's sharply observed account of childhood and manhood, in what I took to be the contemporary world but that was in fact the end of an era.

Stressing epochal change, Churchill spoke of "the doom of war" in a brilliant passage: "Instead of a small number of well-trained professionals championing their country's cause with ancient weapons and a beautiful intricacy of archaic manoeuvre, sustained at every moment by the applause of their nation, we now have entire populations, including women and children, pitted against one another in brutish mutual extermination, and only a set of bleary-eyed clerks left to add up the butcher's bill. I wonder often whether any other generation has seen such astounding revolutions of... values as those through which we have lived."

Having (to this day) a schoolboy's talent for skipping the boring bits, I missed all this. I was in hot pursuit of Churchill's adventures; and he never disappointed me. "What a life," I thought as I closed this volume of reminiscence by an ancient man (sixty-five that year, 1939) who had lived a life of gallant leadership and adventure. There was no one to tell me, since no one knew, that his adventures had barely begun.

It is common enough that the stories we read in childhood plant seeds in us that germinate for a lifetime. In this case, however, it was not just the story that took on new shape with the passage of time, but the storyteller. Churchill went on to lead the fight against fascism, and to begin the global process of accommodating to the Atomic Age. Early life is invariably fascinating. This one more than most.

Matthew Barrett (President and CEO, Bank of Montreal)

Reading *Macbeth* in my teens opened many windows for me. Decades later, I still can see the haunted, blood-stained world that gripped my youthful imagination. The play is often found in high-school Shakespeare courses, yet in many ways it is an odd choice, and not just because the story is far removed from the daily round of twentieth-century life. Young eyes see a stage where evil is far more compelling than good. The men in the white hats win in the end, but they are a dull lot. Duncan has a blandly patronizing benevolence that must have been trying to live with. Malcolm's curious pretendings with Macduff leave an uneasy feeling that Malcolm's subjects in the brave new Scotland would be wise to read the fine print carefully. Only Banquo has a core of dignity and integrity. In contrast Macbeth and Lady Macbeth, traitors, liars, murderers both, are so extraordinarily vivid many people who have never read the play feel they know them well.

Heroes who defy all convention have a natural appeal for the rebellious young. But *Macbeth*'s attraction for me went well beyond that. First, there is the story itself. Uncluttered by sub-plots it moves more swiftly than anything else in Shakespeare, yet it also gives an astonishingly realistic sense of the passage of time that so weighs on the despairing Macbeth. Second, it is the play's atmosphere, darkly luminous, often with an appalling fascination, always so palpable it could almost be cut like so much Scottish turf. And third, of course, is the language. *Macbeth* showed a boy in a small Irish town just how much the English language can do. Actors are said to think that quoting the play is unlucky. Perhaps this is to avoid quoting something so unforgettable all the time. Almost every page has lines that live and grow in the memory. On no grounds at all I like to think the fact that *Macbeth* is the only Shakespeare play with a Celtic setting has something to do with this. (*King Lear* and *Cymbeline* are set in a timeless never-never land rather than an identifiable Celtic Britain.)

Looking back on the play so many years later, I realize that perhaps the people who construct high-school curricula are not so wrong after all. *Macbeth* is an intensely moral play. It creates an image of evil that is so powerful precisely because it reveals the sterility and futility of evil with such dreadful plausibility. Murder makes Macbeth not a king but an automaton. The witches' accurately fulfilled prophecies prove to be far worse than the doubts and hesitations of unaided human knowledge. Encircling them all is the great image of Nature, obeying her own laws, independent of human doings, yet potentially in harmony with them, and defied only at heavy cost. The advantage of reading Shakespeare when young is that such concepts are planted in your mind, and the rest of life shows you their full depth and reach of meaning. I hope *Macbeth* will be read by young people for a long time to come.

Aline Chrétien (wife of Prime Minister Jean Chrétien)

The Tin Flute achieved immediate success when it was published in Canada in 1945. The novel quickly became a best-seller and was made into a film. The author, Gabrielle Roy, was born in Saint-Boniface, Manitoba, on March 22, 1909. I read *The Tin Flute* when I was fifteen and found it engrossing. For one thing, I was about the same age as the central character. And I was truly moved by the image of poverty in the small neighbourhood of Saint-Henri. It affected me very deeply.

Florentine wants to rise out of poverty. She meets a young ambitious man who gets her pregnant and then leaves her. Florentine had wanted a different life than her mother's, but she is soon caught in the mesh of broken dreams and lost illusions. Her mother, Rose-Anna, who seems to be endowed with limitless courage and devotion, is worn out by the menial, endlessly repetitive work she must do. I felt a mixture of tremendous admiration and heart-wrenching pity for her. At the time, women lived in a state of total financial and psychological insecurity, while the men went off to war and often did not return.

As for the father, he is a timeless type, a man of boundless optimism despite the immense difficulties he must confront. I recognized some of my contemporaries in the personality of this engaging character. That is why I found the book so captivating and why I rushed to see the film.

Around the great universal themes of life, death and love, *The Tin Flute* weaves a story of ordinary people, hardworking men and women eking out a hard existence. It is a very rich book in which Gabrielle Roy transports us into the world of an impoverished family that wants to rise out of its condition.

When I was asked to talk about a book which influenced me as a teenager, I thought immediately of *The Tin Flute*. I hope I have made other readers want to find out more about this book, which has been published in seventeen languages, including our country's two official languages. As I myself come from a humble background, I was very sensitive to the difficulties experienced by this family during a period with which I am very familiar. All that misfortune spurred me to do my best all my life to help people who are suffering.

Ben Wicks (writer, cartoonist)

Growing up in a Dickensian area beside London Bridge would, to many, give the impression that little Alfie Wicks (my real name) did little but read in the sandbox. Not true. I did in fact grow up with comics. I was, however, fortunate enough to be living in an area once walked by the great Charles Dickens himself. Actually, the school was built on the site of a house in which, as a child, he and his mother had waited for Dad to be released from the local Marshalsea Jail.

With days spent in the folds of Dickens and evenings in the arms of the Elastic Man, I had the best of all reading. Yet it was neither Little Nell nor the stars of *The Wizard of Oz* that sent me scurrying into the world of books. It was the lodging house that sat at the end of the alley.

For two pennies each, thirty men could hook their arms over a clothes line set at shoulder height and sleep the night away. One such sleeper was W.H. Davies, a Welsh poet and professional tramp who, sitting in the lodging house each night, would write his poems and send them to the giants of the day. Conrad and Shaw both received creased paper on which was scrawled verse of such impressive power that they set the hobo up with free board, with instructions to produce a masterpiece. This he did and *The Autobiography of a Super-Tramp* became more than a classic.

This book was the first to drag a reluctant young reader from the adventures of the wild boy of the jungle into the real world of a remarkable man who, after losing a leg in a train accident, continued to roam the world in search of adventure.

George Bernard Shaw wrote the preface to the book and explained how readers should not be misled into feeling that he was in any way associated with the incredible rogue. I am sure that W.H. Davies felt the same way.

Sandie Rinaldo (broadcaster)

I have several favourite childhood books, but if I had to choose one that stirred my ambitions, one that affected my adolescent dreams, I would choose *Marjorie Morningstar*, by Herman Wouk.

My mother, who was a nurse, used to stop off at the library near the hospital where she worked, and bring home books for me to read. It was a weekly ritual, and I couldn't wait to see what treasures she would unearth. I was a dreamer and loved to lose myself in the characters. In Marjorie Morningstar I saw myself. She was a young girl who dreamed of becoming a performer, and dreamed of pursuing an unconventional romance (he was an actor, not a doctor!!). She was different, an iconoclast, choosing not to follow the traditional path established for women of her generation (to stay home), but still very conventional (she wanted a man in her life), and bound by societal standards (she wouldn't compromise her morality). At the tender age of thirteen, I identified with her ideological soul searching. As for Marjorie, she never did live up to her own youthful expectations (the bright lights!!). She married a dentist, and moved to the U.S. suburb of New Rochelle, where I imagine she raised her children, with conventional wisdom, to reach for their unconventional dreams. The book, and later the film, spoke to me at a time in my life when all childhood goals were attainable, when life made naive promises that always came true. (By the way, I married a lawyer and live in a Toronto suburb.)

Stuart McLean (writer, broadcaster)

I used to read instead of doing my homework when I was a kid. I had an elaborate system worked out so I wouldn't get caught. I would lay the book I was reading in the opened middle drawer of my desk. If my mother or father walked into my room I would lean into the drawer and slide it closed. I had homework arranged on the desk-top in case that happened.

I read a lot of junk. Comics first, then adventures and mysteries. *The Saint*, by Leslie Charteris. The Ken Holt series, by Bruce Campbell, which was a Hardy Boys knock-off about the son of a world-famous foreign correspondent.

I don't remember going to book stores until I was sixteen or seventeen. I don't think there were any in Montreal West. I got my books at the drugstore or the library. When we moved downtown I used to hang around a book store on Ste. Catherine Street called International News the way other kids hung around hockey rinks.

At some point I discovered individual books (as opposed to series). Two that I still own from those days are *Black Like Me* and *The Scalpel, The Sword*.

Black Like Me by John Howard Griffin is the (true) story of a white reporter who, in the autumn of 1959, darkened his skin with chemicals and a sun lamp and travelled through the southern United States as a Negro. *Black Like Me* made me cry when I read it as a teenager.

The Scalpel, The Sword: The Story of Dr. Norman Bethune is a Canadian book that affected me similarly. It is the biography of the radical Canadian doctor who died in China—a chronicle of a Canadian of truly heroic stature.

Richard Ouzounian (Creative Head of Arts, TVO)

The first book that I can remember really falling in love with was *The Great Gatsby*. I had just turned fourteen, it was the spring of 1964, and I remember starting to read it on the subway coming home from the high school I was attending in New York.

I had never read anyone who wrote like F. Scott Fitzgerald. Up until then, I had read my share of Scott, Dumas, Dickens and Cooper, and I thought that all serious fiction was weighty, ponderous, bulky and good for you...like a high-fibre breakfast cereal.

Suddenly, I was faced with a writing style that was light, poetic and ironic. Fitzgerald didn't write the way I actually felt, but the way I wanted to feel. And, at the time, like every fourteen-year-old boy, I was looking for a Daisy who would be worthy of the boundless adolescent love I had to offer.

For the first time, I looked on literature as a partnership: I understood F. Scott Fitzgerald, and I felt he understood me.

After that book, I went on to read everything of his that I could find, and all the biographies, etc., that were available. By the time I got to *The Crack-up*, his famous autobiographical essays written not long before his death, I realized I was in for keeps. People change, authors go in and out of fashion, but I have never stopped being devoted to F. Scott Fitzgerald.

I said that I began reading *The Great Gatsby* on the subway, and I finished it there as well. It was late on a Saturday, I was coming home from a Drama Club rehearsal, and I was riding in the first car, as I always loved to do.

I finished the last page. The train had left the underground, and was now on the elevated tracks, clearing a path home for me through the melancholy twilight. Like Nick, like Daisy, like Gatsby, I stared through the window, searching for that green light in the distance.

Over thirty years later, I'm still searching, thanks to F. Scott Fitzgerald.

Susan Gilmour (actor, singer)

As with music, there are many books I have read that have a strong connection with different times in my life. I have only to think of the book and memories come flooding back to me ... but the one book I remember profoundly affecting me the most, staying in my heart and soul, opening my eyes and awakening my senses, was *The Prophet* by Kahlil Gibran. It was given to me by a dear friend on my sixteenth birthday. I think it was one of those little gifts from heaven that appear when you need them most.

The simple truths found in each chapter on friendships, love, joy and sorrow, prayer, death, forgiveness, marriage, beauty, knowledge (to name only a few) struck a chord deep inside me and my struggling and searching adolescent young soul was calmed. Gibran's sweet words and storytelling opened my heart and mind, taught me many great lessons, inspired thoughts and feelings that were new to me, and confirmed feelings and understandings that I already had. His poetry and wisdom lined that difficult pathway from adolescence to adulthood for me and lives in my heart still. That gentle little book continues to sit at my bedside, an ever faithful companion in my life and in all I do.

Greg Gatenby (writer; artistic director, International Festival of Authors)

When I was twelve years old my curiosity about girls was rampant. I was curious to know what was between their ears as well as what was hidden by their dresses; sometimes the mental mysteries were the more compelling preoccupation; oftentimes, though, the physical questions were all-consuming. This happens a lot when you're twelve.

Keen to learn as much as I could about the opposite sex (hey, let's be honest, I just wanted to learn as much as I could about sex, opposite or not), my ears were ever alert to new sources of information. One day, on the radio, I heard a news story about a book that the government had just decided to allow into the country after having banned it for decades. The book, *Ulysses* by James Joyce, was alleged to be so dirty that even then there were people who thought it should be forbidden. Boy, just hearing about this book made me hot to get it.

I went to my local library and tried to find the book in the Boys' and Girls' Section. In those days, only people who were thirteen years of age or older could use the adult section of the library. Alas, the Boys' and Girls' Section did not have *Ulysses*. But it did have another book by the same author. I figured that if James Joyce wrote one famous dirty book then the chances were good that this other book by him must be hot too. So I checked *A Portrait of the Artist as a Young Man* out of the library, went home with the book hidden in my jacket, and went up to my room prepared for an afternoon of serious and private research into the world of sex.

Well, I didn't find much sex. But I did find a book that changed my life.

Until I read *A Portrait of the Artist*, I always thought that books described things that happened to people who were luckier or smarter or better-looking or more confident than I was. Such books were okay to read but the characters lived lives that were nothing like mine. In those books, the parents never spanked the kids for something they didn't do; the teachers never shouted; the boys always knew how to talk to girls and ask them out on dates; and the girls who were always incredibly beautiful never said they had to do babysitting that night.

What I discovered with James Joyce that afternoon, though, shocked me. Instead of a story full of what the English call "naughty bits," I was reading a story that was a description of my own life! The lead character, Stephen Dedalus, like me, was twelve years old. His parents were devout Catholics but he himself was full of doubts about the Church, and full of dread about what such doubts might bring. And just as I did, he loved books and stories and words and wanted to be a writer.

Until then, I had no idea that writers could sneak right inside your head and put into words your most secret thoughts. And, most assuringly that afternoon, James Joyce convinced me that I wasn't alone in having certain thoughts. Thoughts that I believed were wicked or crazy or outrageous—and was too embarrassed to share even with my best friend—were thoughts that, thanks to James Joyce, I found out many, many people had. In other words, the book taught me that I wasn't crazy, and believe me, when you're twelve years old there are lots of times you wonder if you're crazy.

I spent the whole afternoon reading that book. I was stunned by the way I could recognize myself in one of the characters. I couldn't wait to get my hands on other books by the guy—whether the books had sex in them or not. I wanted to read not only his own books but other books about him. I needed to know how come he was so smart. And reading about James Joyce led me to loads of other writers who also had this magical ability to get right inside your head and put down in words what you were really thinking.

So *A Portrait of the Artist* had a big influence on my life: among many lessons, it taught me a great deal about the good and bad of religion; it taught me that even the most intimate fears and hopes of men and women and boys and girls can be expressed in words; and it also gave me the confidence to become a writer myself.

It has been some years since I last read *A Portrait of the Artist as a Young Man*. But I will always have a special place for the book in my heart. Its effect was that powerful.

Harry J. Boyle (writer, broadcaster)

When I was five I could read adequately but the problem was that we had very few books, and since we lived on a remote sideroad in Western Ontario, with one neighbour, even the great indoor winter pastime of conversation was limited. The telephone had just been installed, but my mother hadn't conquered her inhibitions about listening in on other people's party-line conversation.

On a winter-grey November day I had a choice of reading *The Lives of the Saints*, the Bible, *Home Remedies for Man and Beast*, *Cast up by the Sea* or the latest copy of *The Farmers' Advocate*. Father was reading the *Globe* newspaper, several days old. I knew he would read aloud while mother knitted after supper and I anticipated the comics, but in the meantime I watched as daylight was smothered by the grey clouds.

You could barely see the front gate, but to my amazement someone had opened the gate and was carefully closing it. When I said, "There's somebody coming," Father and Mother came to watch and we saw a tall man, limping, with a sack over his shoulder.

"It's a veteran. He's wearing one of those greatcoats with the badges torn off. Rustle him up something to eat and he can eat it in the back kitchen."

To my surprise my mother said in a firm tone of voice she seldom used, "No! Bring the poor man in where he can get warm and dried off."

This was 1920 and we were used to seeing veterans wearing their army uniforms. When I went with Father to the grist mill there would be several of them sitting there and they invariably asked, "Any chance of a bit of work for grub and tobacco?"

My father would mumble a negative and I knew when he recalled the incident to my mother he would say in a bitter way, "Poor devils were good enough to fight a war but they can't get a day's work now."

I'm a little fuzzy about the sequence, but I know the stranger took off his khaki puttees and coat and dried his feet out in front of the open oven door. He stayed for supper and when he left next morning my father marvelled at how much he had eaten. I fell asleep and was put to bed. When I roused in the morning, he was just leaving. He handed my mother a book and said it was for what he called "the accommodation."

I was desperately hoping Father would keep the book and I missed some of the conversation. I did learn that he was selling books, but as he said, "Money is pretty tough for people to buy books and besides most people want to forget the war."

Finally Mother took some money from the old, cracked teapot on the sideboard and literally pressed it into his hand. I think it was a dollar and something in change.

I didn't see him leave. I was too busy with *The Illustrated History of the Great War, 1914–18.*

Father and Mother didn't get a chance to see what was in the book until after supper. The stark photos of muddy roads and trenches, of exhausted soldiers and dead horses and the gaunt skeletons of houses and in particular, a church where only a fragment of a tower remained to hold a cross aloft, prompted Mother to put the book out of sight. I found the hiding place in the parlour, and pored over it whenever I was alone in the house.

The book had the names of many places I couldn't pronounce. I could appreciate the death and destruction and entertained dreams that were graphic and disturbing. The sense of horror faded. The book was left on a table in the parlour but it was never placed with the other books. A cousin who had served in the war came to visit and he spelled out the names of the places and told stories about being on leave and of the fun the soldiers had. He made it all seem somehow different, but I have never seen a picture of war and the ravages of war without seeing in my mind's eye the tired, limping man who sold us *The Illustrated History of the Great War, 1914–1918*. I shall go to my grave wondering what happened to him.

·9· Words into Action

"Art is an act . . . not an object; a ritual, not a possession"
—Edmund Carpenter

Occasionally books have affected some people's lives in very direct and dramatic ways. They have influenced career choices, political and personal viewpoints and even places of residence.

For some, a book, particularly a children's book, may seem little more than a collection of words or pictures on pieces of paper. They are innocent diversions, a brief foray or excursion, a source of occasional pleasure and not much more. Some people derive considerable satisfaction from books, enjoyment made possible by all kinds of reading, whether casual or purposeful, for diversion, information, escape or many other reasons. But once in a rare while, a book will truly stir a person's soul and actually change them in a memorable and important way.

This book may appear through accidental circumstances, coincidence or recommendation. In any event, the particular book becomes a catalyst, an agent leading to action, growth, or significant personal insight. A book can actually make something happen. However engrossing and fascinating they may be, the stories in most books, even biographies, are fundamentally different from the real and everyday events and experiences in readers' lives. They may shed perspective on our lives but are usually easily separated from direct experience. But when a powerful book hits the mark—the right book at the right time—it can have an enormous impact on a receptive individual.

This has happened to a number of contributors. It was a book that inspired Tony Penikett's love of the north, awakening a lifelong attatchment to the land and its people. A moving and inspirational book encountered in connection with an early acting opportunity encouraged Cynthia Dale to follow her dream of becoming an actor.

Other writers presented crucial role models for Cecil Foster, W.P. Kinsella, Gordon Korman, Barbara Greenwood and numerous others throughout this book. Powerful prose and innovative fiction, along with a hearty appetite for good books, appear to have frequently inspired many a hesitant beginner to first put pen to paper and create their own original stories. Books lead to more books, original work to original works. Pictures and concepts discovered in books helped set high standards and challenging creative goals for artists like Charles Pachter and Toni Onley, influencing them especially forcefully years ago when they were just beginning.

Sometimes ideas and evidence discovered in books and that presented by parents and teachers has been found to be at odds. This may inspire a strong reaction. Andrew Moodie dealt with the dichotomy very directly. Claire Mackay discovered the enormous power of literature to abet and inspire high ideals (and for escape) while her family experienced difficult times. She also developed the creative urge to give something back to society. Bob Rae gained from a powerful writer and social critic a lasting political perspective and a sense of irony.

Edward Greenspan determined his vocation, a career in the legal profession, from a book savoured in his father's study. Revelations from the same book had a huge impact on Ken Thomson. He discovered that the efforts of a single committed and determined person can make a tremendous difference.

The essays in this section are especially exciting because they reveal the power of literature to transport the reader. Most contributors to *Everybody's Favourites* happily admit to being uniquely affected by a book or books, but for some the influence is just that much more palpable and direct.

Tony Penikett (former premier of Yukon)

Ever since first learning to read, I've enjoyed receiving books as Christmas gifts. The first Christmas book to make a real impression on me was a little grey hardback called *Lars in Lapland* by Henry Waddingham Seers. I cannot recall who gave it to me—although it was probably my schoolteacher grandmother. Nor can I remember exactly the year I received it. Yet something about that book made it quite unforgettable.

Decades later, I can still visualize the book's title page, which featured a line-drawing of a little boy in Sami costume and a reindeer with sleigh bells around its neck. Did this drawing fascinate me because of the obvious association between reindeer and Christmas? Or was it something more than that?

After all this time I cannot be sure, but this book was almost certainly my first conscious encounter with the exotic world beyond my family home and the English-speaking community in which I lived. At that age, I had no idea how to locate Lapland; I knew only that it was a wonderful place way up in the far north where a little boy named Lars played with a reindeer.

Many years later, I visited Lapland. At Kiruna, in Swedish Lapland, I became friendly with a man named Lars and at Rovaniemi, in Finland, I learned about an attraction called Santa Claus Land that draws jet loads of British tourists every Christmas holiday. Of course, this was not the Lars, or the Lapland, of my childhood imaginings.

Still, this first visit to Lapland made me realize how much that childhood Christmas book had foreshadowed my future life. In my youth, I went to live in the Yukon Territory. There, I discovered a lifelong interest in the Arctic and sub-Arctic: the homeland of the Dene, the Inuit and the Sami, reindeer and the reindeer's cousin, the barren-ground caribou.

All my adult life, I worked with Yukon aboriginal peoples, settling land claims, trying to reconcile ancient and modern ways of life, and lobbying to preserve the great caribou herds on which some northern communities still depend.

In my time in the north, I have seen some awesome things, spellbinding scenery, and amazing changes, many for the better, some, sadly, for the worse. These experiences are now a part of me, all indelibly etched on my brain. They made me a northerner.

Nowadays, I work in the south, and the Yukon's mountains and rivers seem very far away. But recently a good friend gave me a University of Lapland necktie. Putting the tie on for the first time, I studied its design in the mirror. It showed a small herd of stylized reindeer moving over a rust-coloured tundra, against a skyline of golden light and misty mauves. The tie's design had a strange effect on me. It reminded me of sightings of caribou crossing a hillside in sub-Arctic Yukon twilight. Smiling inwardly at the silken image, my mind wandered, racing backwards through an avalanche of memories.

I remembered sitting beside my youngest brother as he piloted a

Twin Otter, between a heavenly blue sky and endless white ice, over the caribou range and along the Arctic coast. I remembered standing on a mountainside near the Dempster Highway while thousands of caribou milled around me in deep snow. I remembered visiting magical places like Fishing Branch River, which goes underground as it rounds the base of a mountain, then emerges again, so warm that the water just downstream never freezes. This creates an Eden for landlocked salmon, the grizzly bears that feed there year-round and moose who browse nearby. The rush of memories takes me back over my years in territorial politics: aboriginal-rights debates, caribou debates, reindeer-ranching debates. It leads me on to Lapland then, finally, back where it started with little Lars.

So, a word to all grandparents: choose carefully the books you buy for your children's children. You just never know where their reading may take them. Even one little Christmas book may change a person's life.

Cecil Foster (writer)

Growing up on the Caribbean island of Barbados, my daily existence consisted of enduring six solid hours of formal education and about three hours of play. Of course, I very much preferred pitching marbles, playing cricket or just roaming around the village with my roller (an old bicycle wheel which I skilfully guided with a stick) to anything even remotely academic. Only when the sun disappeared like a big red ball drowning in the Caribbean Sea and the island was instantly plunged into darkness would I abandon playing and turn my attention to such things as, maybe, homework.

Then my world changed. It started with a new headmaster at our school, Christ Church Boys Elementary. Mr. Lynch decreed that since the Barbados government was spending so much of its meagre resources on libraries, all the students at his school should show their gratitude and register with the small one-room limestone library in the nearby town, Oistins.

Every two weeks we were required to visit the library. We could borrow a maximum of two books, but I always shunned this generosity and took only one. And it had to be the smallest book, with lots of pictures and white spaces. The fewer the words the better. Then, I would take the book home, throw it on a shelf and set about my real love of pitching marbles, playing cricket and rolling my bicycle wheel. (Of course, I had to take care not to keep the book longer than the maximum fourteen days. The late charge was one cent per day per book. But just one cent in overdue fines would have brought down the wrath of Grandmother on my head.)

One evening I visited the library and it must have been meagre stuff available, for I remember coming across a thin green-back book. It looked new, so I borrowed it. It also was in some dubious category called West Indian literature.

At home, Grandmother was waiting. When I threw the book on the shelf and made as if to leave the house, she asked: "Where you think you going so fast young man? Why you keep borrowing these books from the people's library and then you don't read them?"

She must have been in a bad mood. Or I must have done something to vex her. In any case, I was grounded, under instructions to remain in the house and read this book I had brought from the library only for show. So, sulking, I sat at the table and broke open the book. I was so angry with Grandmother. If only I were a big man and could live my life as I wished. If only...

And then I started to read about a little boy, just like me. This boy lived in a village just like mine, in Barbados. And he lived with a mother, a strict disciplinarian just like Grandmother. And this boy planned to run away from it all... from his mother, the hard life in the village, just how I wished I could run away too, my roller leading the way.

I was simply fascinated. So there were books that spoke about experiences just like mine! Stories about people like all of us in Barbados, not only about people living in England or America! I was hooked.

Within days, I had read the book and returned it to Oistins library. And I started to discover a world of my own as I began an assault on all the writers in this category called West Indian literature. There I was to meet authors like V.S. Naipaul, George Lamming, Sam Selvon and, my favourite at the time, Michael Anthony.

The book that opened up a new world to me was *Amongst Thistles and Thorns* written by Austin Clarke, a fellow Barbadian living in Toronto.

Looking back, I think it was this book that made me realize the importance of stories about life in Barbados and the Caribbean and led me to hope that one day I too would write some of these stories. So if there is some little boy or girl with a strict grandmother, grandfather, mother, father, uncle, aunt, brother, sister, cousin, he or she might run away to some safe and secure corner of the world by breaking open the covers of a book.

Andrew Moodie (actor, playwright)

I will never forget it. I was walking down the stairs of the Ottawa downtown library to the first-floor reading area. I had in my hand a collection of Albert Camus's plays. In grade 12 a girl I knew had turned me on to Camus. I carried *The Fall* with me every day. I was astonished to learn that he had written plays. I thought this was ultra cool. I had always been interested in theatre and this was a major find. I loved the idea that Camus would do the theatre thing. I got to the bottom of the stairs and out of the corner of my eye, I saw the words, "The Africans."

I pull the book off the shelf. *The Africans*, by Basil Davidson; the cover proclaimed that it was An Entry to Cultural History. I opened it to the middle and looked inside. My life was never the same again. The next thing I remembered was the librarian hovering, her way of saying the library had been closed for fifteen minutes. Staring up at me was a chapter on how the seventh-century empires of West Africa had become Muslim and had developed trade with Mecca. I had no idea that there had been empires in West Africa, let alone that they had any contact with the outside world during the seventh century. Soon I was reading about Timbuktu, the legendary city of philosophy, whose houses were rumoured to be roofed with gold, and the warrior women of the Kingdom of Benin. Their ferocity in battle was said to exceed that of any man.

I didn't take the book home. I left it, worried that walking around the halls with a book called *The Africans* would elicit those unwanted comments that grade twelves tend to offer on occasion. The next day, I ran to the library and I was taken away on a journey to ancient, pre-colonial Africa. Strange magical names like Kush and Songhay. Basil Davidson spoke of Kings and Empires, not natives and savages. I had just read Steinbeck's novel on King Arthur's court (a staple of European history) and now I was reading something that told me of a similar plot, only this took place in Africa.

I was amazed but I didn't understand why nothing, NOTHING in my high-school history course had prepared me for this. My English teacher even suggested, without a stitch of irony, that Aliens might have created the Pyramids. When he told the class that the blacks in *Heart of Darkness* had never seen a white man before, I put up my hand and told him that he was wrong; that the people of the Congo had traded with Portugal for at least a hundred and seventy years before Joseph Conrad was even born. And this was not just tribal oral history, this was documented fact, with letters of correspondence from the Emperor of the Congo to the King of Portugal. My statement was greeted with a chorus of derisive laughter. The teacher then informed me that during World War Two he had spent some time in West Africa and the natives there were little more than animals.

It was from that moment on that I knew I could no longer trust this institution to tell me the truth. That I could not trust any institution to tell me the truth. In the search for truth, you must always depend on yourself. And so I did.

Bob Rae (lawyer, former premier of Ontario)

A high-school teacher of mine grew tired of my yakking on about the benefits of the Russian and French revolutions. "For God's sake, Rae. Find a little irony in life. Read Orwell."

And so I did. I started with *1984*, which I found gloomy and brilliant, and then found a second-hand Penguin version of *Animal Farm* in a book store. It looked incredibly thin for a major book. As I read it, it seemed almost too simple, too enjoyable, too much of a pleasure. It made me laugh, and then it made me think. The revolution of Mr. Jones's farm only made life worse. By the end of the book the pigs were walking on their hind legs, and some animals were very clearly more equal than others.

I then devoured everything Orwell wrote, and wasn't satisfied until I had read every single novel and piece of political journalism that I could find. To this day he has remained a touchstone—it is hard to watch governments change without thinking about that farm and those wilful, arrogant pigs, who rewrote history and destroyed the present in the name of a revolutionary ideology. "Common sense?"

It was impossible for me to listen to any political speech, bureaucratic apology or journalistic doublespeak in the same way after reading Orwell and seeing life at least partly through his lens. It still is, which often makes it hard to take even my own words entirely seriously. I found more than a little irony in life. And I'm glad I did.

Claire Mackay (writer)

The favourite book of my childhood, which nobody had ever heard of, was entitled *Og, Son of Fire*. Its author was Irving Crump. (I am not making this up.) It was the twelfth book on the second shelf in the northwest corner of the children's department at Yorkville Public Library in Toronto, and it had a maroon cover with black intaglio printing. I know because I read it seventeen times. I probably dusted it seventeen times, too, because when I was ten years old I worked at the library at a wage slightly below that of a Victorian ratcatcher. I wish I could claim that *The Secret Garden*, or *Anne of Green Gables*, or Oswald Spengler's *The Decline of the West* was my favourite childhood book. Any of those would seem so much more impressive. But no. It was *Og, Son of Fire* (*The Decline of the West* was my second favourite).

Og is—and I use the present tense because, for me, Og lives—a paleolithic prepubescent boy who is the despair of his father, for when it comes to spears and clubs and stone axes, Og is all opposable thumbs. Nor is Og held in high esteem by his peer group—he's always the last to be picked for games like Run, Mammoth, Run. He's an archetypal klutz, a misfit, an outsider. But he's also a quiet revolutionary, a wanderer and a wonderer, with a talent for solitude, a knack for the romantic, and a love for the larger than life. He dreams of noble deeds, of valour, of glory and sacrifice, and of a place in the sun of his father's eyes. Because Og is what he is, to him is granted, courtesy of a serendipitous local lightning bolt, the gift, the transmuting power, and the terrible magic of fire. He brings that gift to his father, to his people.

Why did I love Og so? The answer isn't far to seek. I was Og, no matter that he and I were separated by sex, one hundred millennia of alleged civilization and several other infinities of difference. I was Og—but not nearly so brave. So I was a secret Og, an undercover Og, a closet Og. I dreamed Og dreams of quest and discovery, of astounding bravery, even, when I was feeling especially dramatic or melancholy, of martyrdom. I wanted a place for myself, but, more important, I longed to make a gift to my father, to my people.

And at the time I read—and read and read and read—the book, around 1940, when I was nine, my father (and my people) sorely needed a gift. He had lost his steady well-paying job as bookkeeper in 1930, about a week after I was born, as the Great Depression descended upon the world. Raised to believe that the husband, the father, was the provider and protector of the family, when the means to provide and protect was snatched away, he was at once grievously hurt and deeply bewildered. The loss deformed his life. In an attempt to make sense of it, he began to read the works of Marx and Engels, and soon the whole family underwent political conversion: my grandparents, aunts, uncles, parents—and, willy-nilly, my brother and I—became communists, revolutionaries, idealistic dreamers. Much like Og.

I am convinced that at this point in my childhood the soul-stirring rhetoric of socialism and communism blended with my longing for a life of grand deeds, quest and sacrifice (if absolutely necessary). From this concatenation there grew an almost reflexive sympathy for the powerless (and children are among the most powerless), a delight in being secretly and not-so-secretly subversive (a trait I share with most children's writers), and a pervasive and ill-concealed anti-authority attitude, an attitude reflected in nearly every book I have written. It is not too far a stretch to say that *Og, Son of Fire* determined the course my life would take.

Toni Onley (artist)

I cannot remember ever reading children's books. My father read to me as a child when I was probably three or four. *Treasure Island* was my favourite. Before that I have a very faint memory of my grandmother reading the fairy tales of Hans Christian Andersen, like "The Princess and the Pea," "The Emperor's New Clothes," "The Ugly Duckling" and "The Little Match Girl." The nonsense poems of Edward Lear or Lewis Carroll were recited at the drop of a hat.

When I was born, in 1928, my father was an actor with the Frank Fortesque Repertory Theatre. My parents also ran a boarding house for itinerant actors. Evenings would be taken up with rehearsals; often I would be a reading stand-in. At an early age I was familiar with most of the playwrights of the thirties and forties from John Steinbeck to Tennessee Williams (whom I met much later and for whom I designed a stage set).

By the time I was reading myself I was already actively painting watercolours (from six years on). At fourteen I enrolled in the Douglas School of Art, a school mired in nineteenth-century aesthetics. I spent my time studying illumination, copying the script in the *Book of Kells*. (That has affected my handwriting ever since.)

I can never remember being allowed to be a child; from six on I was dressed in a three-piece Marix Tweed suit. I was expected to have opinions about everything from poetry to politics. In grade 1, I recited Rupert Brooke's "If I Should Die." Life was short and earnest. I was reminded that the ancient stone circles on the island were erected by teenagers. One graveyard on the island contains few who lived beyond twenty-four years, and this was very recent history.

I read Shaw's plays and Shakespeare's *Julius Caesar* and *Hamlet*, in both of which my father acted. My father had committed to memory every book and play he ever read, so was a great help to me in finding nineteenth-century poets of the sublime. I don't think I have changed much in my reading habits from that day to this.

From then on I searched out literature and poetry that would lend expression to what the nineteenth-century painters had done. First there was the aesthetic theory and topographical observations made by the Rev. William Gilpin in 1772. On the correct disposition of hills in a view, or the number of cows permissible in a painting, Gilpin would have shied away from the "unpaintable immensities of the sublime" which interested me.

My home was the Isle of Man where the winters are bad, the seas are high and often the boat from the mainland rides out a storm for days for a trip that usually takes four and a half hours. In early spring a fog rolls in called the "Manamman's Mable" after the Celtic god of the sea. The fog is said to keep out invaders.

A compatible degree of awfulness and solemnity descended on my little world. This world had a connection with literature. If I was able to put it into the context of rhetoric and poetry to parallel what I was trying to do in my paintings, it would all come together for me and I would not be alone. I sought out the most elevated landscape verse from Milton to Wordsworth. I scoured our little public library for anything that would lend expression to my painting. This is what motivated my reading from a very early age.

I left my little world when I was nineteen and came to Canada to paint its unpaintable immensities. My painting and reading have been expanding ever since.

Charles Pachter (artist)

For my tenth birthday, my piano teacher, Rachel Cavalho, presented me with a hefty illustrated book called *The Story of Painting for Young People: From Cave Painting To Modern Times* by H.W. Janson and Dora Jane Janson, published by Harry N. Abrams Inc., New York, 1952. For a long time I kept it by my bedside as an automatic kickstart to vivid dreams.

The frontispiece illustration was one of my favourites—a bold Renaissance portrait by Domenico Ghirlandaio of *An Old Man and His Grandson*. The old man's kind face had a startlingly pocked nose as bulbous as a gourd, in stark contrast to the upturned face of his angelic blond grandson. Through a tall window could be seen a phantasmagorical landscape of meandering river and stylized mountains which would kindle the imagination of any child.

The book had several riveting chapters summarizing human creative output: How Painting Began, The Middle Ages, Explorers and Discoverers, The Age of Genius, The Triumph of Light, The Age of

Machines, and Painting in Our Own Time. Each chapter contained illustrated images and commentaries, from Stone Age cave paintings to religious icons, from the frescoes and sculptures of Michelangelo to the Broadway Boogie Woogie canvases of Mondrian. It was all here between the covers of one book—the Baroque and Rococo painters, Impressionists, Cubists, Abstractionists—a breathtaking sweep of imagery for a young mind to absorb.

I found it challenging, and unsettling, and remember thinking, "I want to do this too!" wondering if I ever could. When I started my first awkward drawings, I would return to my "art bible" for inspiration. Forty-five years later, although I've added hundreds of more comprehensive and specific art books to my library, this one still sits on a special shelf in my studio, never far from my thoughts.

Cynthia Dale (actor)

When I was twelve years old I played the young Emily Carr in a CBC musical based on the artist's life. My mother, thankfully, thought it was important to be familiar with Carr's work, so she brought home everything that had been published. It was in that pile of books I found *Hundreds and Thousands*, or rather, it found me.

Her writing opened up a whole world of wonder. It touched me and spoke to me in such a way that filled me with awe. Her struggles, her passions, her journey gave me the courage to acknowledge my own dreams and taught me to believe that while the life of an artist was not only difficult and full of self-doubt, it was mostly noble, worthy and at times even joyous. I was so blessed to discover her at a time when the world was opening up to me—and inside of me.

I still have my original copy. Certain passages are underlined, many corners are folded back and special papers over the years have been pressed between its pages. I've reread portions of it many, many times, and it always stirs my soul.

Edward Greenspan (criminal lawyer)

Exactly one month after my thirteenth birthday, my father died. Approximately one month after that, I was sitting in our family den, taking a careful look at his library for the first time. I vividly recall removing Irving Stone's biography, *Clarence Darrow for the Defense*, sitting in my father's favourite chair, leafing through the book and noticing that some passages were underlined by my dad. I can see myself turning to page one and starting to read the book.

I was up most of the night and by the next evening I had read the last page. When I closed the book, and I suspect soon after starting the book, I knew what I wanted to do when I grew up.

The book was about an enormous figure in American history, as well as a giant in the courtroom. Clarence Darrow was a legendary criminal lawyer who fought relentlessly against capital punishment. He was a man filled with kindness, charity and infinite pity for the outcast and the weak. He took the minds and hearts of jurors and judges into the realm of great ideas and high values. Darrow was not afraid to demonstrate the absurdity of laws, to uncover the fallacy of their foundations and to attack their unthinking supporters. Darrow often put the law itself on trial as he did in the famous Scopes "monkey trial," in which a high-school teacher in Dayton, Tennessee, was charged with teaching Darwin's legally forbidden theory of evolution rather than the creationist theory of the Bible. He often became frustrated with the rigidity of the law and its resistance to change. The "Attorney for the Damned" had the ability to communicate profound ideas in simple, compelling language and to turn abstractions into immanent realities.

Darrow was a man of action who defended the indefensible, questioned received "truths," instinctively opposed any exercise of government power, and was never willing to sacrifice his own independence of thought. He was a debunker and a demystifier who was always sceptical of every element of the case against his clients, always put the government to the strict proof of its entire case and never accepted anything at face value. His life was dedicated to his clients, freedom of expression and liberty. The stakes were always high: his clients were at risk of losing their liberty or their lives.

As I put the book in its place on the library shelf, I knew that I wanted to be a criminal lawyer. The case for the defence was proven beyond a reasonable doubt.

Kenneth R. Thomson (Chairman, The Thomson Corporation)

I think Irving Stone's *Clarence Darrow for the Defense* was perhaps the book that most impressed and influenced my thinking during my youth. This biography of America's great defence lawyer, who set himself the mission of fighting in the law courts for the protection and rights of the underdog, left a lasting impression on me.

Darrow had great scope to put into practice his personal philosophy and compassion. Fairness to all will always be impossible to achieve and it was certainly far from prevalent in the late nineteenth and early twentieth centuries.

How, I asked myself, could George Pullman, the so-called railway baron, pay his workers subsistence wages, provide them with low- or sub-standard living accommodation, and at the same time charge them high rents which they clearly could not afford to pay? The situation was appalling, as would be obvious to us today, but such conditions did exist a century ago and were accepted by most with what would now be regarded as callous resignation. Darrow was not prepared to accept it. He threw in his lot with the railroad workers and helped to bring about eventual change to more humane conditions.

It was so in other industries as well. Darrow always fought for the groups or individuals that needed his great courtroom skill. And in so doing he helped alleviate human suffering. From very modest beginnings, through his great intelligence, dedication and hard work, he did his job to the fullest and fought for social justice.

Darrow made me realize, earlier than I would otherwise have done, that great injustices exist in this world, that we are all obliged to acknowledge and correct them to the best of our abilities, and that even individuals, through their own efforts, can make a difference. That is why I regard *Clarence Darrow for the Defense* as the book that had perhaps the greatest influence on me at an early stage in my life.

Terry Mosher (Aislin) (cartoonist)

In the early 1960s I was kicked out of high school—Parkdale Collegiate Institute in Toronto—for, admittedly, a very good reason: possession of marijuana.

Someone gave me a copy of Jack Kerouac's *On the Road*, an autobiographical saga about criss-crossing North America on the cheap. Having nothing better to do, I set off in the spirit of Jack, managing to hitch-hike some 24,000 miles throughout Canada, the U.S. and Mexico over the next three years.

Of all the cities I saw, Quebec City won the toss-up over New Orleans as a place to settle down for a bit and go to art school. This eventually led to my move to Montreal, where I've been ever since.

The bottom line? Jack Kerouac got me out of Toronto.

W.P. Kinsella (writer)

The Illustrated Man by Ray Bradbury was a book that gave my own work validity. I discovered the book while I was in high school, a place where the study of fiction was unknown—*Julius Caesar*, and *The Admirable Crichton* by J.M. Barrie were the only literature we studied in high school, and we had no library.

Looking at my own story-writing from those days, as bad as it was, it was full of simile and metaphor. I had no role models. About the only Canadian author was Hugh MacLennan whose novels were didactic treatises that had little to do with fiction.

Reading Ray Bradbury was like walking through a bower of beautiful flowers, his images appealed to sight, sound, taste, touch and smell, things that I had known instinctively as necessary to fiction, but I had never before had my instinct validated.

Writing fiction as a teenager in a society where writing was not valued and generally ridiculed was a very lonely business. Bradbury's work spoke to me, saying, yes, it is all right to create delicate similes and monstrous metaphors.

Bradbury was a living author who was doing with his life exactly what I wanted to do with mine. I still reread *The Illustrated Man* and *The Golden Apples of the Sun*, and marvel at the beauty of the language and the superb imagination that brought about their creation.

Gordon Korman (writer)

As a kid, I was not the voracious devourer of books that some parents would love their children to be. By age eleven, one year before I started to write and sell my own stuff, I was reading almost nothing. That drove my mother (enter the voracious devourer of books) crazy. She scoured book stores for children's material with offbeat titles, and anything funny. If I was going to read, it was a non-negotiable requirement that there had to be laughs.

My problem, aside from laziness, is one that is well known today. Kids' books were simple concept, simple vocabulary. I needed a more complex storyline.

I guess Mom gave up on the children's books (hey, there were no Gordon Korman novels then!) and chose to expose me to Kurt Vonnegut, her own favourite author.

The book was *The Sirens of Titan*, and she started by reading it to me. This was to prevent wandering mind from turning into wandering feet. About halfway through, it wasn't coming quickly enough, so I took over on my own. *The Sirens of Titan* changed my viewpoint, my reading habits, and probably my whole life.

The book is ostensibly science fiction, but it is much much more than that. It is a book on super-serious social, political, inter-personal and ideological themes, certainly not a comedy, yet it is as funny as anything I have ever read. The plot twists and devices break over the reader like tidal waves, shocking and wonderful. It is the kind of book one must regularly put down and digest a bit before reading on. For me some parts had almost a *physical* impact that was very close to joy. For the first time, I met brilliant storytelling, amazing wit and biting irony. It evoked in me, also for the first time, willing suspension of disbelief, and a respect for the author that bordered on worship. I wanted to tell the man how much he moved me; I wanted to meet Vonnegut; I wanted to be Vonnegut.

When I did meet him, it was at an authors' affair, and I simply could not tell him how deeply he and his book had affected me. I wouldn't have wanted him to think I was merely a fan. Such a word would have been inadequate.

But when my first young adult novel, *Don't Care High*, was reviewed in *Quill & Quire* back in 1985 (I was then twenty-one or twenty-two) and Peter Carver wrote that my admiration for the satire of Vonnegut was starting to show up in my work, I was thrilled beyond words. There can be no greater compliment to a writer than to hear that he is arriving at where he has always wished to be.

I read *The Sirens of Titan*, in whole or in part, on a regular basis still.

Barbara Greenwood (writer)

To a child who loves reading, every new book is a box of delights waiting to be explored. I used to hold my breath as I turned to the first page, anticipating the wonders yet to come. Strange, then, how reluctantly I approached the book that made me want to write. In November of my grade 9 year, the librarian at Lawrence Park Collegiate handed out a set of much-used books. Dog-eared, heavily annotated in the unformed handwriting of students who obviously didn't respect books as I felt they should be respected, the copy I received was grubby and unappealing. What's more, this librarian had a poor track record with me. He had previously assigned for reading a book I considered profoundly boring. I, who read the backs of cereal boxes when nothing else was to hand, had hated *The Maneaters of Kumaon*.

So I opened with reluctance his current offering, *Cue for Treason*, by Geoffrey Trease. We were to read two chapters a night and answer the questions that followed. Amid universal groans from my classmates I glanced down the first page. "Weren't we taking the pistol?" caught my eye and then "Why were we creeping out of the house at night like foxes 'round a pen?" I hurried on. By the time Peter had thrown a rock at Sir Philip, fallen in with a band of travelling players and fled to London for a fateful meeting with one William Shakespeare, I was hooked—and not just on *Cue for Treason*. "I want to do this," I thought. "I want to write stories like this, full of vibrant characters, breathtaking adventures, about life long ago. But"—and this was a leap that came from some place other than the book in my hands—"I want to write Canadian stories." My first published novel was almost three decades in gestation, but I know it was conceived the day I reluctantly opened that much-abused copy of *Cue for Treason* and caught writing fever.

·10· An Abundance of Books

"So many books, so little time..."

A fair number of the essays in *Everybody's Favourites* mention more than one book. It seems that when some people begin to reminisce about books that were favourites or that affected them in a special way, the floodgates burst open. They find it almost impossible to restrict themselves to recollecting only one or two. This is the dilemma of the ice-cream parlour—so many flavours to choose from and all of them tempting and delicious. So, even in a short essay, these book-lovers are compelled to graze. They reveal alluring nuggets about several books. For the reader's benefit this simply adds volume to a tantalizing list of recommendations.

It also presented a challenge in the matter of categorizing their submissions. Because there were so many titles, it was extra difficult to place the entry in one section or another. The logical solution was to accommodate these readers and their abundant book selections with a chapter all their own. In some cases, particular groups of books inspired someone in a remarkable way. It was exciting to discover, for instance, that books of information—encyclopedias—could have the same absorbing effect on a hungry reader as works of fiction. The search for knowledge seems to be every bit as powerful as the search for stories.

Books may be ignored or neglected for years. But they are steadfast and patient objects. They stand ready, waiting at attention and all neatly in a row. For the most part they survive in good condition.

They are handily available. But the reader too must be receptive—ready to open both the book and themselves. Ready to hear and see and feel the story. Reading implies taking time away from other activities, listening with your heart. It is, for the most part, as we grow older, very personal and private time. As Frederick Grove has commented, "the effect of a book is the result of a collaboration between writer and audience."

The authors of essays gathered in this section all share at least one important element—a joy of reading. And that, after all, is one of the major goals of this book: to offer good leads and some helpful direction to the many paths and pleasures waiting to be discovered in the world of books.

Lesley Choyce (writer)

The really powerful books in my life happened when I was in my late teens. The long list of books that influenced me around then includes: *Trout Fishing in America* by Richard Brautigan, *Understanding Media* by Marshall McLuhan, *The Wisdom of Insecurity* by Alan Watts, *The Last Temptation of Christ* by Nikos Kazantzakis, *The Politics of Experience* by R.D. Laing, *Summerhill School* by A.S. Neill, *The Dharma Bums* by Jack Kerouac, *Sometimes a Great Notion* by Ken Kesey, and *In God We Trust, All Others Pay Cash* by Jean Shepherd. I was also intrigued by any book that was reported to be "banned" somewhere in North America. Books are banned primarily for ideas, not dirty language. I'm thinking of *Grapes of Wrath*, *Catcher in the Rye*, *Black Like Me*... and many others. While none of the above are really "children's" books, they are books that slam-dunked me into consciousness when I was truly still an adolescent.

But having to make a decision about the best ones—let's say I'm stuck on a desert island with no memory and I can have three books from my distant past, I'd pick *The Magus* by John Fowles, *Pilgrim at Tinker Creek* by Annie Dillard and *How to Keep Your Volkswagen Alive for the Compleat Idiot* by John Muir.

The Magus is a remarkable novel that helped me to understand that my life is shaped by what I believe to be true, not what actually is true. A simple enough discovery but I probably didn't catch on to that one until about 1972. Also, while reading the book, I found certain current events in my life to synchronize with the story to such a point that I figured the book had powers well beyond the usual syntax.

Pilgrim at Tinker Creek has a very simplistic plot: young woman goes out walking around in the woods and sees a bunch of neat stuff, then writes it down. But the way she writes it down! Annie Dillard has an amazing perceptive ability and, in reading her book, I began to learn the mechanisms for seeing better. We live with blinders on. And we miss so much. Annie set me off on the pilgrimage of simple, ever-abundant and unceasing discovery.

And finally, there's *How to Keep Your Volkswagen Alive for the Compleat Idiot*. Now what good would that do me on the desert island? you might ask. I don't even own a VW any more but there was a time where I owned a series of VW Bugs and minibuses, each ranging in purchase price from $50 to $250. They all broke down often and I had little cash, so I learned to fix the contraptions myself. I was a poor mechanic but a good reader. John Muir's classic manual gave me a good attitude, technical advice and a wonderful philosophy about how people and technology might actually survive the presence of each other. My first-edition volume came out in 1969. By 1977 the book was in its nineteenth printing. It's still around and worth a read.

In the intro, John Muir explains the design of his book: "the idea is to never let you get hung up about what to do in any situation." I believe that's the function of most great literature.

Mordecai Richler (writer)

Reading was not one of my boyhood passions. Girls, or rather the absence of girls, drove me to it. When I was thirteen years old, short for my age, more than somewhat pimply, I was terrified of girls. As far as I could make out, they were only attracted to boys who were tall or played for the school basketball team or at least shaved. Unable to qualify on all three counts, I resorted to subterfuge. I set out to call attention to myself by becoming a character. I acquired a pipe, which I chewed on ostentatiously, and made it my business to be seen everywhere, even at school basketball games, pretending to be absorbed by books of daunting significance: say, H.G. Wells's *The Outline of History*, or Paul De Kruif's *Microbe Hunters*, or John Gunther inside one continent or another. I rented these thought-provoking books for three cents a day from a neighbourhood lending library that was across the street from a bowling alley where I used to spot pins four nights a week.

O my God, I would not be thirteen again for anything. The sweetly scented girls of my dreams, wearing lipstick and tight sweaters and nylon stockings, would sail into the bowling alley holding hands with the boys from the basketball team. "Hi," they would call out, giggly, nudging each other, even as I bent over the pins: "How goes the reading?"

The two ladies who ran the lending library, possibly amused by my pretensions, tried to interest me in fiction.

"I want fact. I can't be bothered with *stories*," I protested, waving my pipe at them, affronted.

I knew what novels were, of course. I had read *Scaramouche*, by Rafael Sabatini, at school, as well as *Treasure Island* and some Ellery Queen and a couple of thumpers by G.A. Henty. Before that there had been *Action Comics*, *Captain Marvel*, *Batman* and—for educational reasons—either *Bible Comics* or *Classic Comics*.

Novels, I knew, were mere romantic make-believe, not as bad as poetry, to be fair, but bad enough. Our high-school class master, a dedicated Scot, was foolish enough to try to interest us in poetry. A veteran of World War I, he told us that during the nightly bombardments on the Somme he had fixed a candle to his steel helmet so that he could read poetry in the trenches. A scruffy lot, we were not moved. Instead, we exchanged knowing winks behind that admirable man's back. Small wonder, we agreed, that he drove an ancient Austin and had ended up no better than a high-school teacher.

My aunts consumed historical novels like pastries. My father read *Black Mask* and *True Detective*. My mother would read anything on a Jewish subject, preferably by I.J. Singer or Sholem Asch, though she would never forgive Asch for having written *The Nazarene*, never mind *Mary and the Apostle*. My older brother kept a novel, *Topper Takes a Trip*, secure under his mattress in the bedroom we shared, assuring me that it was placed at just such an angle on the springs that if it were moved so much as a millimetre in his absence he would know and bloody well make me pay for it.

I fell ill with a childhood disease, I no longer remember which, but one obviously meant as a rebuke for those girls in tight sweaters who continued to ignore me. Never mind, they would mourn at my funeral, burying me with my pipe. Too late they would say, "Boy, was he ever an intellectual!"

Aunts, who still took me for a child, brought me really dumb books *in which animals talked*. I was appalled. But the ladies from the lending library also dropped off books for me at our house. The real stuff. Fact-filled. Providing me with the inside dope on Theodore Hertzl's childhood and *Brazil Yesterday, Today, and Tomorrow*. One day they brought me a novel: *All Quiet on the Western Front*, by Erich

Maria Remarque. The painting on the jacket that was taped to the book showed a soldier wearing what was unmistakably a German army helmet. What was this, I wondered, some sort of bad joke?

Nineteen forty-four that was, and I devoutly wished every German on the face of the earth an excruciating death. The invasion of France had not yet begun, but I cheered every Russian counter-attack, each German city bombed and, with the help of a map tacked to my bedroom wall, followed the progress of the Canadian troops fighting their way up the Italian boot. Boys from our street were already among the fallen. Izzy Draper's uncle. Harvey Kugelmass's older brother. The boy who was supposed to marry Gita Holtzman.

All Quiet on the Western Front lay unopened on my bed for two days. A time bomb ticking away, though I hardly suspected it. Rather than read a novel, a novel written by a German, I tuned in to radio soap operas in the afternoons: "Ma Perkins," "Pepper Young's Family." I organized a new baseball league for short players who didn't shave yet, appointing myself commissioner, the first Canadian to be so honoured. Sifting through a stack of my father's back issues of *Popular Mechanics*, I was sufficiently inspired to invent a spaceship and fly to Mars, where I was adored by everybody, especially the girls. Finally I was driven to picking up *All Quiet on the Western Front* out of boredom. I never expected that a mere novel, a stranger's tale, could actually be dangerous, creating such turbulence in my life. About Germans. About my own monumental ignorance of the world. About what novels were.

At the age of thirteen in 1944, happily as yet untainted by English 101, I couldn't tell you whether Remarque's novel was (a) a slice of life, (b) symbolic, (c) psychological or (d) seminal. I couldn't even say if it was well or badly written. In fact, as I recall, it didn't seem to be "written" at all. It just flowed. Now, of course, I understand that writing which doesn't advertise itself is often art of a very high order. It doesn't come easily. But at the time I wasn't capable of making such distinctions.

I also had no notion of how *All Quiet on the Western Front* rated critically as a war novel. I hadn't read Stendhal or Tolstoy or Crane or Hemingway. I hadn't even heard of them. But what I did know was that, hating Germans with a passion, I had read only twenty, maybe thirty pages before the author had seduced me into identifying with my enemy, nineteen-year- old Paul Bäumer, thrust into the bloody trenches of World War I with his schoolmates: Müller, Kemmerich and the reluctant Joseph Behm, one of the first to fall. As if that weren't sufficiently unsettling, the author, having won my love for Paul, my enormous concern for his survival, betrayed me in the last dreadful paragraphs of his book:

> He fell in October 1918, on a day that was so quiet and still on the whole front, that the army report confined itself to a single sentence: All quiet on the Western Front.
>
> He had fallen forward and lay on the earth as though sleeping. Turning him over one saw that he could not have suffered long; his face had an expression of calm, as though glad the end had come.

I felt easier about my affection for the German soldier Paul Bäumer once I had been told by the ladies from the lending library that when Hitler came to power in 1932 he burned all of Erich Maria Remarque's books, and in 1938 took away his German citizenship. Obviously Hitler grasped that novels could be dangerous, something I had learned when I was only thirteen years old. He burned them; I began to devour them. I started to read at the breakfast table and on streetcars, often missing my stop, and in bed with the benefit of a flashlight. It got me into trouble. I understood, for the first time, that I didn't live in the centre of the world but had been born into a working-class family in an unimportant country far from the cities of light: London, Paris, New York. Of course this wasn't my fault; it was my inconsiderate parents who were to blame. But there was, I now realized, a larger world that could be available to me, even though—to my mother's despair—I had been born left-handed, ate with my elbows on the table and had failed once more to come rank one in school.

Preparing myself for the *rive gauche*, I bought a blue beret, which I didn't dare wear even in the house if anybody else was home. I looked at but lacked the courage to buy a cigarette holder. But the next time I took Goldie Zimmerman to a downtown movie and then out to Dinty Moore's for toasted tomato sandwiches, I suggested that, instead of milkshakes, we each order a glass of *vin ordinaire*. "Are you crazy?" she asked.

As my parents bickered at the supper table, trapped in concerns far too mundane for the likes of me—what to do if Dworkin raised the rent again, how to manage my brother's college fees—I sat with, but actually apart from them in the kitchen, enthralled, reading for the first time, "All happy families are alike but an unhappy family is unhappy after its own fashion."

Ted Harrison (writer/illustrator)

The time was the depths of the Great Depression and there was precious little to stir the soul. My father was an ill-paid coal miner and where he got the wherewithal to buy a set of encyclopedias I shall never know.

These magical books entitled *The Wonderland of Knowledge* filled my mind with a world I had never even dreamed of. I read each of them from cover to cover at the age of nine years.

Tansy and Bobbles on Fable Island introduced me to the wisdom of Aesop. Articles about writers led me to such great books as *Treasure Island*, *The Pilgrim's Progress* and *The Call of the Wild*. I became interested in other cultures and studied their religions and environment. Years later when I travelled through India and Africa those early introductions came to life.

When I finally came to the Yukon Territory it was as if Jack London and Robert W. Service had prepared me for the experience. While the Depression raged we were too poor to travel far. When the war came, travelling was an impossibility for most people.

Every month for a full year those wonderful encyclopedias arrived and each created an intensity of great excitement. I was given the key to unlock a door of opportunity to another world more beautiful, more wondrous and much more stimulating than that provided by the reality of the thirties.

Soon the Depression was over only to be exchanged for a war which proved worse than the scourge which had gone before. My encyclopedias became a well of sanity into which I frequently dipped. As my world of reading enlarged and other interests came along, I never forgot those precious volumes which enriched my childhood. Many doors of learning and experience have opened up to me since, but the first door is always the most important and the most memorable.

June Callwood (writer)

I have been embarrassed to respond because I wasn't impressed, wakened, altered, by any one book. My mother, who spoke and read only French when I was born, thought to direct my development as a unilingual Anglophone by her purchase of a set of books, the Harvard Classics, which were the only books in our house. I could read at age four but for years Macaulay's *Essays*, Milton's *Collected Poems* and Alexandre Dumas were incomprehensible. What excited me, age eight, was my Grandfather Callwood's collection called the *Books of*

Knowledge. They included such selections as Knitting, Gibraltar and Epicurus. I could not have grasped much, but what I did learn was that the world is wonderful. My sense of curiosity, which was born in my grandfather's house, led me straight into journalism and into a life that has been infinitely worth the candle.

Camilla Gryski (writer)

Tove Jansson's *Comet in Moominland* is one of the books I still have from my childhood, one of the dozen shabby volumes sitting on the top shelf of a bookcase. I quite often stop and consider this small collection. There are a couple of nurse stories, and one of Enid Blyton's Famous Five adventures. Susan Coolidge's *What Katy Did* and *What Katy Did Next* inscribed to me on my ninth birthday from my English grandparents. And *Peter Pan*, *Alice in Wonderland*, *Gulliver's Travels* and *Comet in Moominland*. Neverland. Wonderland. Lilliput. Moominland: countries of my childhood imagination.

I have known Peter and Wendy, Alice, Gulliver and Moomintroll and Sniff for so long that it is difficult to recapture my first reactions to their stories. Only when I look at the illustrations do I sometimes catch the shadow of an emotion.

Tove Jansson's own illustrations for *Comet in Moominland* must have left a deep impression on me. When I opened the book after many years, probably to read it to one of my own children, it was as though I had never left that world. Moominmamma and the Snork Maiden, the brave Moomintroll and the Muskrat philosopher are all there. Snufkin the traveller plays "All small beasts should have bows in their tails," to an audience of small creatures, water-spooks and tree spirits. The intrepid adventurers use stilts to cross the eerie dry sea bed, while the fiery comet grows ever larger in the darkened sky above them.

Worlds like Moominland, lovingly created with words and pictures, have drawn me into their realities all my life. There are great riches for any traveller willing to suspend disbelief and visit the lands of fantasy. Strange landscapes, wonderful magical happenings, brave quests and fierce battles—these are the riches that glitter. They feed the imagination and beguile the mind's eye. But underneath the otherworldly trappings lie additional riches—truths and perceptions that are at the heart of our own reality. That is why the best children's fantasy resonates for the adult as well as the child. And why we often travel far in space and time only to come face to face with ourselves.

Jean Little (writer)

What a difficult task you have set me! The problem is not, of course, that I can't call a memorable book to mind but that I have dozens crying out to be named.

So here's my best effort. You are at liberty to throw out as much as you like. Remembering was spooky. Remembering myself as a reading child and teenager and talking to Pat about her memories was spooky. Reading is still a great love of mine, even though I now listen to Talking Books, but reading was my ruling passion during those early years. Although I'm still moved by many books, then they were the air I breathed, why I woke up, what I thought about day and night. Such intense joy is only available to me now, I think, when I am writing.

My first thought, on receiving the invitation to write on the one book I read as a child which changed my life and still has power to move me deeply, was to tell, once again, about the love of *The Secret Garden* by Frances Hodgson Burnett. It was and is, for me, a story filled with transforming power and deep delight. It told me that I was not alone in feeling selfish, lonely and ugly, that solitary pleasures could be soul-satisfying and that, if I kept trying to learn, I, like Mary Lennox, might master the language of friendship and find the key to the garden of belonging.

But I have written so much about that book. I decided to tell about another of those I read and reread as a child. But which? The titles which are in contention are many and various. My love of poetry was fostered by the hymns and psalms I sang and read in church and at home but also by my very own copy of Robert Louis Stevenson's *A Child's Garden of Verses* given to me when I was seven. I still have the battered copy and I can recite many of the poems without even having consciously learned them by heart.

But I cannot bear to restrict myself to those poems. Another children's novel which came close to equalling *The Secret Garden* for me was *Jane of Lantern Hill* by L.M. Montgomery. Jane, like me and Mary Lennox, was an outsider. She lived not in magical Prince Edward Island, a place so glorious it was hardly credible that it was within Canada, but in Toronto where I, too, had lived for a year. Her decidedly evil grandmother ran the house where Jane and her mother lived. My grandmother lived with us and, although she was not nearly as malevolent as Jane's, she had her moments. She was angry though and tired, not sweetly poisonous, and I discovered that I was far more fortunate than Jane. Despite her ninny of a mother and her charming but only slightly less stupid father, I thought Jane's story was fine and read it often. Jane had a solid reality which other Montgomery heroines never quite matched, for all their romantic appeal, and she, with Mary, led me, in years to come, to write stories of children who don't fit. My fan-mail tells me that every child alive believes himself or herself to belong in that category.

As a teenager, though, I found other books that wounded me and healed me and imprinted their language on me forever. *Cry the Beloved Country* by Alan Paton, *How Green Was My Valley* by Richard Llewellyn, *Precious Bane* by Mary Webb, and *Jane Eyre* by Charlotte Brontë enlarged my heart and delighted my inner ear. They were such tremendously strong stories and they gave me such vivid friends. If only I could write like that! If only I could read them again for the first time!

Kati Rekai (writer)

When I was born, in Budapest, Hungary, reading was a way of life. This phenomenon was best expressed by my teenage brother, I believe, who, before going to bed at night, would arrange about fifteen books on his blanket. "Why do you do that?" I asked. "You won't be able to read so many books during one night." "I know," he answered, "but it feels so good."

He was right. Books around us feel good. This is why, although I admire school libraries, children should have their own books, so they can turn again and again to their favourite stories.

In Hungary, we started high school at the age of ten. School hours lasted from 8 a.m. to 1 p.m. and we had no afternoon classes. We had plenty of time for homework, sports and mainly for reading. By the time we were ten, we had digested the tales of the Grimm brothers, Hans Christian Andersen, Mark Twain, Jules Verne, Erich Kästner (the original illustration of his series *Emil and the Detectives* can be seen in the Trier collection of the Art Gallery of Ontario) and, of course, the works of Hungarian storytellers.

Among the Hungarian writers whose work ranged from historical to modern, an example is Ferenč Molnár whose play (*The Guardsman*) opened the National Arts Centre in Ottawa; and whose other plays have been included in the Stratford and Shaw Festivals.

Our other reading ranged from Somerset Maugham to Boccaccio, from Goethe to Zola, from Chekhov to Shakespeare, from Mazo de la Roche to Molière, from Shaw to Ibsen. There was also, I confess, the Kurtz Mahler series (forerunner of Harlequin Romances) which we read, or rather girls read, at night, under the covers, away from the eagle eyes of our parents.

I clearly remember being influenced by Russian writers and by the letters of Catherine the Great. For a while I wanted a career similar to hers, as she was my namesake, but later I changed my mind for obvious reasons.

Eberhard H. Zeidler (architect)

As a boy I devoured books which were in rich supply in our home in Germany. I read Wilhelm Busch, who wrote poems that were deceptively simple and easily memorized. They were supposed to be for children, but when I got older I realized they had much wiser and more far-reaching meanings. His cautionary tales about Max and Moritz—two very naughty little boys—were particularly delightful.

One who followed in the footsteps of Busch was Walter Trier whose illustrations I adored. It was uncanny to discover that the aftermath of the war had blown him very near to me in Canada.

Gustav Freitag was a favourite too and so was the North American Jack London; his *The Call of the Wild* touched me deeply.

A favourite writer for young boys was Karl May. His adventure stories were set in the far-off New World of horses, Indians, buffaloes, teepees, canoes and wild untamed forests. The indomitable hero of all these books was an adventurer called Old Shatterhand. The books presented the new World as a place of dramatic colour, high adventure and clever, helpful Native people, most of all Winnetou, the friend of Old Shatterhand.

My father was a teacher and painter. He had wonderfully illustrated books. I remember lying about on the floor, leafing over page after page of reproductions of painters such as Henri Matisse, Caspar David Friedrich, Lovis Corinth and the like.

Among my father's books I also read some that I only partly understood—Goethe, Schiller, Herder and the like. After 1945 Russian soldiers burned them in the backyard of our home, so we were told, but the memory of all those books still remains as irreplaceable baggage which I carry with me to this day.

Matthew Gaasenbeek (businessman)

I started reading in earnest in grade 3 and never stopped. Certainly Jack London's books were an inspiration to me. During World War II, when I was about thirteen, my dad bought me a complete set of his works translated into Dutch. I learned about the North, the Cree Indians, the Hudson's Bay Company, how to start a fire when all is wet and cold (use birch bark) and most importantly, the feeling of the North and its people.

As a result, when I came to Canada it was in a way like coming home!

Another author who deeply influenced my life was Louis Bromfield and his books *Malabar Farm* and *Pleasant Valley*.

These books told how he used his movie and book revenues to purchase worn-out farms in Ohio and restore them.

This became my goal. I too purchased a worn-out and ravaged farm some thirty-five years ago and restored it both as a farm and a nature reserve. The farm became the focal point of our family and the families of my five brothers. Many years later my wife and I made a pilgrimage to Malabar Farm and to Bromfield's grave at his beloved farm in Ohio.

But now that you've got me going, there are so many books which come to mind.

The Heart of the Hunter: This book, by Laurens Van der Post, sensitized me to the depth of feeling and wisdom embedded in ancient religions; in this case the Bushmen, who are probably the most ancient people alive today.

Gone with the Wind: I was sixteen and just learning English. I struggled through this book with a Dutch/English dictionary—it took me weeks. It was a crash course in English and I learned a lot about the South and American history. From then on I became interested in North American history. Having just gotten through the Occupation and the hungry winter of 1944/45, I thought Scarlett O'Hara was a wonderful survivor who looked after her family and herself the best way she knew. It was not until much later that I realized some people thought her terrible.

The Yearling: I could relate to the loneliness of the little boy Jody.

The Well of Loneliness: A painful autobiography of an upper-class British lady who found out she was a lesbian. I was eighteen at the time and it deeply sensitized me forever to the pain of some gay people.

Upon reflection, I think books have the greatest influence on you when you are young and they fill empty quarters of your mind, awareness and being.

From there on, books will still influence you, but not in quite the same deep emotional manner.

Other authors loom in my imagination as ghosts who helped make me what I am today: Toynbee, Schopenhauer, Carl Jung, Socrates, Marcus Aurelius, Prescott, Darwin, the Bible, and so many others. I salute them all as gods who helped me find my way. I could not live without books and would die if I could not read.

Stephen Clarkson (writer)

Although I spent my childhood, youth and adolescence on an Ontario farm, the seventh son of a Toronto-born father, I was brought up English. Along with the rest of my siblings, I had been born in England and though the family "came back" to Canada when I was an infant, our household remained under the cultural hegemony of my British-born mother who saw to it that my mind was stocked with Britannica.

I remember *Our Island Story* with illustrations of Queen Boadicea wreaking havoc among the serried ranks of the invading Romans. I remember sitting in my father's lap as he read me Kipling's Mowgli stories. Later when I could read for myself, I subscribed to *Boy's Own.* I was engrossed by the children's adventure stories written by Arthur Ransome that I inherited from my older brothers. And I plunged into the glories of empire through the heroics gallantly depicted in the G.A. Henty series about Clive in India or Gordon in Khartoum.

One book I remember not for its contents but for its title. My very devout godmother sent me from London for my birthday—probably my eighth as it was just at the end of World War II in which my elder brothers had fought with what their youngest sibling assumed must have been great gallantry—a book which, at first glance, I understood to be *Johnny and the Ten Commandos*. Alas, I did not make it beyond the table of contents where I discovered that the volume was really about *Johnny and the Ten Commandments*. My interest in spiritual uplift being somewhat less than my fascination with military adventure, the gift went unread—no doubt to the everlasting detriment of my spiritual development.

In short, my childhood reading constituted a magnificent mispreparation for life as a Canadian. An upbringing in unreality, it was preparation for a society ruled by a code of values completely foreign to the individualistic, competitive, tough—in short, Americanized—world that I was destined to enter as an adult.

Appendix: Book Lists

I. A Chronology of Important Children's Books

BEFORE 1800

Oral tradition, stories, songs

The Fables of Aesop
Folk-tales, Greek myths, legends
Jack the Giant Killer
Beowolf
Native tales and legends
The Bible
Homer: *The Odyssey* and *The Iliad*
The Legend of King Arthur and the Round Table
Johann Amos Comenius: *Orbis Pictus* (Painted World) (first picture book for children)
John Bunyan: *The Pilgrim's Progress*
Jean de la Fontaine: *Fables*
Charles Perrault: *Tales of Mother Goose*
Arabian Nights Entertainment (first English translation)
Daniel Defoe: *Robinson Crusoe*
Jonathan Swift: *Gulliver's Travels*
Mme. de Beaument: *Beauty and the Beast*
Christian Felix Weiss: *Der Kinderfreund*
John Newbery: *A Little Pretty Pocket Book & Little Goody Two Shoes*

1800-1850

Brothers Grimm: *Fairy Tales* (first English translation)
Sarah and Jane Taylor: *Original Poems for Infant Minds*
Jane Austen: *Sense and Sensibility; Pride and Prejudice*
Johann Wyss: *Swiss Family Robinson*
Sir Walter Scott: *Ivanhoe*
James Fenimore Cooper: *The Last of the Mohicans; The Spy*
Catherine Sinclair: *Holiday House*
Charles Dickens: *Oliver Twist* (1838); *A Christmas Carol* (1843)
Sara Coleridge: *Phantasmion*
Edward Lear: *A Book of Nonsense* (1846); *More Nonsense* (1872); *Laughable Lyrics* (1877)
First great illustrators: Walter Crane, Randolph Caldecott, Kate Greenaway
Hans Christian Andersen: *Fairy Tales*
Robert Browning: *The Pied Piper of Hamelin*
Charlotte Brontë: *Jane Eyre*
Emily Brontë: *Wuthering Heights*

1850-1900

Elizabeth Wetherell: *The Wide Wide World*
Catharine Parr Traill: *Canadian Crusoes* (first Canadian children's book)
Charlotte Young: *The Daisy Chain*
Henry Wadsworth Longfellow: *Hiawatha; Evangeline*

Martha Finley: *Elsie Dinsmore*
Thomas Hughes: *Tom Brown's Schooldays*
Charles Kingsley: *The Water-Babies; Westward Ho!*
Lewis Carroll: *Alice's Adventures in Wonderland* & *Through the Looking Glass*
Mary Elizabeth Mapes Dodge: *Hans Brinker*
Horatio Alger: *Ragged Dick*
Louisa May Alcott: *Little Women; Little Men; Eight Cousins*
Thomas Aldrich: *The Story of a Bad Boy*
George MacDonald: *At the Back of the North Wind*
Susan Coolidge: *What Katy Did*
G.A. Henty: *The Young Settlers*
Mark Twain: *The Adventures of Huckleberry Finn; The Adventures of Tom Sawyer (1876); The Prince and the Pauper*
Anna Sewell: *Black Beauty*
Randolph Caldecott: *The Diverting History of John Gilpin*
Margaret Sidney: *The Five Little Peppers and How They Grew*
Joel Chandler Harris: *Uncle Remus*
Howard Pyle: *The Merry Adventures of Robin Hood*
Oscar Wilde: *The Happy Prince and Other Stories*
Jules Verne: *20,000 Leagues under the Sea; Around the World in 80 Days*
Robert Louis Stevenson: *Treasure Island; Kidnapped; A Child's Garden of Verses; Dr. Jekyll and Mr. Hyde*
Johanna Spyri: *Heidi*
H. Rider Haggard: *King Solomon's Mines*
Carlo Collodi: *The Adventures of Pinocchio* (first English translation)
Joseph Jacobs: *English Fairy Tales*

LATE CENTURY

Frances Hodgson Burnett: *Little Lord Fauntleroy*
Arthur Conan Doyle: *The Adventures of Sherlock Holmes*
Rudyard Kipling: *The Jungle Books*; *Kim*, (1901); *Just So Stories* (1902)
Ernest Thompson Seton: *Wild Animals I Have Known*
Helen Bannerman: *The Story of Little Black Sambo*
E. Nesbit: *The Story of the Treasure Seekers; Five Children and It* (1902); *The Amulet* (1906); *The Railway Children*
Hilaire Belloc: *The Bad Child's Book of Beasts*; or *Cautionary Tales*

1900-1920

L. Frank Baum: *The Wonderful Wizard of Oz* (and sequels)
Beatrix Potter: *The Tale of Peter Rabbit* (and sequels)
L. Leslie Brooke: *Johnny Crow's Garden*
Kate Douglas Wiggin: *Rebecca of Sunnybrook Farm*
Laura Lee Hope: *The Bobbsey Twins* (and sequels)
J.M. Barrie: *Peter Pan*
Gene Stratton Porter: *A Girl of the Limberlost*
Jean Webster: *Daddy Long-Legs*
Howard Garis: *Uncle Wiggly's Adventures*
Lucy Maud Montgomery: *Anne of Green Gables* (1908) (and sequels); *Emily of New Moon* (1923) (and sequels)
Kenneth Grahame: *The Wind in the Willows*
Frances Hodgson Burnett: *A Little Princess* (1905); *The Secret Garden* (1910)
Hugh Lofting: *The Story of Dr. Dolittle*
Eleanor H. Porter: *Pollyanna*

Arthur Rackham (illustrator): e.g., *Mother Goose*; *Peter Pan*; *Rip Van Winkle*
Edgar Rice Burroughs: *Tarzan of the Apes*
O. Henry: *The Ransom of Red Chief*
Norman Lindsay: *The Magic Pudding*

1920-1940

Rupert Bear (illus.) Mary Tourtel (first appears in London's *Daily Express*) (1920)
Carl Sandburg: *Rootabaga Stories*; *Abe Lincoln Grows Up*
Hendrik Willem Van Loon: *The Story of Mankind* (first Newbery medal, 1922)
Margery Williams Bianco: *The Velveteen Rabbit*
Richmal Crompton: *Just William*
Enid Blyton: *Child Whisperers*
A.A. Milne: *When We Were Very Young*; *Winnie-the-Pooh* (and sequels)
Rachel Field: *Hitty, Her First Hundred Years* (1929)
Franklin W. Dixon: *The Tower Treasure* (first Hardy Boys book) (and sequels)
Felix Saltern: *Bambi* (first English trans.)
Wanda Gág: *Millions of Cats*
Arthur Ransome: *Swallows and Amazons* (1930) (and sequels)
Carolyn Keene: *The Hidden Staircase* (1930) (first Nancy Drew book) (and sequels)
Erich Kästner: *Emil and the Detectives* (first English trans.)
Laura Ingalls Wilder: *Little House in the Big Woods* (and sequels)
Jean de Brunhoff: *The Story of Babar*
Marjorie Flack: *The Story about Ping*
Laura Ingalls Wilder: *Little House on the Prairie* (1933) (and sequels)
P.L. Travers: *Mary Poppins*
Enid Bagnold: *National Velvet*
Carol Ryrie Brink: *Caddie Woodlawn*
Munro Leaf: *The Story of Ferdinand* (1936)
Peter and the Wolf: a symphonic story by Sergei Prokofiev (1936)
Dr. Seuss: *And to Think I Saw It on Mulberry Street* (1937); *Green Eggs and Ham*; *The Cat in the Hat*; others
Arthur Ransome: *Pigeon Post* (first Carnegie medal winner, 1937)
Jerry Siegel and Joe Shuster: "Superman" for Action Comics (1938)
"Batman" (1939); "Wonder Woman" (1941)
Noel Streatfeild: *Ballet Shoes*
J.R.R. Tolkien: *The Hobbit*
Walt Disney: (film) *Snow White and the Seven Dwarfs*
T.H. White: *The Sword in the Stone*
Ludwig Bemelmans: *Madeline* (and sequels)
Elizabeth Enright: *Thimble Summer*
Marjorie Kinnan Rawlings: *The Yearling*
Robert L. May: *Rudolph the Red Nosed Reindeer*

1940-1970

Eleanor Estes: *The Moffats* (and sequels)
Eric Knight: *Lassie-Come-Home*
Geoffrey Trease: *Cue for Treason*
Mary O'Hara: *My Friend Flicka*
Walter Farley: *The Black Stallion* (and sequels)
H.A. Rey: *Curious George* (1941) (and sequels)
Robert McCloskey: *Make Way for Ducklings* (1941)
Margaret Wise Brown: *The Runaway Bunny* (1942); *Goodnight Moon* (1947)
Virginia Lee Burton: *The Little House* (1942)

Antoine de Saint-Exupéry: *The Little Prince* (1943)
Esther Forbes: *Johnny Tremain*
Astrid Lindgren: *Pippi Longstocking*
Sydney Taylor: *All-of-a-Kind Family* (and sequels)
Anne Frank: *Diary of a Young Girl* (1947)
George Orwell: *Animal Farm* (1945); *1984* (1948)
William Pène du Bois: *The Twenty-One Balloons* (1948)
C. Day Lewis: *The Otterbury Incident* (1948)
Marguerite de Angeli: *Bright April* (1946); *The Door in the Wall* (1949)
E.B. White: *Stuart Little* (1945); *Charlotte's Web* (1952); *The Trumpet of the Swan* (1970)
Rosemary Sutcliff: *The Eagle of the Ninth* (and sequels); *The Lantern Bearers* (1959); *The Witch's Brat* (1970)
C.S. Lewis: The Narnia books: *The Lion, the Witch and the Wardrobe* (1950) (and sequels)
J.D. Salinger: *The Catcher in the Rye* (1951)
John Wyndham: *The Day of the Triffids* (1951); *The Chrysalids*
Iona and Peter Opie: *The Language and Lore of School Children*
J.R.R. Tolkien: *The Lord of the Rings* (1954)
Shirley Hughes: *Lucy and Tom's Day*
Gene Zion: *Harry, the Dirty Dog*
Beverly Cleary: *Fifteen* (1956); *Ramona* (1952)
Mary Norton: *The Borrowers* (1953) (and sequels)
Fred Gipson: *Old Yeller* (1956)
Jean Craighead George: *My Side of the Mountain* (1959); *Julie of the Wolves* (1972)
Philippa Pearce: *Tom's Midnight Garden* (1958)
Michael Bond: *A Bear Called Paddington* (1960)
Scott O'Dell: *Island of the Blue Dolphin* (1960)
Robert Heinlein: *Stranger in a Strange Land* (1961)
Frank Herbert: *Dune* (1961)
Norton Juster: *The Phantom Tollbooth* (1961)
Madeleine L'Engle: *A Wrinkle in Time* (1962)
Charlotte Zolotow: *Mr. Rabbit and the Lovely Present,* (illus.) Maurice Sendak (1962)
Shel Silverstein: *The Giving Tree* (1964)
Blair Lent: *Tikki Tikki Tembo*
Roger Lancelyn Green: *The Adventures of Robin Hood*
Ezra Jack Keats: *The Snowy Day* (1962)
Maurice Sendak: *Where the Wild Things Are* (1963)
Louise Fitzhugh: *Harriet the Spy* (1964)
Ray Bradbury: *Fahrenheit 451* (1967)
Roald Dahl: *Charlie and the Chocolate Factory* (1964); *The BFG* (1982)
Don Freeman: *Corduroy* (1968)
Samuel Goodrich: *Higglety, Pigglety Pop!,* (illus.) Maurice Sendak (1967)
George Clutesi: *Son of Raven; Son of Deer: Fables of the Tse-Shaht People* (first book of native stories written in English by a First Nations person)
E.L. Konigsburg: *From the Mixed Up Files of Mrs. Basil E. Frankweiler* (1967)
Jill Paton Walsh: *Fireweed* (1969)
William H. Armstrong: *Sounder* (1969)
Theodore Taylor: *The Cay* (1969)
Eric Carle: *The Very Hungry Caterpillar* (1969)

AFTER 1970

John Burningham: *Mr. Gumpy's Outing* (1970)
Betsy Byars: *Summer of the Swans* (1970)
Judy Blume: *Are You There, God? It's Me, Margaret (*1970); *Blubber* (1974)
Virginia Hamilton: *The Planet of Junior Brown* (1971); *M.C. Higgins, The Great* (1974) *The People Could Fly: American Black Folk Tales* (1985)
Richard Adams: *Watership Down*
Robert Newton Peck: *A Day No Pigs Would Die*
Nina Bawden: *Carrie's War* (1973)
Paula Fox: *The Slave Dancer* (1974)
Robert Cormier: *The Chocolate War* (1974)
Shel Silverstein: *Where the Sidewalk Ends* (1974)
Richard Peck: *Are You in the House Alone?* (1976)
Mildred Taylor: *Roll of Thunder, Hear My Cry (*1976)
Katherine Paterson: *Bridge to Terabithia* (1977); *Jacob Have I Loved* (1981)
William Steig: *The Amazing Bone*
David McCord: *Selected Poems* (1977)
Margaret Sidney: *The Five Little Peppers and How They Grew* (1981) (and sequels)
Mordecai Richler: *Jacob Two-Two Meets the Hooded Fang* (and sequels)
Janet and Allan Ahlberg: *Each Peach, Pear, Plum; The Jolly Postman (*1986)
Chris Van Allsburg: *The Garden of Abdul Gasazi* (1979); *The Polar Express* (1986)
Quentin Blake: *Mister Magnolia* (1980)
Robert Munsch: *The Paper Bag Princess* (1980); *Thomas' Snowsuit* (1985)
Maurice Sendak: *Outside Over There*
Lynne Reid Banks: *The Indian in the Cupboard* (1981, sequels)
Nancy Willard: *A Visit to William Blake's Inn* (first poetry book to win Newbery medal)
Walter Myers: *The Young Landlords* (1979); *Fallen Angels* (1988)
Cynthia Voigt: *Homecoming* (1981); *Dicey's Song* (1982)
Joy Kogawa: *Naomi's Road* (1986)
Patricia MacLachlan: *Sarah Plain and Tall* (1985)
Jack Prelutsky: *New Kid on the Block* (1984)
Graeme Base: *Animalia* (1986); *The Eleventh Hour* (1989)
Paul Fleischman: *A Joyful Noise* (1988)
David Macaulay: *The Way Things Work* (1988)
Mary Norton: T*he Borrowers* (1989) (and sequels)
Lois Lowry: *Number the Stars* (1989); *The Giver* (1993)
Anne Fine: *Mrs. Doubtfire* (1987); *Goggle-Eyes* (1989)
Tim Wynne-Jones: *Some of the Kinder Planets* (1994)
Jerry Spinelli: *Maniac Magee* (1990)
Phyllis Reynolds Naylor: *Shiloh* (1991)
Cynthia Rylant: *Missing May* (1992)

II. Notable Early Children's Books about Canada or by Canadians

1800–1900

Philip Henry Gosse: *The Canadian Naturalist* (1840)
Frederick Marryat: *Settlers in Canada* (1844)
Catharine Parr Traill: *Canadian Crusoes*
R.M. Ballantyne: *The Young Fur Traders; Ungava: A Tale of Esquimaux* Land (1856–58)
G.A. Henty: *With Wolfe in Canada*
Miss Grove: *Little Grace*
Mayne Reid: *The Young Voyageurs*
James de Mille: *The B.O.W.C.; Lost in the Fog; The Boys of Grand Pré School*
James Oxley: *Up Among the Ice Floes; The Wreckers of Sable Island*
Margaret Marshall Saunders: *Beautiful Joe*
Egerton Ryerson Young: *Three Boys in the Wild North Land Summer; Children of the Forest: A Story of Indian Love*
C. Phillips-Wolley: *Gold, Gold on the Caribou*
Ernest Thompson Seton: *Wild Animals I Have Known*

AFTER 1900

Charles G.D. Roberts: *The Kindred of the Wild*
Ernest Thompson Seton: *Two Little Savages*
Lucy Maud Montgomery: *Anne of Green Gables* (and sequels); *Emily of New Moon* (and sequels)
Ralph Connor: *Glengarry School Days* (sequels)
Cyrus Macmillan (ed): *Canadian Wonder Tales, Canadian Fairy Tales*
Roderick Haig-Brown: *The Whale People*
Grey Owl: *The Adventures of Sajo and Her Beaver People*
Catharine Anthony Clark: *The Golden Pine Cone*
Farley Mowat: *Lost in the Barrens; The Dog Who Wouldn't Be; Owls in the Family*
William Kurelek: *A Prairie Boy's Summer; A Prairie Boy's Winter*
Edith Lambert Sharp: *Nkwala*
James Houston: *Tikta'liktak: An Eskimo Legend; The White Archer*
Margaret Laurence: *The Olden Days Coat*
Silver Donald Cameron: *The Baitchopper*
Holling Clancy Holling: *Paddle-to-the-Sea*
Sheila Burnford: *The Incredible Journey*
George Clutesi: *Son of Raven; Son of Deer: Fables of the Tse-Shaht People*
Ronald Melzak: *The Day Tuk Became a Hunter and Other Eskimo Stories*
Elizabeth Cleaver (ed.): *The Wind Has Wings; How Summer Came to Canada*
Ruth Nicols: *A Walk Out of the World; The Marrow of the World*
Markoosie: *Harpoon of the Hunter*
Shizuye Takashima: *A Child in Prison Camp*
Emerson and David Coatsworth (ed.): *The Adventures of Nanabush: Ojibway Indian Stories*
Basil Johnston: *Tales the Elders Told: Ojibway Legends*

Favourite 100 (approximately) ent Canadian English Books for nger Children

lderson: *Bonnie athers You're Driving Me ers,* (illus.) Fiona Garrick

Andrews: *The Very Last First Time,* (illus.) Ian Wallace

Warabé Aska: *Who Goes to the Park?*

Jo Bannatyne-Cugnet: *A Prairie Alphabet,* (illus.) Yvette Moore

Michael Bedard: *Emily,* (illus.) Barbara Cooney

Pierre Berton: *The Secret World of Og*

Ann Blades: *Mary of Mile 18*

Jo Ellen Bogart: *Gifts,* (illus.) Barbara Reid

Paulette Bourgeois: *Franklin in the Dark,* (illus.) Brenda Clark

William Roy Brownridge: *The Moccasin Goalie*

Geoff Butler: *The Killick: A Newfoundland Story*

Katherine Burton: *One Grey Mouse,* (illus.) Kim Fernandes

Roch Carrier: *The Hockey Sweater,* (illus.) Sheldon Cohen

Elizabeth Cleaver: *Petrouchka*

Jill Creighton: *Maybe a Monster,* (illus.) Ruth Ohi

Peter Cummings: *Out on the Ice in the Middle of the Bay,* (illus.) Alice Priestly

Virginia Davis: *Simply Ridiculous,* (illus.) Russ Willms

David Day: *The Emperor's Panda,* (illus.) Eric Beddows

Clive Dobson: *Fred's TV*

Ricardo Keens-Douglas: *The Nutmeg Princess*, (illus.) Anouchka Galouchko

Mary Alice Downie: *How the Devil Got His Cat,* (illus.) Jillian Hulme Gilliland

Frank B. Edwards: *A Dog Called Dad* (illus.) John Bianchi

Joan Finnigan: *The Dog Who Wouldn't Be Left Behind*, (illus.) Steve Beinicke

Priscilla Galloway: *When You Were Little and I Was Big,* (illus.) Heather Collins; *Aleta and the Queen; Atalanta: The Fastest Runner in the World*

Marie-Louise Gay: *Moonbeam on a Cat's Ear*

Betty Gibson: *The Story of Little Quack,* (illus.) Kady Macdonald Denton

Don Gillmor: *The Fabulous Song,* (illus.) Marie-Louise Gay

Phoebe Gilman: *Something from Nothing; The Gypsy Princess*

Rachna Gilmore: *WhenIwasalittlegirl,* (illus.) Sally J.K. Davies; *Lights for Gita* (illus.) Alice Priestly

Celia Godkin: *Wolf Island*

Linda Granfield: *In Flanders Fields,* (illus.) Janet Wilson

Nan Gregory: *How Smudge Came,* (illus.) Ron Lightburn

Linda Hendry: *Mrs. Mortifee's Mouse*

Monica Hughes: *Little Fingerling,* (illus.) Brenda Clark

Hazel Hutchins: *Tess*, (illus.) Ruth Ohi

Teddy Jam: *The Year of Fire,* (illus.) Ian Wallace

Sharon Jennings: *When Jeremiah Met Mrs. Ming,* (illus.) Mireille Levert

Dyar Kaur Khalsa: *How Pizza Came to Our Town; Tales of a Gambling Grandma*

Thomas King: *A Coyote Columbus Story,* (illus.) William Kent Monkman

Maryann Kovalski: *Brenda and Edward*

Donn Kushner: *Dinosaur Duster*, (illus.) Marc Mongeau
William Kurelek: *A Prairie Boy's Summer; A Prairie Boy's Winter*
Michael Arvaarluk Kusugak: *A Promise Is a Promise* (with Robert Munsch); *Northern Lights: The Soccer Trails,* (both illus.) Vladyana Krykorka
Julie Lawson: *Whatever You Do Don't Go Near That Canoe*, (illus.) Werner Zimmerman
Loris Lesynski: *Boy Soup or When Giant Caught Cold*
Jean Little: *Jess Was the Brave One*, (illus.) Janet Wilson; *Revenge of the Small Small*, (illus.) Janet Wilson; *Bats about Baseball*, (illus.) Kim LaFave; *Once Upon a Golden Apple*, (illus.) Phoebe Gilman; *Gruntle Piggle Takes Off*, (illus.) Johnny Wales
Celia Barker Lottridge: *The Name of the Tree,* (illus.) Ian Wallace
Berny Lucas: *Brewster Rooster,* (illus.) Russ Willms
Janet Lunn: *Amos's Sweater,* (illus.) Kim LaFave
Hugh MacDonald: *Chung Lee Loves Lobsters,* (illus.) Johnny Wales
Ainslie Manson: *Just Like New*, (illus.) Karen Reczuch
Jim McCugan: *Josepha: A Prairie Boy's Story*, (illus.) Murray Kimber
Sheryl McFarlane: *Waiting for the Whales*, (illus.) Ron Lightburn
Joseph McLellan: *The Birth of Nanabosho*, (illus.) Jim Kirby
Tololwa M. Mollel: *The Orphan Boy*, (illus.) Paul Morin
Irene Morck: *Tiger's New Cowboy Boots*, (illus.) Georgia Graham
Alan Morgan: *The Magic Hockey Skates*, (illus.) Michael Martchenko
Robin Muller: *The Magic Paintbrush*
Robert Munsch: *The Paper Bag Princess*; *Thomas' Snowsuit*; *Mortimer*; *Angela's Airplane*, (all illus.) Michael Martchenko
Janet Munsil: *Dinner at Aunt Rose's*, (illus.) Scot Ritchie
Sheldon Oberman: *The White Stone in the Castle Wall*, (illus.) Les Tait
Joanne Oppenheim: *Have You Seen Birds?,* (illus.) Barbara Reid
Barbara Nichol: *Beethoven Lives Upstairs*, (illus.) Scott Cameron; *Dippers*, (illus.) Barry Moser
P.K. Page: *A Flask of Sea Water*, (illus.) Laszlo Gal
Stéphane Poulin: *Have You Seen Josephine?*
Pierre Pratt: *Follow That Hat!*
Barbara Reid: *Two by Two*, *The New Baby Calf, Zoe* series, *Have You Seen Birds?*
Margriet Ruurs: *Emma's Eggs*, (illus.) Barbara Spurll
Ross Seidel: *The Rats Came Back*, (illus.) Rudolf Curz
Robert W. Service: *The Cremation of Sam McGee*, (illus.) Ted Harrison
Remy Simard: *My Dog Is an Elephant*, (illus.) Pierre Pratt
Ted Staunton: *Puddleman*, (illus.) Brenda Clark
Kathy Stinson: *Red Is Best*; *Big or Little*; (both illus.) Robin Baird Lewis
C.J. Taylor: *How We Saw the World*
Jan Thornhill: *The Wildlife ABC*
Mark Thurman: *One Two Many*
Gilles Tibo: *Simon and the Snowflakes* (and sequels)
William Toye: *The Loon's Necklace,* (illus.) Elizabeth Cleaver
Maxine Trottier: *The Tiny Kite of Eddie Wing*, (illus.) Al Van Mil
Ian Wallace: *Chin Chiang and the Dragon's Dance*
Betty Waterton: *A Salmon For Simon*, (illus.) Ann Blades
W.D. Valgardson: *Sarah and the People of Sand River*, (illus.) Ian Wallace
Tim Wynne-Jones: *Zoom at Sea*, (illus.) Eric Beddows

Paul Yee: *Roses Sing on New Snow; The Ghost Train,* (both illus.) Harvey Chan
Leo Yerxa: *Last Leaf First Snowflake to Fall*
Ludmila Zeman: *Gilgamesh the King*
Zhang Son Nan: *A Little Tiger in the Chinese Night*

IV. My Favourite 100 (approximately) Recent Canadian English Books for Older Children

Barbara Haworth-Attard: *Home Child*
Michael Bedard: *A Darker Magic*; *The Tinder Box*; *Redwork*
William Bell: *Forbidden City*
Geoffrey Bilson: *Death over Montreal*
Marianne Brandis: *The Quarter-Pie Window*; *Fire Ship*
Margaret Buffie: *Who Is Frances Rain?*; *My Mother's Ghost*; *The Dark Garden*
Joan Clark: *The Hand of Robin Squires*; *The Dream Carvers*
Lesley Choyce: *Some Kind of Hero*
John Craig: *No Word for Goodbye*
Peter Cumming: *Mogul and Me*
Brian Doyle: *Angel Square*; *Spud Sweetgrass*; *You Can Pick Me Up at Peggy's Cove*; *Covered Bridge*; *Uncle Ronald*
Sarah Ellis: *Next Door Neighbours*; *Pick Up Sticks*; *Out of the Blue*
Rachna Gilmore: *A Friend Like Zilla*
Martyn Godfrey: *Here She Is, Ms. Teeny Wonderful*; *Mystery in the Frozen Lands*
Marilyn Halvorson: *Let It Go*; *Cowboys Don't Cry*
James Houston: *Tikta'liktak*; *River Runners*; *White Out*
Jan Hudson: *Dawn Rider*; *Sweetgrass*
Monica Hughes: *Hunter in the Dark*; *Blaine's Way*; *Invitation to the Game*; *The Crystal Drop*; *The Castle Tourmandine*
Julie Johnston: *Hero of Lesser Causes*; *Adam-and-Eve-And-Pinch-Me*
Welwyn Wilton Katz: *The Third Magic*; *False Face*; *Whalesinger*; *Out of the Dark*
Joy Kogawa: *Naomi's Road*
Gordon Korman: *The Twinkie Squad*; *The Toilet Paper Tigers*
Paul Kropp: *Moonkid and Liberty*; *Ellen/Elena/Luna*
Donn Kushner: *The Night Voyageurs*
Julie Lawson: *White Jade Tiger*
Jean Little; *Kate*; *From Anna*; *Lost and Found*; *Mine for Keeps*; *Mama's Going to Buy You a Mocking Bird*; *His Banner Over Me*
Celia Barker Lottridge: *Ticket to Curlew*
Janet Lunn: *The Root Cellar*; *Shadow in Hawthorn Bay*
Claire Mackay: *One Proud Summer* (with Martha Hewitt); *The Minerva Program*
Michèle Marineau: *The Road to Chlifa*
Kevin Major: *Dear Bruce Springsteen*; *Hold Fast*; *Blood Red Ochre*; *Eating between the Lines*
Carol Matas: *Lisa*; *Jesper*; *Daniel's Story*; *Sworn Enemies*; *The Burning Time*; *The Primrose Path*; *Sworn Enemies*; *After the War*; *The Freak*
Christie MacKinnon: *Silent Observer*

Suzanne Martel: *The King's Daughter*
Janet McNaughton: To *Dance at the Palais Royale*
Sylvia McNicoll: *Bringing Up Beauty*
O.R. Melling: *The Singing Stone*; *My Blue Country*
Claire Mowat: *The Girl from Away*
Farley Mowat: *Owls in the Family*; *The Dog Who Wouldn't Be*
Barbara Kathleen Nickel: *The Secret Wish of Nannerl Mozart*
Kit Pearson: *The Sky Is Falling* (and sequels); *Awake and Dreaming*; *The Daring Game, A Handful of Time*
Mordecai Richler: *Jacob Two-Two Meets the Hooded Fang* (and sequels)
Ken Roberts: *Past Tense*
Robert Sheward: *A Home in Hastie Hollow*
Barbara Smucker: *Underground to Canada*; *Days of Terror*; *Incredible Jumbo*
Teresa Toten: *The Onlyhouse*
Jan Truss: *Jasmin*; *Red*; *A Very Small Rebellion*
Ann Walsh: *Shabash*
Eric Walters: *Stars*
Diana Wieler: *Last Chance Summer, Bad Boy, Ran Van the Defender* (and sequels)
Budge Wilson: *Thirteen Never Changes, The Leaving, Oliver's Wars*
Tim Wynne-Jones: *The Maestro*
Paul Yee: *The Curses of Third Uncle*; *Tales from Gold Mountain: The Chinese in the New World*, (illus.) Simon Ng; *Breakaway*

V. Some Wonderful Canadian Non-Fiction

Margaret Atwood: *For the Birds*, (illus.) John Bianchi
Michael Bender: *Waiting for Filippo*
Barbara Bondar with Dr. Roberta Bondar: *On the Shuttle: Eight Days in Space*
David Booth: *Images of Nature: Canadian Poets and the Group of Seven*
Paulette Bourgeois: *Changes in You and Me: A Book about Puberty Mostly for Boys*; *Changes in You and Me: A Book about Puberty Mostly for Girls*
Hugh Brewster: *Anastasia's Album*
Harry Bruce: *Maud: The Life of Lucy Maud Montgomery*
David Day: *Noah's Choice*
Terence Dickinson: *Exploring the Night Sky by Day*, (illus.) John Bianchi
Sylvia Funston and Jay Ingram: *The Kids' Guide to the Brain*
Edith Fowke: *Sally Go Round the Sun*, (illus.) Carlos Marchiori
Celia Godkin: *Wolf Island*
Carol Gold (ed.): *How Sport Works*
Linda Granfield: *All about Niagara Falls*, (illus.) Patricia Cupples; *Cowboy: A Kid's Album*
Barbara Greenwood: *A Pioneer Story*, (illus.) Heather Collins
Camilla Gryski: *Let's Play: Traditional Games of Childhood*; *Hands On, Thumbs Up*, (illus.) Patricia Cupples
Lawrence Hill: *Trials and Triumphs: The Story of African Canadians*
Ted Harrison: *Children of the Yukon*
Jay Ingram: *The Science of Everyday Life*
Jean Little: *Little by Little*
Janet Lunn and Christopher Moore: *The Story of Canada*, (illus.) Alan Daniel
Claire Mackay: *Pay Cheques and*

Picket Lines: All about Unions in Canada, (illus.)
Eric Parker, *The Toronto Story*, (illus.) Johnny Wales
Caroline Parry: *Let's Celebrate*
Lynette Roy: *Brown Girl in the Ring: A Biography for Young People*
Bonnie Shemie: *Houses of Bark* (and sequels)
Shirley Sterling: *My Name Is Seepeetza*
David Suzuki: *Looking At* series (Insects, etc.)
Diane Swanson: *Why Seals Blow Their Noses: Canadian Wildlife in Fact and Fiction*; *Coyotes in the Crosswalk: Canadian Wildlife in the City*
Shelley Tanaka: *Discovering the Iceman,* (illus.) Laurie McGaw, *On Board the Titanic,* (illus.) Ken Marschall
Jan Thornhill: *The Wildlife ABC*; *The Wildlife 123*
Valerie Wyatt: *The Science Book for Girls and Other Intelligent Beings*; *Weatherwatch*
Song Nan Zhang: *A Little Tiger in the Chinese Night: An Autobiography*

TWO TERRIFIC CANADIAN ENCYLOPEDIAS

The Canadian Encyclopedia (available as text, on disk, or CD-ROM)
The Canadian Junior Encyclopedia

VI. My Favourite Canadian Poetry Books

David Booth (ed.): *Til All the Stars Have Fallen: Canadian Poems for Children,* (illus.) Kady MacDonald Denton; *Voices on the Wind: Poems for all Seasons*; *Dr. Knickerbocker and Other Rhymes*, (illus.) Maryann Kovalski
Sean Ferris: *Children of the Great Muskeg*
Sheree Fitch: *There Were Monkeys in My Kitchen*
Paul Fleischman (American): *I Am Phoenix*; *Joyful Noise,* (both illus.) Canadian Ken Nutt/Eric Beddows
Robert Heidbreder: *Don't Eat Spiders*
Alice Kane: *The Dreamer Awakes*
Dennis Lee: *Lizzy's Lion*, (illus.) Marie-Louise Gay; *Alligator Pie*, (illus.) Frank Newfeld; *The Ice-Cream Store*, (illus.) David McPhail
Jean Little: *Hey World, Here I Am!*
sean o'huigin : *Ghost Horse of the Mounties*; *Scary Poems for Rotten Kids*
Robert Priest: *A Terrible Case of the Stars*
Robert Service: *The Cremation of Sam McGee*, (illus.) Ted Harrison
Lois Simmie: *Auntie's Knitting a Baby*
Tim Wynne-Jones: *Mischief City,* (illus.) Victor GAD

VII. Notable Canadian Series

Ralph Connor: *Glengarry School Days*
Gordon Korman: *This Can't Be Happening at Macdonald Hall!* (and sequels)
Bernice Thurman Hunter: *That Scatterbrain Booky* (and sequels); *A Place for Margaret* (and sequels)
Roy MacGregor: *Mystery at Lake Placid* (and sequels)
Claire Mackay: *Mini-Bike Hero* (and sequels)
Lucy Maud Montgomery: *Emily of New Moon*; *Emily Climbs*; *Emily's Quest*; *Anne of Green Gables* (and sequels)
Kit Pearson: *The Sky Is Falling* (and sequels)
Mordecai Richler: *Jacob Two-Two Meets the Hooded Fang* (and sequels)
Eric Wilson: *Murder on the Canadian* (and sequels)

VIII. Terrific Short-Story Collections

Martha Brooks: *Paradisé Cafe and Other Stories*; *Traveling On into the Light*
Gillian Chan: *Golden Girl and Other Stories*; *Glory Days*
Sarah Ellis: *Back of Beyond*
Edith Fowke: *Tales Told in Canada*
Vicky Gabereau (intro), The British Columbia Society for the Protection of Cruelty to Animals: *How I Learned to Speak Dog and Other Stories*
Margaret Laurence: *A Bird in the House*
Janet Lunn: *The Unseen: Scary Stories Selected by Janet Lunn*
Eva Martin: *Canadian Fairy Tales*, (illus.) Laszlo Gal
Lucy Maud Montgomery: *Akin to Anne*; *Along the Shore*; *Among the Shadows*; *After Many Days*; *Against the Odds*; *At the Altar*
R.P. MacIntyre: *The Blue Camaro*
Claire Mackay (ed.): *Laughs: Funny Stories* selected by Claire Mackay
Nazneen Sadiq: *Camels Make You Homesick and Other Stories*
Muriel Whitaker (ed): *The Best Canadian Animal Stories* (two volumes); *Great Canadian Adventure Stories*
Tim Wynne-Jones: *Some of the Kinder Planets*; *The Book of Changes*
Paul Yee: *Teach Me to Fly, Skyfighter! and Others Stories*

IX. Children's Book Awards

There are many awards honouring both Canadian and international authors and illustrators of children's books. This is only a partial list.

CANADIAN AWARDS

THE AMELIA FRANCES HOWARD GIBBON ILLUSTRATOR'S AWARD

To the illustrator of an outstanding children's book published during the previous calendar year.

1971 Elizabeth Cleaver. *The Wind Has Wings*. Compiled by Mary Alice Downie and Barbara Robertson. Oxford University Press.
1972 Shizuye Takashima. *A Child in Prison Camp*. Tundra.
1973 Jacques de Roussan. *Au Dela de Soleil/Beyond the Sun*. Tundra.
1974 William Kurelek. *A Prairie Boy's Winter*. Tundra.
1975 Carlo Italiano. *The Sleighs of My Childhood. Les Traineaux de Mon Enfance*. Tundra.
1976 William Kurelek. *A Prairie Boy's Summer.* Tundra.
1977 Pam Hall. *Down by Jim Long's Stage* by Al Pittman. Breakwater.
1978 Elizabeth Cleaver. *The Loon's Necklace* by William Toye. Oxford University Press.
1979 Ann Blades. *A Salmon for Simon* by Betty Waterton. Douglas & McIntyre.
1980 Laszlo Gal. *The Twelve Dancing Princesses* by Janet Lunn. Methuen.
1981 Douglas Tait. *The Trouble With Princesses* by Christie Harris. McClelland & Stewart.
1982 Heather Woodall. *Ytek and the Arctic Orchid* by Garnet Hewitt. Douglas & McIntryre.
1983 Lindee Climo. *Chester's Barn.* Tundra.
1984 Ken Nutt. *Zoom at Sea* by Tim Wynne-Jones. Groundwood.
1985 Ian Wallace. *Chin Chiang and the Dragon's Dance*. Groundwood.
1986 Ken Nutt. *Zoom Away* by Tim Wynne-Jones. Groundwood.
1987 Marie-Louise Gay. *Moonbeam on a Cat's Ear*. Stoddart.
1988 Marie-Louise Gay. *Rainy Day Magic*. Stoddart.
1989 Kim LaFave. *Amos's Sweater* by Janet Lunn. Groundwood.
1990 Kady MacDonald Denton. *Til All the Stars Have Fallen*, ed. David Booth. Kids Can.
1991 Paul Morin. *The Orphan Boy* by Tololwa Mollel. Oxford University Press.
1992 Ron Lightburn. *Waiting for the Whales* by Sheryl McFarlane. Orca.
1993 Paul Morin. *The Dragon's Pearl* by Julie Lawson. Oxford University Press.
1994 Leo Yerxa. *Last Leaf First Snowflake to Fall*. Groundwood.
1995 Barbara Reid. *Gifts* by Jo Ellen Bogart. Scholastic.
1996 Karen Reczuch. *Just Like New* by Ainslie Manson. Groundwood.
1997 Harvey Chan. *Ghost Train* by Paul Yee. Groundwood.

CANADIAN LIBRARY ASSOCIATION BOOK OF THE YEAR FOR CHILDREN AWARD

To the author of an outstanding children's book published in the previous calendar year. Established in 1947, the following are the winners since 1975.

1975 Dennis Lee. *Alligator Pie.* Macmillan.
1976 Mordecai Richler. *Jacob Two-Two Meets the Hooded Fang.* McClelland & Stewart.
1977 Christie Harris. *Mouse Woman and the Vanished Princesses.* McClelland & Stewart.
1978 Dennis Lee. *Garbage Delight.* Macmillan.
1979 Kevin Major. *Hold Fast.* Clarke, Irwin.
1980 James Houston. *River Runners.* McClelland & Stewart.
1981 Donn Kushner. *The Violin Maker's Gift.* Macmillan.
1982 Janet Lunn. *The Root Cellar.* Lester & Orpen Dennys.
1983 Brian Doyle. *Up to Low.* Groundwood.
1984 Jan Hudson. *Sweetgrass.* Tree Frog Press.
1985 Jean Little. *Mama's Going to Buy You a Mockingbird.* Penguin.
1986 Cora Taylor. *Julie.* Western Producer Prairie.
1987 Janet Lunn. *Shadow in Hawthorn Bay.* Lester & Orpen Dennys.
1988 Kit Pearson. *A Handful of Time.* Viking.
1989 Brian Doyle. *Easy Avenue.* Groundwood.
1990 Kit Pearson. *The Sky Is Falling.* Viking.
1991 Michael Bedard. *Redwork.* Lester & Orpen Dennys.
1992 Kevin Major. *Eating between the Lines.* Doubleday.
1993 Celia Barker Lottridge. *Ticket to Curlew.* Groundwood.
1994 Tim Wynne-Jones. *Some of the Kinder Planets.* Groundwood.
1995 Cora Taylor. *Summer of the Mad Monk.* Douglas & McIntyre.
1996 Maxine Trottier. *The Tiny Kite of Eddie Wing.* Stoddart.
1997 Brian Doyle. *Uncle Ronald.* Groundwood.

CANADIAN LIBRARY ASSOCIATION YOUNG ADULT CANADIAN BOOK AWARD

Awarded since 1981 to the author of an outstanding English-language book for young adults (ages 13–18) published in the preceding calendar year.

1981 Kevin Major. *Far from Shore.* Clark, Irwin.
1982 Jamie Brown. *Superbike!* Clarke, Irwin.
1983 Monica Hughes. *Hunter in the Dark.* Clarke, Irwin.
1984 O.R. Melling. *The Druid's Tune.* Penguin.
1985 Mary Ellen Lang-Collura. *Winners.* Western Producer Prairie.
1986 Marianne Brandis. *The Quarter Pie Window.* Porcupine's Quill.
1987 Janet Lunn. *Shadow in Hawthorn Bay.* Lester & Orpen Dennys.
1988 Margaret Buffie. *Who Is Fances Rain?* Kids Can.
1989 Helen Fogwell Porter. *January, February, June or July.* Breakwater.
1990 Diana Wieler. *Bad Boy.* Groundwood.
1991 Budge Wilson. *The Leaving.* House of Anansi.
1992 Susan Lynn Reynolds. *Strandia.* HarperCollins.
1993 Karleen Bradford. *There Will Be Wolves.* HarperCollins.

1994 Sean Stewart. *Nobody's Son*. Maxwell Macmillan.
1995 Julie Johnston. *Adam and Eve and Pinch-Me*. Lester.
1996 Tim Wynne-Jones. *The Maestro*. Groundwood.
1997 Rod McIntyre. *Take*.

ELIZABETH MRAZIK-CLEAVER CANADIAN PICTURE BOOK AWARD

To a Canadian illustrator of a picture book published in Canada, in English or in French, during the previous calendar year.

1986 Ann Blades. *By the Sea*. Kids Can.
1987 Barbara Reid. *Have You Seen Birds?* by Joanne Oppenheim. Scholastic.
1988 Stéphane Poulin. *Can You Catch Josephine?* Tundra.
1989 Ken Nutt (Eric Beddows) *Night Cars* by Teddy Jam. Groundwood.
1990 Ian Wallace. *The Name of the Tree* by Celia Lottridge. Groundwood.
1991 Paul Morin. *The Orphan Boy* by Tololwa Mollel. Oxford University Press.
1992 Ron Lightburn. *Waiting for the Whales* by Sheryl McFarlane. Orca.
1993 Barbara Reid. *Two by Two*. Scholastic.
1994 Leo Yerxa. *Last Leaf First Snowflake to Fall*. Groundwood.
1995 Murray Kimber. Josepha: *A Prairie Boy's Story* by Jim McGugan. Red Deer College.

THE GEOFFREY BILSON AWARD FOR HISTORICAL FICTION FOR YOUNG PEOPLE

To the author of an outstanding work of historical fiction for young people published in the previous calendar year.

1988 Carol Matas. *Lisa*. Lester & Orpen Dennys.
1989 Martyn Godfrey. *Mystery in the Frozen Lands*. James Lorimer. Dorothy Perkyns. *Rachel's Revolution*. Lancelot.
1990 Kit Pearson. *The Sky Is Falling*. Viking.
1991 Marianne Brandis. *The Sign of the Scales*. Porcupine's Quill.
1992 No Award
1993 Celia Barker Lottridge. *Ticket to Curlew*. Groundwood.
1994 Kit Pearson. *The Lights Go On Again*. Viking.
1995 Joan Clark. *The Dream Carvers*. Viking.

THE GOVERNOR GENERAL'S LITERARY AWARDS

The Governor General's Literary Awards were established in 1987. The children's section replaced the Canada Council Children's Literature Prizes. Up to four are awarded each year—to an English-language writer, a French-language writer, an illustrator of a book with English text and an illustrator of a book with French text.

1987 Marie-Louise Gay (illus.). *Rainy Day Magic*. Stoddart. Morgan Nyberg. *Galahad Schwartz and the Cockroach Army*. Groundwood. Darcia Labrosse (illus.). *Venir au monde* by Marie-Francine Hébert. La courte échelle. David Schinkel and Yves

Beauchesne. *Le Don.* Le Cercle du Livre.
1988 Kim LaFave (illus.). *Amos's Sweater* by Janet Lunn. Groundwood.
Welwyn Wilton Katz. *The Third Magic.* Groundwood.
Phillippe Béha (illus.) *Les jeux de Pic-Mots.* Graficor.
Michèle Marineau. *Cassiopée ou l'été.* Québec-Amérique.
1989 Robin Muller (illus.). *The Magic Paintbrush.* Doubleday.
Diana Wieler. *Bad Boy.* Groundwood.
Stéphane Poulin (illus.). *Benjamin et la saga des oreillers.* Annick.
Charles Monpetit. *Temps mort.* Paulines.
1990 Paul Morin (illus.). *The Orphan Boy* by Tololwa Mollel. Oxford University Press.
Michael Bedard. *Redwork.* Lester & Orpen Dennys.
Pierre Pratt (illus.). *Les fantaisies de l'oncle Henri* by Benedicte Froissart. Annick.
Christiane Duchesne. *La vraie histoire du chien de Clara Vic.* Québec-Amérique.
1991 Joanne Fitzgerald (illus.). *Dr. Kiss Says Yes* by Teddy Jam. Groundwood.
Sarah Ellis. *Pick-Up Sticks.* Groundwood.
Sheldon Cohen (illus.). *Un champion* by Roch Carrier. Tundra.
François Gravel. *Deux heures et demie avant Jasmine.* Boréal.
1992 Ron Lightburn (illus.). *Waiting for the Whales* by Sheryl McFarlane. Orca.
Julie Johnston. *Hero of Lesser Causes.* Lester.
Gilles Tibo (illus.). *Simon et la ville de carton.* Tundra.
Christiane Duchesne. *Victor.* Québec-Amérique.
1993 Mireille Levert (illus.). *Sleep Tight Mrs. Ming* by Sharon Jennings. Annick.
Tim Wynne-Jones. *Some of the Kinder Planets.* Groundwood.
Stephane Jorisch (illus.). *Le monde selon Jean de...* by André Vandal. Doutre et Vandal.
Michele Marineau. *La route de Chlifa.* Québec-Amérique.
1994 Murray Kimber (illus.). *Josepha: A Prairie Boy's Story* by Jim McGugan. Red Deer College.
Julie Johnston. *Adam and Eve and Pinch-Me.* Lester.
Pierre Pratt (illus.). *Mon chien est un éléphant* by Rémy Simard. Annick.
Suzanne Martel. *Une belle journée pour mourir.* Fides.
1995 Ludmila Zeman (illus.). *The Last Quest of Gilgamesh.* Tundra.
Tim Wynne-Jones. *The Maestro.* Groundwood.
Anouchka Gravel *Galouchko* (illus.). *Shõet les dragons d'eau.* Annick.
Sonia Sarfati. *Comme une peau de chagrin.* La courte échelle.
1996 Eric Beddows (illus.). The Rooster's Gift. Groundwood.
Paul Yee. *Ghost Train.* Groundwood.
Gilles Tibo (text). *Noémie-Le Secret de Madame Lumbago.* Québec/Amérique.

INFORMATION BOOK AWARD

This award is sponsored by the Children's Roundtables of Canada and recognizes an outstanding information book published the previous year for young people from 5 to 15 years of age.

1987 David Suzuki. *Looking at Insects.* Stoddart.
1988 Caroline Parry. *Let's Celebrate.* Kids Can.

1989 Terence Dickinson. *Exploring the Night Sky by Day*. Camden House.
1990 Celia Godkin. *Wolf Island*. Fitzhenry & Whiteside.
1991 Camilla Gryski. *Hands On, Thumbs Up*. Kids Can.
1992 Jan Thornhill. *A Tree in a Forest*. Greey de Pencier.
1993 Janet Lunn & Christopher Moore. *The Story of Canada*. Key Porter.
1994 Barbara Bondar. *On the Shuttle: Eight Days in Space*. Greey de Pencier.
Linda Granfield. *Cowboy: A Kid's Album*. Groundwood.
1995 Barbara Greenwood. *A Pioneer Story*. Kids Can.

THE MR. CHRISTIE'S BOOK AWARD

This award was established in 1990 by Christie Brown & Co. to reward excellence in the writing and illustrating of both French and English children's books published in Canada in the previous calendar year. Originally there were four prizes, two for text and two for illustration. Since 1993 there have been six, for the best book in three age categories (7 and under, 8 to 11, and 12 and over).

1989 Ian Wallace (illus). *The Name of the Tree* by Celia Lottridge. Groundwood.
Kit Pearson. *The Sky Is Falling*. Viking.
Philippe Béha (illus.). *Mais que font les fées avec toutes ces dents?* Raton Laveur.
Ginette Anfousse. *Rosalie s'en va-t-en guerre*. La courte échelle.
1990 Kady MacDonald Denton (illus.). *The Story of Little Quack* by Betty Gibson. Kids Can.
Brian Doyle. *Covered Bridge*. Groundwood.
Pierre Pratt (illus.). *Les fantasies de l'oncle Henri* by Bénédict Froissart. Annick.
Francois Gravel. *Le Zamboni*. Boréal.
1991 Barbara Reid (illus.). *Zoe* (series). HarperCollins.
Dennis Lee. *The Ice Cream Store*. HarperCollins.
Stéphane Poulin (illus.). *Un voyage pour deux*. Annick.
Christiane Duchesne. *Bibitsa, ou, l'étrange voyage de Clara Vic*. Québec-Amérique.
1992 Yvette Moore (illus.). *A Prairie Alphabet*. Tundra.
Dominique Jolin (illus.). *C'est pas juste!* Raton Laveur.
Sheree Fitch. *There Were Monkeys in My Kitchen*. Doubleday.
Gilles Gauthier. *Le gros problème du petite Marcus*. La courte échelle.
Janet Lunn and Christopher Moore. *The Story of Canada*. Key Porter.
Dominique Demers. *Un hiver de tourmente*. La courte échelle.
1993 Berny Lucas, Russ Willms (illus.). *Brewster Rooster*. Kids Can.
Joceline Sanschagrin, Hélène Desputeaux (illus.). *Caillou-La petit soeur & le petit pot*. Chouette.
Co-Winners: Song Nan Zhang. *A Little Tiger in the Chinese Night*. Tundra, Leo Yerxa. *Last Leaf First Snowflake to Fall*. Groundwood.
Christiane Duchesne. *La 42e soeur de Bébert*. Québec-Amérique.
Diana Wieler. *RanVan the Defender*. Groundwood.
Dominique Demers. *Les grands sapins ne meurent pas*. Québec-Amérique.
1994 W.D. Valgardson, Ange Zhang (illus.). *Thor*. Groundwood.

Rémy Simard & Pierre Pratt (illus.). *Mon chien est un éléphant.* Annick.
Barbara Greenwood & Heather Collins (illus.). *A Pioneer Story.* Kids Can.
Denis Côté. *Le parc aux sortilèges.* La courte échelle.
Sarah Ellis. *Out of the Blue.* Groundwood.
Raymond Plante. *L'étoile a pleuré rouge.* Boréal.

1995 Nan Gregory, Ron Lightburn (illus.). *How Smudge Came.* Red Deer College.
Pierrette Dubé, Yayo (illus.). *Au lit, au lit, princesse Émilie.* Raton Laveur.
Mordecai Richler, Norman Eyolfson (illus.). *Jacob Two-Two's First Spy Case.* McClelland & Stewart.
Christiane Duchesne. *La bergère de chevaux.* Québec-Amérique.
Joan Clark. *The Dream Carvers.* Viking.
Jean Lemieux. *Le trésor de Brion.* Québec-Amérique.

1996 Don Gillmor & Marie-Louise Gay (illus.). *The Fabulous Song.* Stoddart.
Shelley Tanaka & Laurie McGaw (illus.). *Discovering the Iceman.* Scholastic.
Brian Doyle. *Uncle Ronald.* Groundwood.
Danielle Marcotte & Stéphane Poulin (illus.). *Poil de serpent dent d'araignée. Laval: Les 400 coups.*
Robert Davidts, Francis Back (illus.). *Jean-Baptiste, coureur des bois.* Boréal.
Jacques Lazure. *Le rêve couleur d'orange.* Les éditions Québec.

RUTH SCHWARTZ CHILDREN'S BOOK AWARD

This prize recognizes authors and illustrators who demonstrate artistic excellence in Canadian children's literature. Winning books, published the previous year, are selcted by juries of children from two Toronto public schools.

1976 Mordecai Richler. *Jacob Two-Two Meets the Hooded Fang.* McClelland & Stewart.
1977 Robert Thomas Allen. *The Violin.* McGraw-Hill.
1978 Dennis Lee. *Garbage Delight.* Macmillan.
1979 Kevin Major. *Hold Fast.* Clarke, Irwin.
1980 Barbara Smucker. *Days of Terror.* Clarke, Irwin.
1981 Suzanne Martel. *The King's Daughter.* Groundwood.
1982 Marsha Hewitt and Claire Mackay. *One Proud Summer.* Women's Press.
1983 Jan Truss. *Jasmin.* Groundwood.
1984 Tim Wynne-Jones. *Zoom at Sea.* Groundwood.
1985 Jean Little. *Mama's Going to Buy You a Mockingbird.* Penguin.
1986 Robert Munsch. *Thomas' Snowsuit.* Annick.
1987 Barbara Reid. *Have You Seen Birds?* Scholastic.
1988 Cora Taylor. *The Doll.* Western Producer Prairie.
1989 Janet Lunn. *Amos's Sweater.* Groundwood.
1990 Diana Wieler, *Bad Boy.* Groundwood.
1991 William Bell. *Forbidden City.* Doubleday.
1992 Paul Yee, (illus.) Harvey Chan. *Roses Sing on New Snow.* Groundwood.
1993 Phoebe Gilman. *Something from Nothing.* Scholastic.

1994 Michael Kusugak, (illus.) Vladyana Krykorka. *Northern Lights: The Soccer Trails*. Annick.
O.R. Melling. *The Hunter's Moon*. HarperCollins.
1995 Barbara Greenwood, (illus.) Heather Collins. *A Pioneer Story*. Kids Can.
Julie Johnston. *Adam and Eve and Pinch-Me*. Lester.
1996 Geoff Butler. *The Killick: A Newfoundland Story*. Tundra.
Welwyn Wilton Katz. *Out of the Dark*. Groundwood.
1997 Kit Pearson. *Awake and Dreaming*. Viking.
Paul Yee. *Ghost Train*, (illus.) Harvey Chan. Groundwood.

THE SILVER BIRCH AWARD

The Silver Birch Award is part of a reading program developed by the Ontario Library Association. Students select winners (both fiction and non-fiction) from books published the previous year.

1994 Carol Matas. *Daniel's Story*. Scholastic.
1995 Daisy Corning Stone Spedden, (illus.) Laurie McGaw. *Polar, the Titanic Bear*. Little, Brown.
1996 Sylvia McNicoll. *Bringing Up Beauty*. Maxwell Macmillan.
Annouchka Gravel Galouchka. *Sho and the Demons of the Deep*. Annick.
1997 Shelley Tanaka (non-fiction). *On Board the Titanic,* (illus.) Ken Marschall. Scholastic.
Eric Walters (fiction). *Stars*. Stoddart.

VICKY METCALF AWARD

This award is presented annually by the Canadian Authors Association to a Canadian writer in recognition of a body of work (more than three books) appealing to children aged 7 to 17.

1963 Kerry Wood
1964 John F. Hayes
1965 Roderick Haig-Brown
1966 Fred Swayze
1967 John Patrick Gillese
1968 Lorraine McLaughlin
1969 Audrey McKim
1970 Farley Mowat
1971 Kay Hill
1972 William Toye
1973 Christie Harris
1974 Jean Little
1975 Lyn Harrington
1976 Suzanne Martel
1977 James Houston
1978 Lyn Cook
1979 Cliff Faulknor
1980 John Craig
1981 Monica Hughes
1982 Janet Lunn
1983 Claire Mackay
1984 Bill Freeman
1985 Edith Fowke
1986 Dennis Lee
1987 Robert Munsch
1988 Barbara Smucker
1989 Stéphane Poulin
1990 Bernice Thurman Hunter
1991 Brian Doyle
1992 Kevin Major
1993 Phoebe Gilman
1994 Welwyn Wilton Katz
1995 Sarah Ellis
1996 Margaret Buffie
1997 Tim Wynne-Jones

VICKY METCALF SHORT-STORY AWARD

This award is presented by the Canadian Authors Association to the Canadian writer of the best children's short story published in Canada the previous year.

1979 Marina McDougall. "The Kingdom of Riddles," in *Ready or Not*, ed. Jack Booth. (Language Patterns Impressions Reading Series) Holt, Rinehart and Winston.
1980 Estelle Salata. "Blind Date," in *Time Enough*, ed. Jack Booth. (Language Patterns Impressions Reading Series) Holt, Rinehart and Winston.
1981 James Houston. "Long Claws," in *The Winter Fun Book*, ed. Laima Dingwall and Annabel Slaight. Greey de Pencier.
1982 Barbara Greenwood. "A Major Resolution," in *Contexts*. Nelson.
1983 Monica Hughes. "The Iron Barred Door," in *Anthology* 2. Nelson.
1984 P. Colleen Archer. "The Dog Who Wanted to Die." *JAM* Magazine 4, no. 1 (Sept./Oct. 1983).
1985 Martyn Godfrey. "Here She Is, Ms. Teeny-Wonderful!" *Crackers* Magazine, no. 12 (Spring 1984).
1986 Diana Wieler. "The Boy Who Walked Backwards," in *Prairie Jungle*. Coteau.
1987 Isabel Reimer. "The Viking Dagger," in *Of the Jigsaw, a Multicultural Anthology for Young Readers*. Peguis.
1988 Claire Mackay. "Marvin and Me and the Flies." *Canadian Children's Annual* No. 12 (1987).
1989 Martha Brooks. "A Boy and His Dog," in *Paradise Café & Other Stories*. Thistledown.
1990 Patricia G. Armstrong. "Choose Your Grandmother," in *Jumbo Gumbo*, ed. Wenda McArthur and Geoffrey Ursell. Coteau.
1991 No Award
1992 Edna King. "Adventure on Thunder Island," in *Adventure on Thunder Island*. James Lorimer.
1993 Rod McIntyre. "The Rink," in *The Blue Jean Collection*. Thistledown.
1994 Tim Wynne-Jones. "The Hope Bakery," in *Some of the Kinder Planets*. Groundwood.
1995 No Award
1996 Bernice Friesen. "The Seasons Are Horses," in *The Seasons Are Horses*. Thistledown.
1997 No Award

AMERICAN AND INTERNATIONAL AWARDS

RANDOLPH CALDECOTT MEDAL

Established in 1938 and named in honour of the famous nineteenth-century British artist, this prize is awarded to the illustrator of the most distinguished picture book for children, published in the United States the preceding year. Following are the winners since 1975.

1975 *Arrow to the Sun* by Gerald McDermott (Viking)
1976 *Why Mosquitoes Buzz in People's Ears* retold by Verna Aardema, (illus.) Leo & Diane Dillon (Dial)
1977 Ashanti to Zulu: *African Traditions* by Margaret Musgrove, (illus.) Leo & Diane Dillon (Dial)

1978 *Noah's Ark* illus. by Peter Spier (Doubleday)
1979 *The Girl Who Loved Wild Horses* by Paul Goble (Bradbury)
1980 *Ox-Cart Man* by Donald Hall, (illus.) Barbara Cooney (Viking)
1981 *Fables* by Arnold Lobel (Harper)
1982 *Jumanji* by Chris Van Allsburg (Houghton)
1983 *Shadow* by Blaise Cendrars, (illus.) Marcia Brown (Scribner)
1984 *The Glorious Flight: Across the Channel with Louis Blériot* by Alice & Martin Provensen (Viking)
1985 *Saint George and the Dragon* retold by Margaret Hodges, (illus.) Trina Schart Hyman (Little, Brown)
1986 *The Polar Express* by Chris Van Allsburg (Houghton)
1987 *Hey, Al* by Arthur Yorinks, (illus.) Richard Egielski (Farrar)
1988 *Owl Moon* by Jane Yolen, (illus.) John Schoenherr (Philomel)
1989 *Song and Dance Man* by Karen Ackerman, (illus.) Stephen Gammell (Knopf)
1990 *Lon Po Po: A Red-Riding Hood Story from China*, trans. and illus. by Ed Young (Philomel)
1991 *Black and White* by David Macaulay (Houghton)
1992 *Tuesday* by David Wiesner (Clarion)
1993 *Mirette on the High Wire* by Emily Arnold McCully (Putnam)
1994 *Grandfather's Journey* by Allen Say (Houghton)
1995 *Smoky Night* by Eve Bunting, (illus.) David Diaz (Harcourt)
1996 *Officer Buckle and Gloria* by Peggy Rathmann (Puttman)
1997 *Golem* by David Wisniewski (Clarion)

JOHN NEWBERY MEDAL

Since 1922 this award, named for the renowned eighteenth-century British publisher and bookseller, has been conferred by the American Library Association. It is awarded to the author of the most distinguished contribution to literature for children, published in the United States during the preceding year.

1922 *The Story of Mankind* by Hendrik Willem Van Loon (Liveright)
1923 *The Voyages of Doctor Dolittle* by Hugh Lofting (Lippincott)
1924 *The Dark Frigate* by Charles Hawes (Atlantic–Little, Brown)
1925 *Tales from Silver Lands* by Charles Finger (Doubleday)
1926 *Shen of the Sea* by Arthur Bowie Chrisman (Dutton)
1927 *Smoky, The Cowhorse* by Will James (Scribner)
1928 *Gayneck, The Story of a Pigeon* by Dhan Gopal Mukerji (Dutton)
1929 *The Trumpeter of Krakow* by Eric P. Kelly (Macmillan)
1930 *Hitty, Her First Hundred Years* by Rachel Field (Macmillan)
1931 *The Cat Who Went to Heaven* by Elizabeth Coatsworth (Macmillan)
1932 *Waterless Mountain* by Laura Adams Armer (Longmans)
1933 *Young Fu of the Upper Yangtze* by Elizabeth Lewis (Winston)
1934 *Invincible Louisa* by Cornelia Meigs (Little, Brown)
1935 *Dobry* by Monica Shannon (Viking)
1936 *Caddie Woodlawn* by Carol Ryrie Brink (Macmillan)
1937 *Roller Skates* by Ruth Sawyer (Viking)
1938 *The White Stag* by Kate Seredy (Viking)

1939 *Thimble Summer* by Elizabeth Enright (Rinehart)
1940 *Daniel Boone* by James Daugherty (Viking)
1941 *Call It Courage* by Armstrong Sperry (Macmillan)
1942 *The Matchlock Gun* by Walter D. Edmonds (Dodd)
1943 *Adam of the Road* by Elizabeth Janet Gray (Viking)
1944 *Johnny Tremain* by Esther Forbes (Houghton)
1945 *Rabbit Hill* by Robert Lawson (Viking)
1946 *Strawberry Girl* by Lois Lenski (Lippincott)
1947 *Miss Hickory* by Carolyn Sherwin Bailey (Viking)
1948 *The Twenty-One Balloons* by William Pène du Bois (Viking)
1949 *King of the Wind* by Marguerite Henry (Rand McNally)
1950 *The Door in the Wall* by Marguerite de Angeli (Doubleday)
1951 *Amos Fortune, Free Man* by Elizabeth Yates (Dutton)
1952 *Ginger Pye* by Eleanor Estes (HBJ)
1953 *Secret of the Andes* by Ann Nolan Clark (Viking)
1954 *...And Now Miguel* by Joseph Krumgold (Crowell)
1955 *The Wheel on the School* by Meindert DeJong (Harper)
1956 *Carry On, Mr. Bowditch* by Jean Lee Latham (Houghton)
1957 *Miracles on Maple Hill* by Virginia Sorensen (HBJ)
1958 *Rifles for Watie* by Harold Keith (Crowell)
1959 *The Witch of Blackbird Pond* by Elizabeth George Speare (Houghton)
1960 *Onion John* by Joseph Krumgold (Crowell)
1961 *Island of the Blue Dolphin* by Scott O'Dell (Houghton)
1962 *The Bronze Bow* by Elizabeth George Speare (Houghton)
1963 *A Wrinkle in Time* by Madeleine L'Engle (Farrar)
1964 *It's Like This, Cat* by Emily Cheney Neville (Harper)
1965 *Shadow of a Bull* by Maia Wojciechowska (Atheneum)
1966 *I, Juan De Pareja* by Elizabeth Borten de Treviño (Farrar)
1967 *Up a Road Slowly* by Irene Hunt (Follett)
1968 *From the Mixed-Up Files of Mrs. Basil E. Frankweiler* by E.L. Konigsburg (Atheneum)
1969 *The High King* by Lloyd Alexander (Holt)
1970 *Sounder* by William H. Armstrong (Harper)
1971 *Summer of the Swans* by Betsy Byars (Viking)
1972 *Mrs. Frisby and the Rats of Nimh* by Robert C. O'Brien (Atheneum)
1973 *Julie of the Wolves* by Jean Craighead George (Harper)
1974 *The Slave Dancer* by Paula Fox (Bradbury)
1975 *M.C. Higgins, The Great* by Virginia Hamilton (Macmillan)
1976 *The Grey King* by Susan Cooper (McElderry)
1977 *Roll of Thunder, Hear My Cry* by Mildred D. Taylor (Dial)
1978 *Bridge to Terabithia* by Katherine Paterson (Crowell)
1979 *The Westing Game* by Ellen Raskin (Dutton)
1980 *A Gathering of Days: A New England Girl's Journal, 1830–32* by Joan W. Blos (Scribner)
1981 *Jacob Have I Loved* by Katherine Paterson (Crowell)
1982 *A Visit To William Blake's Inn: Poems for Innocent and Experienced Travelers* by Nancy Willard (HBJ)
1983 *Dicey's Song* by Cynthia Voigt (Atheneum)
1984 *Dear Mr. Henshaw* by Beverly Cleary (Morrow)

1985 *The Hero and the Crown* by Robin McKinley (Greenwillow)
1986 *Sarah, Plain and Tall* by Patricia MacLachlan (Harper)
1987 *The Whipping Boy* by Sid Fleischman (Greenwillow)
1988 *Lincoln: A Photobiography* by Russell Freedman (Clarion)
1989 *Joyful Noise: Poems for Two Voices* by Paul Fleischman(Harper)
1990 *Number the Stars* by Lois Lowry (Houghton)
1991 *Maniac Magee* by Jerry Spinelli (Little, Brown)
1992 *Shiloh* by Phyllis Reynolds Naylor (Atheneum)
1993 *Missing May* by Cynthia Rylant (Orchard)
1994 *The Giver* by Lois Lowry (Houghton)
1995 *Walk Two Moons* by Sharon Creech (HarperCollins)
1996 *The Midwife's Apprentice* by Karen Cushman (Clarion)
1997 *The View from Saturday* by E.L. Konigsburg (Jean Karl/Atheneum)

EDGAR ALLAN POE AWARDS

The Mystery Writers of America honours exceptional work in the mystery, crime, suspense and intrigue fields in several media each year. An award for "Best Juvenile Novel" was introduced in 1962, "Best Young Adult Novel" in 1989. J *indicates juvenile,* Y/A *indicates young adult. Following are the winners since 1985.*

1985 *Night Cry* by Phyllis Reynolds Naylor (Atheneum)
1986 *The Sandman's Eyes* by Patricia Windsor (Delacorte)
1987 *The Other Side of Dark* by Joan Lowery Nixon (Delacorte)
1988 *Lucy Forever* and *Miss Rosetree, Shrinks* by Susan Shreve (Holt)
1989 J: *Megan's Island* by Willo Davis Roberts (Atheneum)
Y/A: *Incident at Loring Groves* by Sonia Levitin (Dial)
1990 J: No Award
Y/A: *Show Me the Evidence* by Alane Ferguson (Bradbury)
1991 J: *Stonewords: A Ghost Story* by Pam Conrad (HarperCollins)
Y/A: *Mote* by Chap Reaver (Delacorte)
1992 J: *Wanted...Mud Blossom* by Betsy Byars (Delacorte)
Y/A: *The Weirdo* by Theodore Taylor (Harcourt)
1993 J: *Coffin on a Case!* by Eve Bunting (HarperCollins)
Y/A: *A Little Bit Dead* by Chap Reaver (Delacorte)
1994 J: *The Twin in the Tavern* by Barbara Brooks Wallace (Atheneum)
Y/A: *The Name of the Game Was Murder* by Joan Lowery Nixon (Delacorte)
1995 J: *The Absolutely True Story...How I Visited Yellowstone Park with the Terrible Rubes* by Willo Davis Roberts (Atheneum)
Y/A: *Toughing It* by Nancy Springer (Harcourt)
1996 J: *Looking for Jamie Bridger* by Nancy Springer (Dial)
Y/A: *Prophecy Rock* by Rob MacGregor (Simon & Schuster)
1997 J: *The Clearing* by Dorothy Reynolds Miller
Y/A: *Twisted Summer* by Willo Davis Roberts (Atheneum)

CARNEGIE MEDAL

Established in 1936 by the (British) Library Association for a children's book of outstanding merit written in English and first published in the United Kingdom in the preceding year. The following are the winners since 1985.

1985 *Storm* by Kevin Crossley-Holland (Heinemann)
1986 *Granny Was a Buffer Girl* by Berlie Doherty (Methuen)
1987 *The Ghost Drum* by Susan Price (Faber)
1988 *A Pack of Lies* by Geraldine McCaughrean (Oxford)
1989 *Goggle-Eyes* by Anne Fine (Hamish Hamilton)
1990 *Wolf* by Gillian Cross (Oxford)
1991 *Dear Nobody* by Berlie Doherty (Orchard)
1992 *Flour Babies* by Anne Fine (Hamish Hamilton)
1993 *Stone Cold* by Robert Swindells (Hamish Hamilton)
1994 *Whispers in the Graveyard* by Theresa Bresling (Methuen)
1995 *Northern Lights* by Philip Pullman (Scholastic)
1996 *Junk* by Melvin Burgess (Penguin)

KATE GREENAWAY MEDAL

Awarded by the (British) Library Associaton to the most distinguished work in the illustration of children's books first published in the United Kingdom in the preceding year. Following are the winners since 1985.

1985 *Sir Gawain and the Loathly Lady* by Selina Hastings, (illus.) Juan Wijngaard (Walker)
1986 *Snow White in New York* by Fiona French (Oxford)
1987 *Crafty Chameleon* by Mwenye Hadithi, (illus.) Adrienne Kennaway (Hodder & Stoughton)
1988 *Can't You Sleep, Little Bear?* by Martin Waddell, (illus.) Barbara Firth (Walker)
1989 *War Boy: A Country Childhood* by Michael Foreman (Pavilion)
1990 *The Whale's Song* by Dyan Sheldon, (illus.) Gary Blythe (Hutchinson)
1991 *The Jolly Christmas Postman* by Janet & Allan Ahlberg (Heinemann)
1992 *Zoo* by Anthony Browne (Julia MacRae)
1993 *Black Ships Before Troy* by Rosemary Sutcliff, (illus.) Alan Lee (Frances Lincoln)
1994 *Way Home* by Libby Hawthorne, (illus.) Gregory Rogers (Anderson)
1995 *The Christmas Miracle of Jonathan Toomey* by P.J. Lynch (Walker Books)
1996 *The Baby Who Wouldn't Go to Bed* by Helen Cooper (Doubleday)

SMARTIES BOOK PRIZE

This award is designed to stimulate interest in children's books. Prizes are given in three age categories from books published in the United Kingdom the preceding year. One of the three receives a Grand Prize (and that book is listed first).

1985 *Gaffer Samson's Luck* by Jill Paton Walsh (Viking)
It's Your Turn, Roger! by Susanna Gretz (Bodley Head)
Watch It Work! The Plane by Ray Marshall and John Bradley (Viking Kestrel)
1986 *The Snow Spider* by Jenny Nimmo (Methuen)

The Goose That Laid the Golden Egg retold & illus. by Geoffrey Patterson (Deutsch)
The Mirrorstone by Michael Palin, Alan Lee and Richard Seymour (Cape)
Village Heritage by Miss Pinnell & the Children of Sapperton School (Alan Sutton)
1987 *A Thief in the Village* by James Berry (Hamish Hamilton)
The Angel and the Soldier Boy by Peter Collington (Methuen)
Tangle and the Firesticks by Benedict Blathwayt (Julie MacRae)
1988 *Can't You Sleep Little Bear?* by Martin Waddell, (illus.) Barbara Firth (Walker)
Can It Be True? by Susan Hill, (illus.) Angela Barrett (Hamish Hamilton)
Rushavenn Time by Theresa Whistler (Brixworth Primary School)
1989 *We're Going on a Bear Hunt* by Michael Rosen, (illus.) Helen Oxenbury (Walker)
Bill's New Frock by Anne Fine (Methuen)
Blitzcat by Robert Westall (Macmillan)
1990 *Midnight Blue* by Pauline Fisk (Lion)
Six Dinner Sid by Inga Moore (Simon & Schuster)
Esio Trot by Roald Dahl, (illus.) Quentin Blake (Cape)
1991 *Farmer Duck* by Martin Waddell, (illus.) Helen Oxenbury (Walker)
Josie Smith by Magdalen Nabb, (illus.) Pirkko Vainio (HarperCollins)
Krindlekrax by Philip Ridley (Cape)
1992 *The Great Elephant Chase* by Gillian Cross (Oxford)
Nice Work, Little Wolf by Hilda Offen (Hamish Hamilton)
The Story of the Creation by Jane Ray (Orchard)
1993 *War Game* by Michael Foreman (Pavilion)
Hue Boy by Rita Phillips Mitchell, (illus.) Caroline Binch (Gollancz)
Listen to the Dark by Maeve Henry (Heinemann)
1994 *The Exiles at Home* by Hilary McKay (Gollancz)
So Much by Trish Cooke, (illus.) Helen Oxenbury (Walker)
Dimanche Diller by Henrietta Branford, (illus.) Lesley Harker (Young Lions)
1995 *Double Act* by Jacqueline Wilson (Doubleday)
Weather Eye by Elizabeth Howarth (Walker)
The Last Noo-Noo by Jill Murphy (Walker)
Thomas and the Tinners by Jill Paton Walsh (Macdonald)
1996 *The Firework-Maker's Daughter* by Philip Pullman (Yearling)

WHITBREAD BOOKS OF THE YEAR

To acknowledge outstanding books, including children's literature, "not only for the qualities accorded to them by the critics of the day, but for popular qualities which in the opinion of the judges make them readable on a wide scale." Established in 1972, the following are the winners since 1985.

1985 *The Nature of the Beast* by Janni Howker (Julia MacRae)
1986 *The Coal House* by Andrew Taylor (Collins)
1987 *A Little Lower than the Angels* by Geraldine McCaughrean (Oxford)
1988 *Awaiting Developments* by Judy Allen (Julie MacRae)

1989 *Why Weeps the Brogan?* by Hugh Scott (Walker)
1990 *AK* by Peter Dickinson (Gollancz)
1991 *Harvey Angell* by Diana Hendry (Julie MacRae)
1992 *The Great Elephant Chase* by Gillian Cross (Oxford)
1993 *Flour Babies* by Anne Fine (Hamish Hamilton)
1994 *Gold Dust* by Geraldine McCaughrean (Oxford)
1995 *The Wreck of the Zanzibar* by Michael Morpurgo (Methuen)

INTERNATIONAL BOARD ON BOOKS FOR YOUNG PEOPLE (IBBY)

Each national section of IBBY selects two books (one for text, one for illustration) that are representative of the best in children's literature from each country. They must also be considered suitable for publication throughout the world. In 1978 a third category was added to the IBBY Honour List, translation. While recommendations are made from several countries, the following is the Canadian English-language list since 1986.

IBBY AWARDS—CANADA

1986 (text) *Sweetgrass* by Jan Hudson (Tree Frog Press)
(illus.) *Chin Chiang and the Dragon's Dance* by Ian Wallace (Groundwood)
1988 (text) *Shadow in Hawthorn Bay* by Janet Lunn (Lester & Orpen Dennys)
(illus.) *The Emperor's Panda* by David Day, illus. by Eric Beddows (McClelland & Stewart)
1990 (text) *Bad Boy* by Diana Wieler (Groundwood)
(illus.). *Could You Stop Josephine?* by Stéphane Poulin (Tundra)
1992 (text) *Redwork* by Michael Bedard (Lester & Orpen Dennys)
(illus.) *The Orphan Boy* by Tolowa M. Mollel, illus. by Paul Morin (Oxford)
1994 (text) *Ticket to Curlew* by Celia Barker Lottridge (Groundwood)
(illus.) *Un voyage pour deux* by Stéphane Poulin (Annick)
1996 (text) *Traveling into the Light and Other Stories* by Martha Brooks (Groundwood)
(illus.) *Gifts* by Jo Ellen Bogart illus. by Barbara Reid (North Winds)
(trans.) Susan Ouriou, *La route de Chlifa* by Michèle Marineau (Québec-Amérique)

x. MORNINGSIDE CHILDREN'S BOOK LIST—CBC RADIO

A panel of experts appeared regularly on the CBC radio program "Morningside" to discuss children's books with the host, Peter Gzowski. These are the titles and authors they recommended in various age categories from November 1992 to May 1997.

NOVEMBER 1992—AGES 7–11

A Coyote Columbus Story, Thomas King (Groundwood)
The Steadfast Tin Soldier, Hans Christian Andersen, (illus.) Fred Marcellino, (HarperCollins)
The Story of Canada, Janet Lunn and Christopher Moore (Lester)
Fish House Secrets, Kathy Stinson (Thistledown)
The Twinkie Squad, Gordon Korman (Scholastic)
Hero of Lesser Causes, Julie Johnston (Lester)
Ellen/Elena/Luna, Paul Kropp (Maxwell Macmillan)
Ticket to Curlew, Celia Barker Lottridge (Groundwood)
Words of Stone, Kevin Henkes (Greenwillow)
The Stinky Cheese Man and Other Fairly Stupid Tales, Jon Scieszka/Lane Smith (Viking)
The True Confessions of Charlotte Doyle, Avi (Avon)
Wolf, Gillian Cross (Puffin)

OCTOBER 1993—AGES 6 AND UNDER

We Are All in the Dumps, With Jack and Guy, Maurice Sendak (HarperCollins)
The Longest Home Run, Roch Carrier (Tundra)
Board Books—*Everyday Children; Town; House; Pets; Cynthia Rylant* (Bradbury Press)
Martha Speaks, Susan Meddaugh, (Houghton Mifflin)
Ten Small Tales, Celia Barker Lottridge (Groundwood)
The Happy Hocky Family, Lane Smith (Viking)
Go Away, Big Green Monster, Ed Emberley (Little, Brown)
Northern Lights: The Soccer Trails, Michael Kusugak (Annick)
Last Leaf First Snowflake to Fall, Leo Yerxa (Groundwood)
Pot Luck, Tobi Tobias (Lothrup, Lee & Shepard)
I Went to the Zoo, Rita Golda Gelman (Scholastic)
Stories by Firelight, Shirley Hughes (Random House)
Hue Boy, Rita Phillips Mitchell, (illus.) Caroline Binch (Gollancz)
Out on the Ice in the Middle of the Bay, Peter Cumming (Annick)
Victor and Christabel, Petra Mathers (Knopf)

NOVEMBER 1993—AGES 10 AND OVER

A Short Walk Around the Pyramids, Philip Isaacson (Knopf)
The Giver, Lois Lowry (Houghton Mifflin)
RanVan the Defender, Diana Wieler (Groundwood)
Haveli, Suzanne Fisher Staples (Knopf)
Missing Angel Juan, Francesca Lia Block (HarperCollins)

Cowboy: A Kid's Album, Linda Granfield (Douglas & McIntyre)
The Man in the Ceiling, Jules Feiffer (HarperCollins)
Champions: Stories of Ten Remarkable Athletes, Bill Littlefield (Little, Brown)
The Lights Go On Again, Kit Pearson (Viking)
The Sword in the Stone, T.H. White (Philomel)
I Had Seen Castles, Cynthia Rylant (Harcourt Brace)
Daniel's Story, Carol Matas (Scholastic)
City of Light, City of Dark, Avi (Orchard)
Some of the Kinder Planets, Tim Wynne-Jones (Groundwood)
The Science Book for Girls and Other Intelligent Beings, Valerie Wyatt (Kids Can)

DECEMBER 1993—AGES 6–10

ABC Dinosaurs, Jan Pienkowski (Heinemann)
Mieko & the Fifth Treasure, Eleanor Coerr (Putnam)
Dr. Knickerbocker & Other Rhymes, David Booth & Maryann Kovalski (Kids Can)
Baby, Patricia MacLachlan (Delacourt)
A Small Tall Tale from the Far Far North, Peter Sis (Knopf)
Time Detectives: Clues from Our Past, Donalda Badone (Annick)
Black Ships Before Troy, Rosemary Sutcliff (Lester)
A Child's Garden of Verses (Everyman's Library), Robert Louis Stevenson, (illus.) Charles Robinson (Knopf)
The Princess and the Goblin (Everyman's Library), George MacDonald (Knopf)
Beethoven Lives Upstairs, Barbara Nichol, (illus.) Scott Cameron (Lester)
Oxford Book of Children's Stories, Jan Mark, ed. (Oxford University Press)
It Was a Dark and Stormy Night, Janet & Allan Ahlberg (Viking)
Boondoggle—Making Bracelets with Plastic Lace, Camilla Gryski (Kids Can)
Ship, David Macaulay (Houghton Miffin)
Charles Dickens: The Man Who Had Great Expectations, Diane Stanley/Peter Vennema (Morrow)
The Stone Wife, Bob Barton, (illus.) Georgi Yudin (Quarry)
The Iron Woman, Ted Hughes (Faber)

OCTOBER 1994—AGES 6 AND UNDER

My Painted House, My Friendly Chicken and Me, Maya Angelou (Clarkson Potter)
Gifts, Jo Ellen Bogart, (illus.) Barbara Reid (Scholastic)
Mother Goose: A Canadian Sampler, Celia Barker Lottridge, ed. (Groundwood)
The Three Golden Keys, Peter Sis (Doubleday)
Lyle at the Office, Bernard Waber (Houghton Mifflin)
The Wise Old Woman, Yoshiko Uchida, (illus.) Martin Springett (McElderry Books)
How Night Came from the Sea: A Story from Brazil, Mary-Joan Gerson, (illus.) Carla Golembe (Little, Brown)
Something Might Be Hiding, Celia Barker Lottridge, (illus.) Paul Zwolak (Groundwood)
Eagle Dreams, Sheryl McFarlane, (illus.). Ron Lightburn (Orca)
What Am I? Looking Through Shapes at Apples & Grapes, N.N.

Charles, (illus.) Leo & Diane Dillon (Blue Sky)
The Big Book of Things That Go (Scholastic)
Josepha: A Prairie Boy's Story, Jim McGugan, (illus.) Murray Kimber,
The First Christmas, Robbie Trent, (illus.) Marc Simont (HarperCollins)
Pat the Dog, Gus Clarke (Anderson)
EIEIO, Gus Clarke (Red Fox)
Three Little Pigs, Marie-Louise Gay (Groundwood)

NOVEMBER 1994—AGES 10 AND OVER

The Art Pack, Christopher and Helen Frayling (Knopf)
Out of the Blue, Sarah Ellis (Groundwood)
The Unseen: Scary Stories, Janet Lunn (Lester)
The Root Cellar, Janet Lunn (Lester)
Catherine Called Birdy, Karen Cushman (Houghton Mifflin)
The Wheel of Surya, Jamila Gavin (Mammoth)
The Eye of the Horse, Jamila Gavin (Methuen)
Traveling On into the Light, Martha Brooks (Groundwood)
The Glory Field, Walter Dean Myers (Scholastic)
Lives of the Writers, Kathleen Krull (Harcourt Brace)
Golden Girl and Other Stories, Gillian Chan (Kids Can)
The Frozen Waterfall, Gaye Hicyilmaz, Faber and Faber/Penguin
Troubling a Star, Madeleine L'Engle (Farrar, Straus and Giroux)
A Pioneer Story, Barbara Greenwood (Kids Can)
The Macmillan History of the World, Plantagenet Somerset Fry (Macmillan)
Ratface, Garry Disher (Ticknor and Fields)
Cordelia Clark, Budge Wilson (Stoddart)

DECEMBER 1994—AGES 6–10

For Sale: One Brother, Patti Stren (Scholastic)
Guests, Michael Dorris (Hyperion)
Thor, W.D. Valgardson (Groundwood)
The Charlotte Stories, Teddy Jam (Groundwood)
A Caribbean Dozen: Poems from Caribbean Poets, John Agard and Grace Nichols (Candlewick)
The Magic Schoolbus: In the Time of Dinosaurs, Joanna Cole (Scholastic)
Lights for Gita, Rachna Gilmore, Second Story Press
The Daydreamer, Ian MacEwan (Knopf)
Mouse TV, Matt Novak, Orchard Books/Macmillan Canada
Why Did the Underwear Cross the Road? Gordon Korman (Scholastic)
The Enchanted Castle, E. Nesbit (Puffin)
Stig of the Dump, Clive King/Judy Ann Sadler (Puffin)
Christmas Crafts, Judy Ann Sadler (Kids Can)
Beads, Judy Ann Sadler (Kids Can)
Gifts a Kid Can Make, Sheila McGraw (Firefly)
Tchaikovsky Discovers America, Esther Kalman (Lester)
Reaching for the Stars (Kingfisher)
Amber Brown Is Not a Crayon, Paula Danziger (Putnam)
The Always Prayer Shawl, Sheldon Oberman (Boyds Mills Press)

MAY 1995—GENERAL BOOKS DISCUSSED, VARIETY OF AGES

How the Eagles Got Their Eyes (Willowisp Press)
The Flea Story, Leo Lionni (Knopf)
So Much, Trish Cook, (illus.). Helen Oxenbury (Candlewick)
Would They Love a Lion? Kady MacDonald Denton (Kingfisher)
His Banner Over Me, Jean Little (Viking)
Bats About Baseball, Clarie Mackay (Viking)
The Good Fortunes, Margaret Mahy (Dell)
RanVan: A Worthy Opponent, Diana Wieler (Groundwood)
The Kids' Guide to the Brain, Sylvia Funston and Jay Ingram (Owl Books)
The Mennyms; The Mennyms in the Wilderness, Sylvia Waugh (Random House)
Lady Bug Garden, Celia Godkin (Fitzhenry & Whiteside)
Uncanny; Undue; The Gizmo, Paul Jennings (Puffin)
In Black and White and Other Stories, Jan Mark (Puffin)
Frogs in Clogs, Sheila White Samton (Crown)
The Dream Carvers, Joan Clark (Viking)
A Bone from a Dry Sea, Peter Dickinson (Laurel Leaf)
The Midwife's Apprentice, Karen Cushman (Houghton Mifflin)
Spud in Winter, Brian Doyle (Groundwood)
Big Bear's Treasury (Candlewick)

OCTOBER 1995—AGES 6 AND UNDER

Too Much Talk, Angela Shelf Medearis, (illus.) Stefano Vitale (Candlewick)
The White Stone in the Castle Wall, Sheldon Oberman, (illus.) Les Tait (Tundra)
Clown, Quentin Blake, Jonathan Cape
Good Zap Little Grog, Sarah Wilson, (illus.) Susan Meddaugh (Candlewick)
The Moccasin Goalie, William Roy Brownridge (Orca)
Just Like New, Ainslie Manson, (illus.) Karen Reczuch (Groundwood)
Grunt: The Primitive Cave Boy, Timothy Bush (Crown)
Selina and the Bear Paw Quilt, Barbara Smucker, (illus.) Janet Wilson (Lester)
The Big Red Bus, Judy Hindley, (illus.) William Benedict (Candlewick)
The Night Is Like an Animal, Candace Whitman (HarperCollins)
Bone Button Borscht, Aubrey Davis, (illus.) Dusan Petricic (Kids Can)
Simply Ridiculous, Virginia Davis, (illus.) Russ Willms (Kids Can)
In the Woods: Who's Been Here?, Lindsay Barrett George (Greenwillow)
Flood Fish, Robyn Eversole, (illus.) Sheldon Greenberg (Crown)
Supper for Crow: A North West Indian Tale, Pierre Morgan (Crown)
The Gypsy Princess, Phoebe Gilman (Scholastic)
Tess, Hazel Hutchins, (illus.) Ruth Ohi (Annick)

NOVEMBER 1995—AGES 10 AND OVER

The First Time: True Stories, Charles Montpetit (Orca)
The Toll Bridge; *Dance On My Grave*; *Now I Know*; *Breaktime*, Aidan Chambers (Red Fox)
In Flanders Fields: The Story of the

Poem by John McCrae, Linda Granfield (Lester)
Truly Grim Tales, Priscilla Galloway (Lester)
Aleta and the Queen, Priscilla Galloway (Annick)
Atalanta, The Fastest Runner in the World, Priscilla Galloway (Annick)
The Illustrated Book of Myths, Neil Philip, ed. (H.B. Fenn)
In My Room: Teenagers in Their Bedrooms, Adrienne Salinger (Raincoast)
The Onlyhouse, Teresa Toten (Red Deer College)
The Maestro, Tim Wynne-Jones (Groundwood)
Her Stories, Virginia Hamilton, ed. Leo and Diane Dillon (illus.) (Scholastic)
The Night Voyagers, Donn Kushner (Lester)
Out of the Dark, Welwyn Wilton Katz (Groundwood)
White Wave, Mary Razzell (Groundwood)
The Diary of a Young Girl (The Definitive Edition) Anne Frank (Doubleday)
The Acting Bug, Kathryn Ellis (Boardwalk)

NOVEMBER 1995—AGES 6–11

The Meadow Mouse Treasury (Groundwood)
Lassie-Come-Home, Rosemary Wells, (illus.) Susan Jeffers (Henry Holt)
The Thirteenth Floor: A Ghost Story, Sid Fleischman, (illus.) Peter Sis (Greenwillow)
Images of Nature: Canadian Poets and the Group of Seven, David Booth, ed. (Kids Can)
Stand Up Mr. Dickens: A Dickens Anthology, Edward Blishen, (illus.) Jill Bennett (Orion)
Kashtanka, Anton Chekhov, (illus.) Gennady Spirin (Harcourt Brace)
Jenny and the Hanukkah Queen, Jean Little, (illus.) Suzanne Mogensen (Viking)
The Gift, Joseph Kertes, (illus.) Peter Perko (Groundwood)
Let's Play: Traditional Games of Childhood, Camilla Gryski (Kids Can)
The Ear, the Eye, and the Arm, Nancy Farmer (Puffin)
The Castle Tourmandyne, Monica Hughes (HarperCollins)
Talking with Artists, Vol. 2, Pat Cummings, ed. (Maxwell Macmillan)
Dog Heaven, Cynthia Rylant (Scholastic)
The Illustrated Father Goose, Shelley Tanaka, (illus.) Laurie McGaw (Little, Brown)
In a Circle Long Ago, Nancy Van Laan, (illus.) Lisa Desimini (Random House)
The Way Life Works, Mahlon Hoagland and Bert Dodson (Times)
From Far Away, Robert Munsch, (illus.) Michael Martchenko (Annick)
Gutenberg's Gift, Nancy Willard, Bryan Leister (illus.) (Harcourt, Brace)
The Oxford Book of Story Poems (Oxford University Press)

MAY 1996—GENERAL BOOKS DISCUSSED, VARIETY OF AGES

Bad Girls, Cynthia Voigt (Scholastic)
How Smudge Came, Nan Gregory (illus.) Ron Lightburn (Red Deer College)
Bibi and the Bull, Carol Vaage, (illus.) Georgia Graham (Dragon Hill)
Yo! Yes? Chris Raschka (Orchard)
Keri, Jan Andrews (Groundwood)

The Secret Wish of Nannerl Mozart, Barbara Kathleen Nickel (Second Story)
Step by Wicked Step, Anne Fine (Hamish Hamilton)
The Kids Campfire Book: The Official Book of Campfire Fun, Jane Drake and Ann Love, (illus.) Heather Collins (Kids Can)
The Wanderings of Odysseus: The Story of the Odyssey, Rosemary Sutcliff, (illus.) Alan Lee (Frances Lincoln)
The Middle Passage, Tom Feelings (Dial)
Too Many Suns, Julie Lawson, (illus.) Martin Springett (Stoddart)
The Golden Compass, Philip Pullman (Knopf)
Edward Unready for School: *Edward in Deep Water*; *Edward's Overwhelming Overnight*, Rosemary Wells (Dial)
Cybersurfer: The Owl Internet Guide for Kids, Nyla Ahmad (Owl)
Cougar Cove, Julie Lawson (Orca)
When Vegetables Go Bad!, Don Gillmor, (illus.) Marie-Louise Gay (Doubleday)
On Board the Titanic, Shelley Tanaka, (illus.) Ken Marschall (Scholastic)
Market, Ted Lewin (Lothrop)
Feathers for Lunch, Lois Ehlert (Harcourt Brace)

OCTOBER 1996—10 AND UP

A Girl Named Disaster, Nancy Farmer (Orchard)
What I Did for Roman, Pam Conrad (HarperCollins)
Glory Days and Other Stories, Gillian Chan (Kids Can)
Uncle Ronald, Brian Doyle (Groundwood)
Metropolis: Ten Cities, Ten Centuries, Albert Lorenz (Abrams)
Back of Beyond, Sarah Ellis (Groundwood)
Awake and Dreaming, Kit Pearson (Viking)
Little Sister, Kara Dalkey (Harcourt Brace)
Martha Black, Gold Rush Pioneer, Carol Martin (Douglas and McIntyre)
Shadows on a Sword, Karlene Bradford (HarperCollins)
Weapons and Warfare: From the Stone Age to the Space Age, Milton Meltzer (HarperCollins)
After the War, Carol Matas (Scholastic)
To Dance at the Palais Royale, Janet McNaughton (Tuckamore)
Robin Hood, Louis Rhead (McMillan U.S.)
So You Love to Draw, Michael Seary (Douglas & McIntyre)
The Ballad of Lucy Whipple, Karen Cushman (Clarion)
This Same Sky: A Collection of Poems from Around the World, Naomi Shihab Nye (Aladdin)

NOVEMBER 1996—AGES 7 AND UNDER

Ghost Train, Paul Yee, (illus.) Harvey Chan (Groundwood)
The Rooster's Gift, Pam Conrad, (illus.) Eric Beddows (Groundwood)
Cock-A-Doodle-Moo, text & illus. by Bernard Most (Harcourt Brace)
The Best Children's Books in the World: A Treasury of Illustrated Stories, ed. Byron Preiss (Abrams)
The Dust Bowl, David Booth, (illus.) Karen Reczuch (Kids Can)
Jacob's Best Sisters, Teddy Jam, (illus.) Joanne Fitzgerald (Groundwood)

Freight Train, text & illus. by Donald Crews (Tupelo Books)
Good Night, Gorilla, Peggy Rathmann (Putnam)
Eating the Alphabet, Lois Ehlert (Harcourt Brace)
The Token Gift, Hugh William McKibbon, (illus.) Scott Cameron (Annick)
The Story of Little Babaji, Helen Bannerman, (illus.) Fred Marcellino (HarperCollins)
A Mountain Alphabet, Margriet Ruurs, Andrew Kiss (illus.) (Tundra)
Boy Soup, or, When Giant Caught Cold, written and illus. by Loris Lesynski (Annick)
Goose, Molly Bang (Blue Sky)
Hush, A Thai Lullaby, Minfong Ho, (illus.) Holly Meade (Orchard)
Melody Mooner Takes Lessons, Frank B. Edwards, (illus.) John Bianchi (Bungalo)
My Very First Mother Goose, Iona Opie ed., (illus.) Rosemary Wells (Candlewick)
The Patchwork House, Sally FitzGibon, (illus.) Dean Griffiths (Orca)
Whatever You Do, Don't Go Near That Canoe! Julie Lawson, (illus.) Werner Zimmerman (Scholastic)

DECEMBER 1996—AGES 6–12

You Asked? Over 300 Great Questions and Astounding Answers (Owl)
Shoebag Returns, Mary James (Scholastic)
Tiger's New Cowboy Boots, Irene Morck, (illus.) Georgia Graham (Red Deer College)
The Very Hungry Lion, Gita Wolf, Indrapramit Roy (Annick)
The War between the Vowels and the Consonants, Priscilla Turner, (illus.) Whitney Turner (Farrar, Straus and Giroux)
The Phantom Tollbooth, Norton Juster, (illus.) Jules Feiffer (Random House)
How Can a Frozen Detective Stay Hot on the Trail?, Linda Bailey (Kids Can)
North Star to Freedom, Gena Gorrell (Stoddart)
Antastasia's Album, Hugh Brewster (Penguin)
Discovering the Ice Man, Shelley Tanaka, (illus.) Laurie McGaw (Scholastic)
The Creation, Brian Wildsmith (Millbrook)
When the World Was New, Jurg Schubiger, (illus.) Rotraut Susanne Berner (Annick)
Tiktala, Margaret Shaw-McKinnon and Laszlo Gal (Stoddart)
The Starry Messenger, Peter Sis (HarperCollins)
The Puffin Treasury of Children's Stories (Puffin)
Necklace of Stars, Veronika Martenova Charles (Stoddart)

MAY 1997—GENERAL BOOKS DISCUSSED, VARIETY OF AGES

A Seed Grows; A New Butterfly; Hungry Animals, Pamela Hickman, (illus.) Heather Collins (Kids Can)
The Eye-to-Eye Books: Insects and Spiders, Snakes and Lizards (Somerville House)
Rumpelstiltskin's Diary, Diane Stapley (Morrow)
The Belonging Place, Jean Little (Viking)
Laughs, Funny Stories, ed. by Claire Mackay (Tundra)
Ella Enchanted, Gail Carson (Harper Collins)
Promise Song, Linda Holeman (Tundra)

Rebellion, Marianne Brandis (Porcupine's Quill)
Wings to Fly, Celia Barker Lotteridge (Groundwood)
Open Me: I'm a Dog, Art Spiegelman (HarperCollins)
Cloudland, John Burningham (Crown)
A Fly Named Alfred, Don Trembath (Orca)
The Forest Wife, Theresa Tomlinson (Dell)
Silver Wing, Kenneth Oppel (HarperCollins)